The Christian Religion

An Introduction

Thomas E. Helm

Western Illinois University

PRENTICE HALL, Englewood Cliffs, New Jersey 07632

Library of Congress Cataloging-in-Publication Data

Helm, Thomas Eugene, (date)
  The Christian religion : an introduction / by Thomas E. Helm.
    p. cm.
  Includes bibliographical references.
  ISBN 0-13-133513-8
  1. Christianity. I. Title.
BR121.2.H3582 1991
200—dc20   90-31064
                                                               CIP

Editorial/production supervision and
  interior design: Louise Capuano and Jan Stephan
Cover design: Lundgren Graphics, Ltd.
Manufacturing buyer: Herb Klein

Photo Credits: Page 64—Gift of Friends of the Cleveland Musem of Art, 27.197; page 92—
Reprinted with permission of the British Library; page 99—Ewing Galloway; page 132—
A/P World Wide Photos.

Scripture quotations are from the Revised Standard Version of the Bible, copyright 1946
1952, 1971 by the Division of Christian Education of the National Council of Churches o
Christ in the USA and used by permission.

Printed in the United States of America

10 9 8 7 6 5 4 3 2 1

ISBN   0-13-133513-8

Prentice-Hall International (UK) Limited, *London*
Prentice-Hall of Australia Pty. Limited, *Sydney*
Prentice-Hall Canada Inc., *Toronto*
Prentice-Hall Hispanoamericana, S.A., *Mexico*
Prentice-Hall of India Private Limited, *New Delhi*
Prentice-Hall of Japan, Inc., *Tokyo*
Simon & Schuster Asia Pte. Ltd., *Singapore*
Editora Prentice-Hall do Brasil, Ltda., *Rio de Janeiro*

To my father, Eugene Thomas Helm
and
to the memory of my mother,
Ruby Ashcraft Helm (1927–1989)

Contents

II THE SHAPE OF CHRISTIAN HISTORY

PREFACE

This book had its beginnings in my teaching of undergraduate students at a state university. The students who have enrolled in my courses on Christianity have over the years come from diverse religious and cultural backgrounds. I have come to expect a fairly even mix of Roman Catholic and traditional Protestant students in the rows facing the lectern at the start of the fall and spring semesters. I know too that there will be students with no religious loyalties as well as others with a very high level of religious commitment and conviction. In recent years these Christian and secular students have been joined with increasing frequency by Muslim, Buddhist, and Hindu students in my course "The Christians." Yet it has been my experience that whatever the mix of students there is a shared curiosity about the Christian religion. The curiosity is not so much about church or denominational history or the history of Christian doctrine. The students I teach are interested rather in religious experience and meaning, in religious worship and practice, in religious life and community. Their interest in Christianity, I believe, focuses on the forms of the Christian religion and on the ways the Christian religion has shaped and continues to shape human existence.

It was this particular set of interests that led me first to think of writing a comprehensive introduction to the *religion* of Christians. With an emphasis on the religious character of Christianity, this book is designed for college and university level programs in religious studies. Broadly defined, its purpose is to present an objective account of Christianity's religious foundations, its formative histories, and its diverse forms of worship, belief, practice, community, and life. In the sense that our narrative is descriptive and seeks to represent the forms of the Christian religion in a manner that is faithful to the experience and convictions of Christians, we can say that the method we use is phenomenological. The book's emphasis is comparative in that it discusses the forms of Christian religious experience, worship, belief, community, and life in relation to the religious forms of other religions. This comparative emphasis often gives new or fresh perspectives on familiar Christian features, and it provides a reminder that in our contemporary world it is no longer possible and certainly not desirable to talk about cultures or religions in a vacuum. And, though our study is not a history of Christianity, its character is inevitably historical and cultural. Its character is historical in part because Christians think of religious realities in historical terms. As my former teacher G. Ernest Wright was fond of putting it, the God of Christians is a God who acts in history. Our study is historical and cultural too because religions both are shaped by and shape the societies of which they are a part. The story of Christianity is not then simply a history of Christian people. It is a story of the history and cultural heritage of Europeans, and today it is becoming the story also of women and African Americans whose experience has been relegated to the margins of Western culture. And, as the population of the Christian world shifts from Europe and North America, Christians of Africa and Asia and South America are discovering ways of telling the story in terms of their own histories and cultures.

Our study of Christianity is arranged in three major sections. It begins with an examination of Christianity's biblical foundations and world view, a discussion of the historical Jesus whom Christians came to recognize as the decisive revelation of God's nature and purpose, and a survey of the formative period of the early Christian churches. The center section of the book narrates the heritage and history of the Christian religion, the emergence of its diverse traditions, and the transformations of its forms of worship and belief and its patterns of organization and life. The last section takes a synchronic approach to discrete Christian traditions. Here we look at the forms and meaning of Christian diversity. We examine the character of the several forms of Catholic and Protestant Christianity as well as the forms Christianity is taking in the world today among groups historically on the margins of the traditional churches.

The preparation of the book also reflects a pedagogical orientation that comes from the teaching of undergraduate students. A glossary of key terms is found at the end of the book. These terms are indicated in the body of the text; in most cases important terms or ideas are also explained or defined in the text as they occur. A bibliography is provided at the end of each chapter as a guide to further reading. In the chapter bibliographies, I have listed the books and articles which are generally regarded as standard references or which are otherwise lively, interesting, and accessible. Study questions at the end of each chapter are useful for review of the chapter's central themes, movements, and figures.

Finally, it is my hope to capture in the writing and style of narrative something of the excitement, drama, and importance of the Christian story. After all, what is true about Christianity—what is true about all the great religions of the world—is its capacity to empower and transform human lives and to shape human culture and history.

ACKNOWLEDGMENTS

I have come to believe that one should not begin a book without prior approval of one's family and friends. Not only their support and patience but also their time and energy are required for the project to get done. And so for the innumerable ways that I have received encouragement and help from those around me, thanks.

Among those to whom I owe so much in the preparation of this book, for their reading of the manuscript and their generous offer of good counsel and thoughtful criticism, I wish to thank in particular Rowland Sherrill of Indiana University at Indianapolis; Bryant Keeling of Western Illinois University; Reo Christenson of Miami University of Ohio; Susan Henking of Hobart and William Smith Colleges. Thanks also for the helpful and constructive suggestions of George Saint-Laurent of California State University at Fullerton and Lawrence Cunningham of Notre Dame University. Because of their careful reading and insight, the final text was much improved. The staff at Prentice Hall and especially Helen Brennan deserve mention too for their encouragement and help. They have been good people with whom to work. Finally, to my wife Virginia who often put her own research and writing aside to help me with mine, my special gratitude and thanks.

Thomas E. Helm

1 Introduction: The Study of Christianity in Religious Perspective

The Christian religion is the largest of the world religions with a varied and immensely complex history reaching back in time nearly two thousand years to the age of its founder, a first-century Jew named Jesus of Nazareth. Christians claim in fact that their sacred history reaches still farther back to the time of Israel's kings and prophets and back still farther to Moses and Jewish beginnings, back even to the time of Abraham, the historically distant figure at the beginning of the second millennium to whom Jews, Christians, and Muslims all trace the origins of their respective faiths. The task, then, of disentangling Christianity's history from the history it shares with other religions is a formidable one. So too, is the job of tracing the threads of the Christian story which are a part of the fabric of European history and culture. Our job is still more complicated today by the emergence of indigenous Christianity among peoples in Asia, Africa, and South America—peoples endeavoring to make Christianity authentically their own.

At the outset, therefore, we are confronted with difficulties in telling our story of the Christian religion, and we understand the need for boundaries. Let's start with the understanding that our account of this religion is introductory. That does not mean that it is my purpose to write a survey of Christianity. What follows is rather a selection of characters, events, symbols, and themes woven together into something like a tapestry. My object is to direct the reader to the patterns that emerge—patterns that give form to what is characteristically Christian in Christianity's history and among its diverse traditions.

Our study is secondly intended as a contribution to the academic study of religion. It is a study of the Christian *religion*. Our interest in Christianity focuses on its character as one of the important forms human religiousness has taken. And so in what follows, we attempt to situate Christianity in relation to other religions and especially in relation to that nonordinary reality called the holy. Because religion is also a system of meaning, a way humans have of giving form and value to their lives and experiences, our study also endeavors to situate Christianity in relation to culture and society. These constitute Christianity's context, if not its ultimate meaning.

Terms for the Study

Represented on every continent of the globe, Christianity is the largest of the world religions. Yet Christianity, though sprung originally from the part of the world that we know as the Middle or Near East, has been a predominately western religion. In the words of a Yale University church historian, it was "as a religion of Europe that [Jesus'] message came to the nations of the world and the islands of the sea—a religion of Europe both in the sense of a religion from Europe and, often, a religion about Europe as well." [1] At the end of the last century, however, changes in the religious and cultural insularity of the West were already apparent. The interreligious dialogue that characterized the 1893 World's Parliament of Religions in Chicago was to become in the twentieth century a permanent feature of the religious landscape. The conversation initiated in Chicago among Protestants, Roman Catholics, and Jews, and between the religious traditions of the West and the East, would gain momentum in this century. The stimulus supplied by the Parliament of Religions for the development of the comparative study of religion in major American academic centers would also contribute to significant contact and understanding among representatives of the world's religions. Above all, the parliament established by example that religious plurality in this century would be an important context for the study and the practice of religion.

In recent years, recognition of the rapidly pluralizing world that we live in has prompted religious scholars to establish forums for discussing the meaning of this religious diversification. And few of these forums have been more useful for thinking about religion amidst a sometimes bewildering diversity of religions and cultures than the one held in Lexington, Virginia. There, on the campus of Washington and Lee University, the Department of Religion sponsored jointly with Harvard University's Center for the Study of World Religions a symposium appropriately titled, "The Christian Faith in a Religiously Plural World." [2]

Symposium participants came from widely divergent religious backgrounds, from major Christian groups, both Protestant and Catholic, as well as from Judaism, Islam, Hinduism, and Buddhism, self-consciously to tackle the problem of religious pluralism. All agreed that the time had come to face the theological, intellectual, and moral challenge of living in a religiously and culturally diverse world. All further agreed that diversity is a positive development, and the presence of others of differing religious persuasions is the best context for reflecting on one's own way of being religious. The only remaining question was how to begin conversation that would preserve the differences in religious points of view without sacrificing the possibility of communication. One participant proposed that the symposium's special quandary might be formulated in terms of that special kind of puzzle that Zen Buddhists know as the koan. [3] He proposed that the symposium give thought to what he called a koan for Christians. The proposed koan might be stated thus: How is it possible to preserve loyalty to the truth of one's own religious tradition and at the same time be open to the truth in the lives of other people of faith?

This koan is a challenge to those who are exploring what it means to be religious at this stage in human religious history. It is also relevant for those interested in the academic study of religion where religious pluralism is a given of the study itself. Whether a person is studying Christianity as one already convinced of Christianity's essential rightness or as one who approaches from the outside, the koan for Christians may provide insight into what it means to think about the Christian religion and its many diverse expressions. As was true of the symposium at Washington and Lee, it is not expected here that everyone is religious in the same way or to the same degree—or even religious at all. What is basic in approaching our study of Christianity, however, is an appreciation that religion involves a special way of being human and that the study of religion entails the study of what I like to call *vital truths*, truths that are not necessarily our own but truths that people live by.

Our capacity to understand points of view different from our own and answers to questions that are not our questions is in part dependent on an awareness of diversity. Our capacity to appreciate another's religious truth as a vital truth may even depend on a capacity to ask questions as others might ask them, as when, for example, the Christian writer and Islamicist Wilfred Cantwell Smith seriously asks: "Is the Qur'an the Word of God?" [4] For the student with loyalty to another religion or to no religion at all, a process like this questioning will be required if he or she is to appreciate the religion of the Christians. But a similar process of questioning will be required of Christians as well. In the study of Christianity, the Christian will find that Christianity itself is diverse in form and that many of its traditions will seem quite foreign. An American Baptist looking at Orthodox Christianity in Romania or Zulu Zion in South Africa may be surprised at how strange Orthodoxy's adoration of the icon or Zulu Zion's blend of native African traditions with New Testament faith seems when viewed with Baptist eyes.

To return to the koan for Christians. Is it possible to be open to the religious truth another lives by without diminishing loyalty to one's own truth? Is it possible to steer between a relativism that diminishes and an exclusivism that insulates and provincializes religious experience? Once more, the Washington and Lee symposium provides us with a model for thinking through this apparent dilemma. The symposium participants recognized the limitations of reasoning to bring about an abstract resolution of the paradox. Rather than being content with simple, unequivocal answers, they trusted instead to the dynamics of personal encounter, conversation, and dialogue.

Dialogue and conversation also provide us with a serviceable model for the *academic study of religion*. Commitment to a process like the one we have been discussing is essential for understanding if the Catholic is to grasp the significance of Luther's reformation or the Protestant the role of the pope as a religious symbol for Roman Catholics or a contemporary American the import of the fourth-century desert monks who withdrew to the Egyptian desert to struggle with desire and demons. We will approach, then, the study of religion as we might approach a conversation with an engaging stranger from another culture. As we talk about things of importance, points of view will be compared, similarities discovered, differences noted. And, when confidence in the conversation builds, we may find too that the basic questions each of us asks are not the same questions, that the interpretational frames each uses for thinking about the world are not the same frames, and that the world views each brings to the conversation are not the same. At that point, we may find that for further understanding it will be necessary to suspend our presuppositions, be patient, and attend to what the other has to show or tell us. Something like this procedure is involved in what scholars call the *phenomenological method*. It is a descriptive method that requires disciplined looking and listening, and it is a set of attitudes that encourage an empathetic approach to religious phenomena. In the process of conversational encounter, however, it may be discovered that thinking about the interpretational frame of another forces us to reflect more thoughtfully on our own. And so the questions asked by others of themselves may stimulate us to reflect and clarify the meanings and values that inform our lives. The process also holds promise that the meanings we live by, the values we hold—our own vital truths—will find new affirmation as our sympathies for the expressions of others' faiths are enlarged.

The Nature of Religion

At the heart of religion is the experience of *sacred mystery*. But what is "mystery" and how are we to use it? Originally a Greek word, *mystery* designated that which is hidden, secret, or esoteric, hence our association of mystery with something that is unexplained, unknown, or puzzling. Similarly in religion, mystery refers to that which is puzzling, beyond our comprehension, has no place in our ordinary scheme of things, to that which historian of religion Rudolph Otto speaks of as the holy. Following Otto, historians of religion today often use the word *mystery* to refer to the holy or the experience of awe and wonder associated with the divine or numinous presence of the divine. We too will use the word in this wider sense. Mystery will be our way of referring to holy, numinous, divine reality or to those ruptures in ordinary time and space wherein humans become aware of the holy or of that reality named by prophets, religious seers, and mystics with names like Tao, Brahma, and Nirvana. The history of religion demonstrates that the experience of the holy has power to arouse the human heart. These experiences also provide impetus to religion's attempt to understand sacred mystery and to speak of it through symbol, myth, and ritual. It is to these experiences, which reside at the heart of religion, that we point when we use the word *mystery*.

Such experiences as these are elemental to religious expression and practice, and yet they are to be looked at from without, as well as within, the context that we usually think of as religious. Devout religious persons are made aware of sacred mystery while bathing in the Ganges or awaiting the first light from the Church of the Holy Sepulchre on Easter morning, while chanting sacred Scripture or reciting the Jesus Prayer, while praying before the Western Wall of the Jerusalem Temple or in a Pentecostal service awaiting the baptism of fire. But such encounters are also reported outside the formal context of worship and devotion. The Book of Exodus records that, while tending sheep, Moses came upon a bush that burned but was not consumed, and from the bush he heard a voice call to him, "Moses, Moses." The Acts of the Apostles in the New Testament describes a sudden noise from the sky like the sound of wind and tongues of fire that appeared and rested over the head of each apostle. The American novelist Walker Percy reminds us that mystery is even apprehended in ways that by usual definition appear not to be religious at all. Thus Binx Bolling in Percy's *The Moviegoer* speaks of the change in his life on first becoming conscious of mystery while on a tour of duty in Korea. Awakening under a chindolea bush, Binx says that "six inches from my nose a dung beetle was scratching around under the leaves. As I watched there awoke in me an immense curiosity. I was on to something, and I vowed that if I ever got out of this fix, I would pursue the search." [5] Binx's experience under the chindolea bush awakens him to the fact that in addition to ordinary, profane reality there is another reality, a reality that stands out from the ordinary routines of everyday life as something unexpected, unfamiliar, and extraordinary. Whatever forms the encounters of this mysterious reality take, religion is a witness to it.

Yet religion is not just the experience of sacred mystery. *Religion is the human response to sacred mystery. It is the attempt to comprehend that mystery in symbol, ritual, story, and theology, to give expression to its moral authority in patterns of behavior, and to stabilize, preserve, and transmit its meaning in canonical writings and sacred tradition.* When, for example, the nineteenth century Hindu teacher Sri Ramakrishna experienced sacred power, he was performing priestly duties in a temple dedicated to the goddess Kali. It was to Kali, the Divine Mother, that he called for understanding. "I don't understand what is happening to me," he prayed. "Please teach me yourself how to know you." This encounter with sacred mystery was intensely personal, yet its cultic setting in a Hindu temple and the symbols for deity appealed to were intimately related to Ramakrishna's interpretation of its meaning. Similarly, when the sixteenth-century Spanish Catholic nun Saint Theresa experienced holy power, she discovered its meaning in the tradition of devotion and in the symbols for God familiar to her. The mystery—described as "a force beneath my feet so powerful that I know nothing to which I can compare it"—she identified as Lord, Majesty, and King. Before this reality, her response was obedient submission, for "we have not the capacity" for understanding it. Thus, while the encounter with mystery is at the heart of religion, religion is also about what religious people say and do to understand and express the meaning of mystery, and how they seek to communicate its power to others who would share in it.

Sacred Mystery and the Christian Religion

Christianity takes the encounter with sacred mystery, the mystery of God revealed in Jesus the Christ, as the elemental religious experience. In many places the New Testament records the extraordinary effect that Jesus had on those who came into contact with him. The cycle of miracle stories found in Mark 5–7, for example, tells of Jesus casting out a legion of demons from the Gerasene demoniac, bringing Jairus's daughter back to life, healing the woman with the hemorrhage, freeing the Syrophoenician woman's daughter from demon possession, and healing the man with a speech impediment. In these encounters the response was one of amazement and in the case of the woman with the hemorrhage "fear and trembling." Biblical scholar Norman Perrin writes that these miracles express "an aura of divine presence" [6], a presence best described as *numinous*.

Making use of this term popularized by Rudolph Otto, we can say that Jesus was experienced as a numinous reality—a reality whose character is strangely and inexplicably incommensurate with ordinary human reality and before which ordinary humans are overcome with feelings of wonder and awe. [7] Thus he was also portrayed in the Transfiguration. As Matthew recounts the event, Peter, James, and John accompanied Jesus to "a high mountain apart" where Jesus appeared before them as a heavenly person radiant with light like that of the sun and as a divine presence experienced in an overshadowing cloud. Here again, the narrative describes Jesus as the focus and manifestation of sacred reality and his disciples as overwhelmed and filled with awe by his numinous presence.

Like other religions, however, Christianity is not just an encounter with but also a response to sacred mystery. It is the attempt to interpret, express, and communicate the meaning and power of divine reality in symbols, stories, rituals, codes of conduct, patterned behavior, and sacred community. The account of Jesus' Transfiguration illustrates this point. In the Transfiguration story, Jesus appears as a numinous presence, exalted above all historical reality. But in associating the Transfiguration (which scholars think may have been a postresurrection appearance account) with the passion and suffering of Jesus, the Gospel writers placed Jesus' epiphany within an interpretive theological frame behind which we cannot go. Among other purposes, the Gospel narratives affirm that God's purpose and power are made known most fully in the historical events of Jesus' Passion and death, that sacred mystery manifests itself decisively in the form of human vulnerability and suffering.

Buddhist teaching about suffering provides an instructive comparison with this Christian view that ultimate mystery manifests itself decisively in the midst of suffering. According to traditional legend about the origin of Buddhism, Gautama, the future Buddha, converted from a life of pleasure, luxury, and ease after seeing three striking manifestations of pain and suffering. Witnessing sickness, old age, and death in successive visions or apparitions, Gautama was profoundly impressed by the stark fact that everything is suffering: "Birth is Ill [Suffering], decay is Ill, sickness is Ill, death is Ill: likewise sorrow and grief, woe, lamentation and despair." [8] And the Buddha believed that the acknowledgement of the truth of suffering was the beginning of wisdom. We should mark, however, that suffering in Buddhist teaching is not limited to physical or psychological discomfiture. Its meaning also includes the idea of impermanence. Everything restricted to time and space is subject to change; all things that have a beginning lamentably have an end. This too is suffering and in Buddhist teaching is the source of the "unsatisfactoriness" of human existence. The consciousness that nothing lasts prompted Siddhartha Gautama to an act known in Buddhist folklore as the great renunciation. Cutting his hair and beard, stripping off his princely robes, and putting on the yellow robe of a mendicant monk, the future Buddha set out on a quest that led ultimately to a place called Bodhgaya. There under a bodhi tree Gautama became aware in his enlightenment that the ultimate mystery, for which Buddhists use the word *nirvana,* is in the extinction of suffering.

Yet for Christians, time and space are not essentially problematic, and suffering is not identified as the source or cause of the unsatisfactoriness of human existence. With roots deep in the religious heritage of Judaism, early Christianity resisted the temptation to disentangle the revelation of ultimate mystery from the vagaries of human history. Christian doctrine teaches that the created world is the proper arena of human existence; the kerygma or message of the New Testament church holds that the Passion and crucifixion of Jesus is the decisive disclosure of the mystery of God's love. Christian apostles preached about the person of Jesus, and the primitive Christian church confessed him as Lord. Martyrs imitated his sacrificial crucifixion in blood. Fellowship with one another and with the risen Lord was made possible through the ritual act of baptism and in the celebration of a sacred meal. By these and other religious forms, Christians from the first century to the present endeavored in diverse ways—for Christianity is not one but many interpretive responses to Jesus Christ—to mediate between an embodied, historically manifest mystery and the world that makes humans what they are.

Overview

The earliest expression of Christian faith affirmed that Jesus was born of Mary, suffered under Pontius Pilate, was crucified, died, buried, and resurrected from the dead. Here was the essence of the good news—the *gospel*—preached by the early Christians: The life and teaching of Jesus reveals the truth that redeems humans from sin and death; his suffering and death bring forgiveness of sin and reconciliation with God; and his resurrection is a sign of new life in God's eternal Kingdom. If we ask what is distinctive about Christian understanding of sacred mystery, it is to this gospel faith that we must point. This faith expresses the center of the Christian awareness of sacred mystery and the essential features of the Christian perspective on salvation, its *religious vision.* This vision is the subject of Chapter 3. And, because this chapter is an introduction to the time, circumstance, and character of Jesus' historical ministry, this chapter might be a good place to begin after the Introduction. Chapter 2 on the Christian world view might then be read in connection with the discussion of the Christian traditions in Part III. Yet, for the reason that Chapter 2 presents religious beliefs about the world that Christianity inherited from Judaism, I have located it at the beginning of our narrative of the Christian story. Chapter 3 takes up another foundational theme. It deals with the beginning of the church and the formation of the church's tradition, with the emergence of the church's ministry, its *canon* of sacred writings, and its formulas of belief and creeds.

One of the lessons history teaches is that there are many ways of being human; a lesson of *Christian* history is that there are many ways of being Christian. Part II examines the evolving character of Christianity in time and in relation to the historical horizons that change with changing political, social, cultural, and intellectual circumstances. In this historical section we also explore the themes that broadly speaking give a unity of focus in our study of Christian history. As we look at central figures and pivotal events in Christianity's past, we are especially concerned with issues that have challenged Christians in the context of their societies and cultures. We examine the idea of sacred order, and papal and imperial authority in the Constantinian church, the ideal of Christian culture in the Middle Ages, the character of reform and reformation in the Western church culminating in the Catholic and Protestant Reformations of the sixteenth century, the relation of church and state in American society, and the question of religious authority in a modern secular world. Through this approach, we are introduced to the persons, ideas, and events that shaped Christian history as well as to major themes that give unity to our understanding of that history.

The history of a religion is always more than a record of the past. A religion's history offers insight into the human response to sacred mystery—the attempt, as we have suggested, to mediate between our world and a timeless reality that summons and transforms. For that reason the academic study of religion uses what can be called a *diachronic* approach which finds in the historical narratives of religious experience evidence of the human response to sacred mystery. The approach in Part III of the text, however, presents Christianity *synchronically*, as if in a moment of time without reference to historical influences. A major focus of this approach is *religious tradition*, with the rites and symbols that have been faithfully and authoritatively transmitted to and received by religious communities that find in those rites and symbols access to sacred mystery. For our purposes we speak of two broadly defined forms of Christianity and discuss individual church traditions as expressions of one or the other of those forms. In Chapter 10 we investigate the diversity of religious perspective and practice of the church traditions of Catholic Christianity; in Chapter 11 we look at the unity and diversity within Protestant Christianity. The concluding Chapter 12 gives us an opportunity to evaluate some of the new forms Christianity is taking as a result of new challenges and circumstances in the world today. From within its churches, for example, we hear voices of Christian women and Christian peoples of the Third World. From without, religious peoples of non-Christian faiths challenge the Christian traditions with the paradox with which we began, the challenge of preserving loyalty to one's own tradition without sacrificing openness to others with whom the globe is shared.

REVIEW AND REFLECTION

1. What implications do religious and cultural diversity have for the academic study of religion?
2. Describe the approach to religion that we recommend and indicate how it is possible to balance the needs of openness and fairness and personal commitment.
3. Explain what was meant when we said that sacred mystery is at the heart of religion.
4. Summarize the features of religion in our definition of religion.
5. How did we use our discussion of religion in general to talk about the Christian religion?

END NOTES

1. Jaroslav Pelikan, *Jesus Through the Centuries: His Place in the History of Culture* (New Haven and London: Yale University Press, 1985), pp. 221–222.

2. Papers of the conference have been collected and edited by Donald G. Dawe and John B. Carman in the volume, *Christian Faith in a Religiously Plural World* (Maryknoll, NY: Orbis Books, 1978).

3. Minor Lee Rogers proposed this idea in his introduction to Dawe and Carman, eds., *Christian Faith in a Religiously Plural World,* pp. 5ff.

4. Wilfred Cantwell Smith explores the affirmative of this question in "Is the Qur'an the Word of God?" found in Willard G. Oxtoby, ed., *Religious Diversity: Essays by Wilfred Cantwell Smith* (New York, Hagerstown, San Francisco, London: Harper & Row, Publishers, 1976).

5. Walker Percy, *The Moviegoer* (New York: Farrar, Straus and Giroux, 1960), p. 11.

6. Norman Perrin and Dennis C. Duling, *The New Testament: An Introduction,* 2nd ed. (New York: Harcourt, Brace, Jovanovich, Publishers, 1982), p. 245.

7. Rudolph Otto, *The Idea of the Holy,* 2nd. ed., trans. John W. Harvey (Oxford, London, and New York: Oxford University Press, 1971), p. 28.

8. Smart, Ninian and Richard D. Hecht, eds. *Sacred Texts of the World: A Universal Anthology,* (New York: The Crossroad Publishing Company, 1982), p. 236.

SUGGESTED FURTHER READING

BARRACLOUGH, GEOFFREY. *The Christian World: A Social and Cultural History*. New York: Harry N. Abrams, 1981.

CHIDESTER, DAVID. *Patterns of Action: Religion and Ethics in a Comparative Perspective*. Belmont, CA: Wadsworth Publishing Company, 1987.

CLEBSCH, WILLIAM A. *Christianity in European History*. New York: Oxford University Press, 1979.

JONES, CHESLYN, GEOFFREY WAINWRIGHT, and EDWARD YARNOLD, eds. *The Study of Spirituality*. New York and Oxford: Oxford University Press, 1986.

LATOURETTE, KENNETH SCOTT. *A History of Christianity*. rev. ed. by Ralph D. Winter. New York: Harper & Row, Publishers, 1975.

MAGILL, FRANK N. and IAN P. MCGREAL, eds. *Christian Spirituality: The Essential Guide to the Most Influential Spiritual Writings of the Christian Tradition*. San Francisco: Harper & Row, Publishers, 1988.

MARTY, MARTIN E. *A Short History of Christianity*. Cleveland and New York: Meridan Books, The World Publishing Company, 1959.

MANSCHRECK, CLYDE L. *A History of Christianity in the World: From Persecution to Uncertainty*. Englewood Cliffs, NJ: Prentice-Hall, Inc. 1974.

PELIKAN, JAROSLAV. *The Christian Tradition: A History of the Development of Christian Doctrine*. Chicago: University of Chicago Press, 1971–1989.

PELIKAN, JAROSLAV. *Jesus through the Centuries: His Place in the History of Culture*. New Haven and London: Yale University Press, 1985.

SMART, NINIAN. *In Search of Christianity*. New York: Harper & Row, 1979.

WIGGINS, JAMES B. and ROBERT S. ELLWOOD. *Christianity: A Cultural Perspective*. Prentice-Hall Series in World Religions. Englewood Cliffs, NJ: Prentice Hall, Inc., 1988.

2 | The Christian World View in Comparative Perspective

INTRODUCTION

The idea of *world view* is familiar to most of us, though we usually use it in connection with points of view that differ from our own. By world view, we have in mind those basic convictions that a person or a people have about the world. We usually don't refer to our own world view for the simple reason that the axial principles shaping the way we think about reality are so much a part of our way of seeing that we take them for granted. But even this tells us something about world view. The axial assumptions on which all our other views turn are for the most part taken for granted and are rarely, if ever, subject to examination.

It is our purpose here to discuss only the world view of Christians, a task that on the surface admittedly appears impossible. After all, there is to be found among Christians of different historical periods and cultural backgrounds seemingly irreconcilable differences on fundamental matters of belief and practice. Yet the diverse traditions of *normative Christianity* are understandably Christian and make sense within a common horizon of religious value and meaning. Within the horizon of normative Christianity, for example, the different Christian traditions all regard the time of Jesus and the first-century church as a sacred time with special importance for belief, worship, and practice. It is to this time that Christians trace their central symbols, rituals, and stories. And it is to this time that we need to look for the basic elements of the Christian world view.

Christianity's Jewish Heritage—Key Dates

DATES	EVENT
2nd millennium B.C.E.	Babylonian *Enuma elish* (or Epic of Creation) about the world's creation and the origin of human beings
c. 2000 B.C.E.	epic poem *Gilgamesh*, a Babylonian myth containing a story of the flood
c. 2000–1500 B.C.E.	Abraham and the patriachal age
c. 1200 B.C.E.	Moses, the Exodus from Egypt, the Sinai Covenant
1000–922 B.C.E.	time of Israel's great kings: David and Solomon; the building of the first Temple by Solomon
621 B.C.E.	Josiah's reform; Israel's covenant renewal
587/6 B.C.E.	Jerusalem falls to the Babylonians; the Temple is destroyed; the period of Israel's exile begins; age of Israel's great prophets
538 B.C.E.	the edict of Cyrus allowing the Jews to return to Palestine
520–515 B.C.E.	the second temple is built
c. 400 B.C.E.	the Torah (i.e. Pentateuch) accepted as authoritative
168–164 B.C.E.	Maccabean revolt; rededication of the temple defiled by order of Antiochus IV; the Book of Daniel and its apocalyptic hope reflects this period
c. 180 B.C.E.	writings called the Prophets accepted as authoritative
1st century C.E.	the third section of Hebrew Scripture known as Writings accepted
90 C.E.	the Council of Jamnia (or Jabneh), establishes the standard Jewish canon

A second important source for our discussion of Christianity's fundamental beliefs and values is found in the Old Testament. The first Christian Scripture, these writings which Christians adopted from Judaism tell of the formative experiences and sacred history of the ancient Jewish nation called Israel. Above all else, this ancient Scripture records Israel's experience of God. It was this experience of God as Lord of history and creation that Christians interpreted anew in the light of their own experience of Jesus of Nazareth. In Jesus, they held, God was manifest in a decisive way and his purpose for creation was made known once and for all time. Yet the God Christians worship as the Father of Jesus Christ is worshipped also as the same God who made known his purposes to Abraham and Moses—Israel's God of creation and the covenant. And so what is true of this God is true also of the Christian experience of God and of the Christian belief regarding the world of his making.

And it is for this reason in particular that we give special attention to the creation story of Genesis. This account—which scholarly consensus takes to be, in fact, the work of two anonymous writers called the *Priestly Writer* and the *Yahwist*—gives us in brief narrative form the essential biblical understanding of nature, time, self, society, and human evil. Yet, like all else, the creation story is filtered through the Christian experience of Jesus, and this experience will guide our world-view analysis.

CHRISTIAN UNDERSTANDING OF GOD

God and the World

What we do reflects what we believe. The reason is not difficult to discover. We behave in conformity with our understanding of reality. This is true of individuals and societies. It is true of religious communities. And it was true of the Christians whose lives we glimpse in the earliest Christian writings, the letters of the apostle Paul. In his famous first letter to the Corinthians, Paul was responding to reports concerning, among other things, conduct that he thought inconsistent with Christian love and disruptive of the community's unity. He expressed earnest concern about the ethical indifference of a "spiritual" elite who believed themselves above the moral regulations governing other so-called weaker brethren. One man, contrary to law, boasted of living with his stepmother; others went to Corinth's notorious houses of prostitution; still others ate meat sacrifices offered to pagan gods. Others of the Corinthians adopted *asceticism*, and they taught a sexual abstinence that extended even to husbands and wives. What is puzzling is the essentially negative image of material existence implied in the conduct of the libertines and the ascetics. It is puzzling because Christianity accepted the Hebrew doctrine of the goodness of creation. And so the question arises: How was it that certain members of the church in that Greek city arrived at such different conclusions about the gospel that Paul had taught them? Had they simply misunderstood Paul when he opposed the spirit to the law? Had his teaching about grace encouraged moral license? Could Paul's view of celibacy and the single life in service of God's Kingdom be interpreted as an endorsement of an ascetic contempt of the body? We may not be in the position to answer these questions, but one thing is clear. A version of salvation that set the spirit in opposition to the world and the body had serious ramifications for the fundamental Christian affirmations about God, the world, and the self. A doctrine of salvation that called into question the essential goodness of creation made doubtful the goodness or power of the God whom Christians worshipped as Creator.

Normative Christianity's understanding of God and the world met with an even more serious challenge during the second century from *Gnosticism* and *Marcionism*. According to the syncretistic religious movement known as Gnosticism, the world originated with a precosmic disaster and the tragic imprisonment of particles of divine light—the stuff of human souls—in material bodies. Confined in bodies and living in an alien world created by an inferior creator or demiurge, these divine sparks remained in a state of forgetfulness, waiting for a revealer-redeemer to awaken them through a secret, mystical knowledge or gnosis to the possibility of escape from the material world. Some forms of Gnosticism were openly hostile to Christianity, others thought of Christ as a Gnostic redeemer. But in either case Gnostics did not conceive of salvation as a transformation of creation. They thought of it rather as the soul's liberation and flight from the world.

The Roman Christian Marcion posed a similar, and in many ways more serious threat to Christianity. Like the Gnostics, Marcion thought of reality in dualistic terms, as divided between flesh and spirit. In his teaching, the God of the Old Testament was an inferior creator—a demiurge who created the world and a lawgiver who ruled it arbitrarily. As for the relation or resemblance of the demiurge of Genesis and the true God and Father of Christ, there was none. In Marcion's view, Christ was not tainted by the flesh, not born a man, not subject in any way to the dominion of the Creator. He had descended from the true God, moved as a phantom on earth, revealed God's purpose to deliver humans from the power of the demiurge, and through grace promised to establish men and women in a spiritual kingdom above. The church's belief that Christ was born of Mary and that there is a resurrection of the body were, according to Marcion, misrepresentations or falsehoods.

By repudiating the beliefs central to the Hebrew Scripture, Marcion perhaps presented Christianity with its most serious challenge. At one level, of course, his proposal to substitute Christian writers for ancient Jewish ones was not unreasonable in view of the fact that Christianity had already begun a process of adaptation to Hellenistic culture, values, and thought. Yet, at a level that the church may only have become aware of in the crucible of controversy, the challenge went to the heart of Christianity's understanding of the sacred mystery as revealed in relation to the world of time and space and in the person of Jesus of Nazareth. At question in the confusion and controversy that embroiled the early Christians was its basic understanding of the relation between creation and redemption.

Biblical Account of Creation

There are a great many different creation stories among the world's religions, nor do all of them conceive of creation and redemption as one activity. In the African myth of Uganda, for example, the high god Kabezya-Mpnugu creates the sky and the earth and two human beings and then announces that he will hide himself "so that Man can no longer see me." Among the Torajanese of Indonesia, the sky god Puang Matua is angered by the thief of his flint and breaks the stone stairway leading to his abode. And so the first humans were cut off from access to the Creator who thus became removed from ordinary life on the earth. Yet, when we turn to the biblical world, we see that even its word for creation—*bara*—serves to describe both the making of the world and divine activity in history and in the affairs of human beings. In the biblical world,

> The Lord is the everlasting God,
>   the Creator of the ends of the earth.
> He does not faint or grow weary,
>   his understanding is unsearchable.
> He gives power to the faint,
>   and to him who has no might he increases strength. (Isaiah 40:27–29)

In these verses Isaiah echoes the first chapter of Genesis where God is presented as a transcendent being whose power is without challenge or limitation. There is no need for this Creator to subdue primal chaos as the Babylonian creator Marduk had to conquer the sea serpent Tiamat in order to fabricate a world. Nor is there a concern in the biblical story that the primal material might be difficult to work with as it was in the creation story of Plato's *Timaeus*. In the beginning of Genesis, we hear of the spirit of God moving over the waters of the deep and of the effortless speaking of the divine word: "Let there be." By divine fiat, the primal waters submit, the heavens appear above, the earth below; and on successive days the earth brings forth plants, the waters teem with sea creatures, the air multiplies with birds and likewise the land with plants and animals. And all this world God blesses with a blessing of fertility: "Be fruitful and multiply" (Genesis 1:22).

More prominent in Isaiah, however, is the emphasis on the personal, caring presence of holy reality—a theme that is also central to the New Testament and the teachings of the Jesus. Familiar, for example, is Jesus' saying: "Look at the birds of the air . . . Consider the lilies of the field, how they grow; they neither toil nor spin; yet I tell you, even Solomon in all his glory was not arrayed like one of these. But if God so clothes the grass of the field, which today is alive and tomorrow is thrown into the oven, will he not much more clothe you, O men of little faith?" (Matthew 6:26–30) What is interesting about Jesus' sayings is that the unity of creation and redemption is so much taken for granted that they appear almost to be one rather than two themes.

God is the creative source of the world and all its creatures, but what is basic to the biblical perspective is that God's creative activity is not exhausted in a single act of origination. The ultimate source of existence is believed also to be a sustaining, even a solicitous reality, concerned for the continued well-being of creation. The God who calls the world into being in six days is the same God who delivers the Hebrews from slavery in Egypt and forms them into a people in the wilderness. And for Christians the God of Genesis is the same God whose purpose and concern for creation were revealed conclusively in the person of Jesus of Nazareth. According to the Gospel of John, Jesus is in fact the very incarnation of the creative Word uttered in the beginning. "In the beginning"—John wrote in the prologue of his Gospel.

> In the beginning was the Word [Logos], and the Word was with God, and the Word was God. He was in the beginning with God; all things were made through him, and without him was not anything made that was made. . . . And the Word became flesh and dwelt among us, full of grace and truth; we have beheld his glory, glory as of the only Son from the Father. (John 1:1–3, 14)

The God whom Christians worship and who was revealed in the person of Jesus of Nazareth is at once the source and salvation of creation. And we might say of his attributes what the great English mystic Julian of Norwich said: "The first is that God made [the world], the second is that he loves it, and the third is that God preserves it."

THE CREATED WORLD

Christian View of Nature

The idea of nature is not as prominent in Christianity as in many of the other great religions of the world. Not that Christianity assigns no value or importance to the physical world or material existence. The puritanical John Calvin sees God's glory in the immensity, symmetry, and beauty of the universe. "Wherever you cast your eye," he writes, "there is no particle of the world in which some sparks at least of His glory cannot be observed to shine." In the *Canticle of Brother Sun*, the ascetic Saint Francis of Assisi praises God through creation and addresses the moon as sister, the wind as brother, and at his last hour he greeted Sister Death. The Orthodox theologian Gregory Palamas spoke of the "blessed passions" and held that the body like the soul experiences the uncreated divine light and like the soul is the source of sanctification. Christians worship with bread and wine and with oil, wax, and incense. And, though the Christian drama is anchored in time and history, nature's seasonal progression is assimilated to the Christian calendar and the cycle of the liturgical year.

English Archbishop William Temple accurately observed of Christianity that it is "the most avowedly materialistic of all the great religions." Certainly, this is true when comparing it with the religions of India. The Christian attitude toward the physical world exhibits none of the Buddhist rejection of the senses. There is nothing in Christian art quite comparable to the great statue of the seated Buddha of Gandhara dating from the third century of the *common era* (henceforth C.E.; *before the common era*, B.C.E.). Legs folded in the yoga position, back erect, eyes closed, senses shut to the world, mind turned inward, the stone Buddha teaches suspicion of what is seen and heard. By contrast, the Christian view, rooted in Genesis, sees nature as integral to the divine purpose and as a sign of divine generosity. And, based on a belief in the Incarnation, the Christian view even assigns nature a positive role in the drama of salvation.

Yet, however positive nature's role in biblical religion, reverence for nature is not a characteristic Christian attitude. Just as one finds no real analogues to contemplative Buddhas in Christian sculpture, Christian culture produced nothing quite comparable to the portrayals of nature encountered in the familiar Chinese ink-on-silk landscapes of mountains, trees, clouds, and water. These paintings invest nature with an aura of mystery. In and behind nature one senses a divine principle—the Chinese call this Tao—from which the myriad of things arise, a primordial, though by no means menacing, reality before which humans appear small and inconspicuous. To be sure, Christian mystics discover in nature vestiges of

God. Saint Bonaventure affirmed that in "the things that are made" one sees clearly "the invisible things of God." Nevertheless, even the mystics refrain from going beyond Genesis's presentation of the world's dependency on a transcendent, self-sufficient, and independent Creator who is the true referent of glory and mystery. And, as bearers of the divine image, humans also enjoy authority over the natural world. They are expressly charged by the Creator to "fill the earth and subdue it" (Genesis 1:28) and are given permission to enjoy its bounty. The aspiration to equilibrium and harmony with nature so prevalent in Chinese religion was never a dominant theme where Christianity's influence prevailed. In the Christian world, the human—not the natural—is the central concern expressed in art, literature, philosophy, and science.

Though nature is valued and enjoyed, it is of value not because of any intrinsic good that it might possess. In biblical perspective, nature's worth derives in part from its usefulness for satisfying human need, in part from its stability as a reliable context for human life and work. In these emphases too, the biblical story stands in bold relief to the creation stories of other religions and their surrounding cultures. Humans are not made to serve the gods as they are in the Babylonian creation epic, the *Enuma elish*, nor is nature thought to teeter on the brink of chaos, which, like the Babylonian sea serpent Tiamat, threatens to draw the world back into itself. In what may have been a deliberate demythologizing of this popular Near Eastern myth, the writer of Genesis neutralizes the myth's principle of chaos and writes simply that, "The earth was without form and void, and darkness was upon the face of the deep" (Genesis 1:2). Mention is even made of "the great sea monsters" (Genesis 1:21) in what may well be an oblique reference to the sea serpent of Near Eastern myth, though here the sea monsters are but one of many fish that fill the sea. And, as a culminating act, the Genesis writer confers authority for the natural order on humans as a blessing: "Be fruitful and multiply, and fill the earth and subdue it; and have dominion over the birds of the air and over the fish of the sea and over every living thing that moves upon the earth" (Genesis 1:28). We may infer that in part the human transcendence of nature is what is meant by the human likeness to God.

Early in Christian history, however, an essentially unbiblical suspicion of the body and human sexuality gained ascendency in Christian thought and culture through the influence in particular of the great North African theologian Augustine of Hippo. Much later, the sixteenth-century Elizabethan poet Edmund Spenser summarized in a line of poetry what for centuries had been a prevailing Christian understanding of the fall: "In the flesh at first the guilt committed was." Spenser did not doubt that God was the sovereign source of the material world, yet he was convinced that, if there was a primal sea serpent that bore watching, surely it was female sexuality. But Spenser's denunciation of sexuality was moderate, no doubt because his career depended in large measure on the good favor of a woman, England's Queen Elizabeth I. Augustine was less reserved in naming the cause of sin. "I know of nothing," wrote Augustine of Hippo, "which brings the manly mind down from the heights more than a woman's caresses and that joining of bodies without which one cannot have a wife." Encouraged by Augustine and other early Christian writers, an antifemale tradition took root in medieval thought and theology, in a popular hysteria over witches, and in religious practice. We can even see Augustine's view of sin and sexuality having an influence on the rise and popularity of monasticism as the surest path to heaven. So influential, in fact, was the ideal of celibacy that we find that even the doughty Sir Lancelot of King Arthur's Round Table renounced his amour, Arthur's Queen Guinevere, as a condition of the quest and a mystical vision of the holy grail. Yet Christian asceticism was not fully able to subvert the biblical doctrine of creation. Even the Christian Middle Ages thought of asceticism as a measure not for liberating the soul from the body but only of disciplining the body in the service of the soul.

Christian View of Time

Just as different religions conceive nature differently, so the world's religions have differing understandings of time and human existence in time. Religions of the East like Buddhism, for example, think of time as a series of impermanent, short-lived states with no ultimate meaning. And they teach that salvation is a freeing of the soul from its entanglement in temporal existence. Yet Christianity, like Judaism from which it sprung, discovers sacred meaning within the unfolding drama of human history and in connection with concrete historical events. Christians believe that salvation is from a God who is revealed in connection with the saga of the Old Testament patriarchs and again at the time of the Exodus and in the affairs of the nation of Israel. But what differentiates Christianity from Judaism is that Christians also teach that God entered human history as the person Jesus of Nazareth in order to restore the created world and deliver human beings once and for all from the evil that besets their existence. According to John's Gospel, God's eternal Word, the divine *Logos*, "became flesh and dwelt among us, full of grace and truth" (John 1:14). Luke's Gospel is more circumstantial than John's in situating Jesus' birth and the drama of the *Incarnation* within a definite historical and geographical horizon. Luke's gospel story begins:

> In those days a decree went out from Caesar Augustus that all the world should be enrolled. This was the first enrollment, when Quirinius was governor of Syria. And all went to be enrolled, each to his own city. And Joseph

also went up from Galilee, from the city of Nazareth, to Judea, to the city of David, which is called Bethlehem, because he was of the house and lineage of David, to be enrolled with Mary, his bethrothed, who was with child. And while they were there, the time came for her to be delivered. And she gave birth to her first-born son and wrapped him in swaddling cloths, and laid him in a manger, because there was no place for them in the inn. (Luke 2:1–7)

If we study just John's Gospel, we might conclude that the Christian teaching of the Incarnation was but another variation on an important theme in the history of religions. Here, it might be thought, is but another instance of the descent and incarnation of the god, a pattern familiar in the popular devotional Hindu text, the *Bhagavadgita*. There we read of the miraculous appearing of Krishna, the incarnation of the great god Vishnu, to the epic's troubled hero, Arjuna. Krishna, we are told, comes "into being age after age to offer protection to the good, destroy evildoers, and establish justice." We find this pattern also among the Gnostics of whom we spoke earlier. The Gnostic revealer appears in the world like Krishna to impart spiritual wisdom and then returns again to the supratemporal realm. Pictured in this manner in the Gnostic *Gospel of Thomas*, Jesus appears in human form, teaches a divine wisdom, summons souls trapped in material bodies to a heavenly destiny, and then ascends once more to the world of spirit.

Yet this pattern of the god or Gnostic revealer who enters the phenomenal world while remaining untouched by it, does not fit the New Testament picture of Jesus. As we have already seen, Luke anchors the birth narratives in geography and external history. Matthew provides Jesus a genealogy and a history—relating him to the Davidic kings and still farther back in Israel's history to Abraham. And John's Gospel, in spite of its similarity in important respects to the narratives of the Gnostic revealer, recounts the career of a real person and a savior whose exaltation was most clearly manifest at the moment of his suffering and death. For John, as for the synoptic Gospels, the meaning of Jesus' life and mission is revealed amidst—not apart from—the risk and vicissitudes of temporal existence.

Early in its development, therefore, Christianity sought to differentiate its teaching of the descending Logos from the idea of a redeemer whose appearance in the world was essentially untouched by the conditions of earthly existence in time and the body. The Christian view of time differed also from the Greek notion that temporal existence is devoid of enduring meaning or significance. [1] And, though Christianity went a long way in accommodating its thought to Greek and Roman philosophy, the Platonic opinion that time is ephemeral and the aristocratic Stoic idea that temporal existence is a dreary repetition of itself were only to color Christianity's biblical understanding of history. They were not, however, to alter the basic belief that history is the arena of a drama of ultimate significance. It was in connection with great historical events: with the Exodus, the constitution of Israel as God's chosen nation, the conquest of Canaan, the foundation of Israel's monarchy, even the destruction of the nation at the hand of the Babylonians, that God's eternal purpose was revealed. And it was in "the fullness of time" that God made plain his purpose to rescue creation. That rescue, Christians believe, was announced in the gospel of Jesus Christ.

Those early Christians believed that here was the turning point of human time, the key in fact that unlocked the meaning of all history, the sacred history of the Jews and the secular history of the gentiles. And it seemed to these Christians, as a logical extension of this belief, quite natural to look to the Hebrew Bible and to the ancient Hebrew experience recorded there for signs and prefigurations of the Christ whom they worshipped. Since Christ is the end of Scripture, as the church reasoned, Scripture speaks of Christ. It speaks of Christ symbolically with types or figures. The prophets and the Psalms spoke of him; the great events that shaped Israel's history beginning with the Exodus were shadows of Christ's life and work. The early Christian biblical exegete Melito of Sardis, for example, saw in the slaying of Abel, the binding of Isaac for sacrifice, and the suffering of the prophets the prefiguration of Christ's suffering and sacrifice. And he discerned in the events of the Old Testament a shadow of things that were perfectly accomplished by Christ. Jonah's being swallowed by the great fish prefigured Christ's entombment typologically, and the lamb's blood on the doors that spared the Hebrews of the Exodus from the Angel of Death announced in advance of the Incarnation Christ's blood that rescues sinners from death.

Using an interpretative method known as *typology* to discover in Jewish Scripture a foreshadowing of the New Testament, Christians soon made the Hebrew Bible a Christian one. Christians made Israel's understanding of history a Christian heritage as well. Those Christian theologians whom Christians call *Apologists* sought to assimilate secular history and thought into Christian truth much as Christianity's early biblical exegetes turned Hebrew Scripture into Christianity's Old Testament. The Apologists accomplished this by demonstrating that what the ancient philosophers believed about an eternal wisdom—a divine Logos—had become a historical reality in Jesus, the Logos made flesh. Thus Justin Martyr, one of the most famous of the Christian apologists, argued that the Platonists knew the Christian Logos as a creative World-Soul; the Stoics knew the Logos as a divine Reason permeating all reality. In these forms, Justin believed, even the ancient poets and philosophers held in esteem the truth now fully revealed in the Christian savior. It was by this means too that Justin was able to show that even secular history anticipates and is fulfilled in the obscure life of a Jewish carpenter who was crucified during the reign of Tiberius.

It is one of the significant facts of Western civilization that this view—of Christ as Alpha and Omega, the beginning and end, the point on which human history converges—prevailed not only among Christians but was triumphant in the ancient Roman world where it gained enduring formulation as a Christian philosophy of history in Augustine's *City of God* (c. 413–426). This Christian belief that history's meaning is to be discovered in the life and ministry of Jesus of Nazareth even prompted Christians to create a new calendar. Counting years from "Our Lord's Incarnation" (A.D., *anno Domini*), the sixth-century Scythian monk Dionysius Exiguus devised a way of numbering years still in use.

The Christian view of history had one further important consequence. It assumed that humans are essentially historical creatures and that existence in time is the appropriate context of human existence. Augustine put it very well in his famous *Confessions* (c. 397). There he said that God caused time to have a beginning and "man, whom He had previously made, He made in time [and] gave him existence in time." And for biblical faith, existence in time is primarily thought of as a faithfulness directed toward a promised future. It is perhaps for this reason that Abraham is so often taken to be the Christian exemplar of faith lived in hope. In the biblical account Abraham certainly does not stand as a model of faith because of character, courage, or heroic deed. Abraham and his wife Sarah are people of faith because they believe in God's promise of a future blessing. To put it another way, Abraham and Sarah are people of faith because they know that "what [God] has said he will do." [2] Yet their confidence does not remove the uncertainty and ambiguity of historical existence. The biblical story has them journeying toward a future promise dogged at every step by the perennial human problem of doubt and uncertainty and "fear and anxiety."

THE IMAGE OF GOD

The Christian View of Self

Visitors to the Sistine Chapel of the Vatican Palace see on the chapel's ceiling the work of one of the great artists of the Renaissance. There Michelangelo Buonarroti covered an area of approximately fourteen yards by forty with 343 separate figures representing scenes from Genesis. Many believe that the most arresting of those scenes is that of Adam's Creation.

The recumbent Adam, with a body remarkable for beauty and grace, stretches a hand upward so that a raised finger almost touches the extended finger of God. One almost feels the creative power pass between the figures.

Undoubtedly, here is a vivid and penetrating interpretation of the Christian view of the human self. Here is a creature—according to Genesis 1, an androgynous figure inclusive of both male and female—whose essential nature is revealed in relation to the divine. [3] As Michelangelo's Adam with finger extended but not touching the divine finger, the human is raised toward its creative source and mirrors the divine glory. Yet the story, like Michelangelo's image in oil, envisions a distance between creature and Creator. How different from this Christian perspective is the view of Upanishadic Hinduism that ultimate mystery is discoverable within the self, that Atman (the true self) is but an interior aspect of Brahman (universal Spirit). Equally alien to the biblical world view was the ancient Babylonians' belief that humans were the afterthought of the gods, destined in the cosmic scheme for subservience to divine beings. Genesis imagines instead a divine transcendence without a diminution of the human self or its dignity.

For Christianity, then, humans are unique in creation, creatures mysteriously linked to the ultimate source of mystery on which all existence depends, beings created in the image and likeness of the Creator. And, to the *Psalmist's* question, "What is man that thou art mindful of him?", Christians characteristically have answered as the writer of the eighth Psalm.

> Yet thou hast made him less than God,
>   and dost crown him with glory and honor.
> Thou hast given him dominion over the works of thy hand;
>   thou hast put all things under his feet,
> all sheep and oxen,
>   and also the beasts of the field,
> the birds of the air, and the fish of the sea,
>   whatever passes along the paths of the sea. (Psalm 8:3-7)

Like Michelangelo's Adam at the moment of creation, the Psalmist imagines the human crowned with a glory that suggests both an external beauty and an inward dignity. The prophet Ezekiel also writes that the first humans appeared with "perfect beauty" (Ezekiel 8:12). The Psalmist recognizes too that human life has a sanctity that nature does not have, that the human is clarified in relation to the divine image, while nature's significance appears largely in relation to the sphere of human existence. Finally, the Psalmist, in what is a poetic replica of Genesis 1, connects the image with its consequence, namely, a godlike sovereignty that sets humans apart from and above the natural order. To this, we add the naming of the animals in the Yahwist's creation narrative of Genesis 2 to complete the biblical and Christian conception of the created self. The commission in Genesis 1:19 to have dominion over the animal kingdom transfers God's authority to humans as God's vice-regents on earth. The naming episode represents humans as co-creators, beings endowed with a capacity for language that Adam uses as an instrument for bringing conceptual order to existence and that determines his nature as a social being not only capable of but requiring linguistic relatedness.

As sovereign and creative, the self in Christian perspective is a free agent, responsible for the natural world and capable of making purposive decisions about the future. Yet Christianity has tended not to idealize either human autonomy or human self-sufficiency. Nor have Christians inclined to the view that human freedom is best conceived as the unrestricted exercise of the will. As we have already seen, commission and responsibility are the immediate context of human will in the original, paradisal state for which the first pair were created. Commissioned by the Creator, humans are responsible for the animals, for the cultivation and maintenance of the garden of Eden, and for incorporating, through naming, the animals into the human world. Responsibility, that uniquely human capacity to answer for what one does, in the Hebrew-Christian creation story may even be thought of as the equivalent of the biblical meaning of freedom. We should add too that responsible, purposive work seems to be a condition of the free enjoyment of the garden.

In the Yahwist's account, the only external restriction on human freedom is the divine command: "And the Lord God commanded the man, saying, 'You may freely eat of every tree of the garden; but of the tree of good and evil [the Hebrew equivalent of omniscience] you shall not eat, for in the day that you eat of it you shall die" (Genesis 2:16–17). We will hear more of this commandment in the next section. Here we only want to comment on the possible biblical significance of a prohibition. As a prohibition, of course, the commandment sets boundaries and is restrictive. But from another angle, the commandment establishes a context apart from which the exercise of human freedom would be trivial or pointless. Thus, precisely because the prohibition makes choosing a matter of profound importance, the Yahwist's paradise—which is remarkable for its difference from the gardens of sensual pleasure and ease of other ancient oriental paradisal myths—assumes a heightened seriousness. Finally, the prohibition of the forbidden tree situates the human will in a direct and personal relation to the divine will. This, of course, explains in part the significance biblical religions attach not only to obedience but also to personal loyalty in human dealings with God.

Biblical scholars, with the prohibitive commandment of Genesis 2 in mind, have held, in fact, that the question of this garden narrative consists in obedience and loyalty and that the essential meaning of being human in relation to God is revealed in the unfolding drama of loyalty and disloyalty to God, the divine commandments, and the covenant of Sinai. It is important, of course, that our modern, post-Enlightenment view of the individual as self-legislating is not allowed to prejudice our appreciation of the biblical world where obedience does not entail either passivity or a violation of persons. The biblical notion of obedience is rather related to the ideas of freedom and loyalty and is predicated on a voluntary response to what is right and just. Indeed, in the Old Testament, where authentic humanness manifests itself in an attending and responding to the divine word, the act of obedience perhaps is best conceived as one of hearing.

The biblical heroes of faith are those who obey, who are faithful in "keeping" and "observing," by listening and heeding. God calls and sends; Israel's patriarchs and prophets hear and do. The pattern is simple but characteristic of Scripture where hearing, sending, and doing characterize God's dealing with those whom he chooses. When the patriarch Abraham is tested, God calls him: " 'Abraham!' And he said, 'Here am I.' He said, 'Take your son, your only son Isaac, whom you love, and go to the land of Moriah, and offer him there as a burnt offering upon one of the mountains of which I shall tell you' " (Genesis 22:1–2). When Moses is charged to go to Egypt to bring the Hebrews forth from bondage, he hears a call from the burning bush: " 'Moses, Moses!' And he said, 'Here I am.' " "Come, I will send you to Pharaoh that you may bring forth my people, the sons of Israel, out of Egypt" (Exodus 2:4, 10). And, when Isaiah in a vision before the throne of God receives his prophetic commission, a voice speaks to him: " 'Whom shall I send, and who will go for us?' Then I said, 'Here I am. Send me' " (Isaiah 6:8). Go, send, do—the pattern is repeated in the New Testament as well, as when Paul on the road to Damascus is addressed by a heavenly voice: " 'Saul, Saul, why do you persecute me?' And he said, 'Who are you, Lord?' And he said, 'I am Jesus, whom you are persecuting; but rise and enter the city, and you will be told what you are to do' " (Acts 9:4–6).

Common to all these commissioning episodes is the assumption that knowledge of God is not discovered in nature or within the self but is revealed in a personal relationship with God and accompanies a knowledge of one's own vocation or calling to "walk" in God's ways. The balance or equilibrium essential for genuine humanness in Taoism becomes in Judaism and Christianity a perfection of the human will in harmony with God's will. For Judaism, that balancing of will is fulfilled most perfectly in loyalty to the divine covenant and in the obedient observance of the Torah. In the New Testament, Christian vocation is inseparably connected with Jesus Christ whose life of spontaneous and humble obedience to God's will prompts Paul to identify him as the New Creation, the Second Adam, and the true likeness of God.

For Christianity, "to be conformed to the image of the Son" (Romans 8:28) is the profoundest meaning of obedience and the truest sense of humanness. We perhaps need to remind ourselves at this point that Christianity, beginning with its struggle against the Gnostics, resists the tendency to individualize this central religious insight at the expense of its social content. In normative Christian belief, humans are essentially—and not incidentally—social and are destined, according to the creation narratives of Genesis, for personal relatedness. Imitation of Christ, therefore, means the exercise of freedom within community and above all on behalf of others in service and selfless love. As the Christian ethicist Paul Ramsey summarizes it, "existence within the image of God is the same as existence for another."

The Human Condition

We examined the axial assumptions basic to the Christian world view and found that the Christian understanding of nature, time, and the self is intimately related to the Christian view of ultimate mystery. We have seen in particular that the Hebrew-Christian account of origins conceived of that relationship as one of dependency in relation to a transcendent creator of the world. Even the human creature, though more nearly like the Creator in freedom and in a self-transcendence evident in the human capacity for responsible choice, creativity, and personal relatedness, was thought of in terms of creaturely dependency. Acknowledgment of this dependency in the Old Testament was expressed as Israel's covenant fidelity and in the New Testament as a conformity to Christ whose perfect, spontaneous responsiveness to God's will established the conditions of a new covenant. We have seen too that the idea of creation affirms not only the reality of finite existence in relation to a transcendent Creator but its essential goodness. Before the fall of Adam and Eve, the Bible posits no evil. Nature harbors no secret, hidden malevolence; time holds only the promise of fulfillment for a creature whose very freedom is a summons to the future. How then do Christians account for the fact of evil and what might be called the *unsatisfactoriness* of the human condition?

Since death and immortality are prominent in Christian thinking, one answer might be that time itself is the source of the unsatisfactoriness that troubles the human spirit. In an earlier part of this chapter, we observed that the Greek and Roman philosophers did in fact think of temporal existence as problematic. Time overcomes all things in its everlasting coming into being and passing away, and wisdom for those ancient sages was the despising of everything that perishes. More poignantly still, the ancient ~~Sumerian~~ *Akkadian* *Epic of Gilgamesh* portrays death as a threat to life and its fundamental meanings. In the epic, the hero-king's companion and friend, Enkidu, dies, and his dying pierces Gilgamesh to the heart with terror. "How can I rest," as the epic's central theme runs, "how can I be at peace? Despair is in my heart. What my brother [Enkidu] is now, that shall I be when I am dead." Here is not the philosopher's calm meditation on time. The epic lays bare the fact of death and decay as an inescapable human reality. Though its hero initially denies this fact, Enkidu's putrefying flesh forces Gilgamesh to relinquish his friend to the earth. And, though Gilgamesh sets out in search of immortality, the hero's quest ends in despair, and the epic concludes on a note of resignation.

Yet these answers, in spite of their philosophical appeal or existential power, do not typically characterize normative Christianity's attitude toward existence. For one thing, the Christian doctrine of creation, based on the Hebrew creation narratives of Genesis, affirms the positive character of both material and temporal existence. And, though Christianity regards death as a serious problem, Christians point neither to time nor to nature to explain death's meaning. The New Testament rather treats death and other related ills of mortality as merely symptomatic, a consequence— not a cause—of the primeval disobedience in Eden. What Christianity regards as most profoundly problematic about human existence is not death but the estrangement of Creator and creation caused by a human failure to keep God's commandment. The Christian word for this condition is sin. And yet this word itself translates a variety of meanings for Christians, everything from the vaudevillian personification of the Seven Deadly Sins in medieval morality plays to the philosophically sophisticated conception of sin as the privation of good. In the New Testament, sin often translates the idea of "missing the mark," a falling short of what the law requires which Jesus summarized as the great commandment to love God and the neighbor (Mark 12:29–31).

As far back as Augustine's *Confessions*, Christians have attempted to penetrate the mystery of evil and the causes of sin. Yet most Christians agree that attempts to penetrate the mystery of evil and the origination of sin must start with Genesis and the story of Adam's fall. The plot of the narrative is simple and familiar. Having been prohibited the tree of the knowledge of good and evil, Adam and Eve are tempted by a serpent to eat of its fruit. Then, overcome with shame, the couple hide themselves from God's sight, are found out, endeavor to shift the blame for their disobedience (the man to the woman and the woman to the serpent), are rebuked by the Creator, and, in spite of the transgression and before they are sent forth from paradise, are given garments of skin in what may well have been a sign of God's concern for human well-being.

Perhaps the simplicity of the story explains its power; its subtlety in presenting human motivation accounts for its appeal to writers and poets since the beginnings of European literature. We might add to these qualities the Yahwist's unflinching realism when it comes to assessing the circumstance and the nature of sin. According to this narrative, humans are made to bear the responsibility for the transgression against the tabooed tree. The original couple are at fault for this first sin. To be sure, some Christians explain the motivation of sin by favoring a view that the serpent is Satan or an instrument of Satan. Yet, even dualistic explanations of the fall, which see evil as a larger-than-life reality external to the human mind and heart, retain the story's essential concern with human accountability. [4]

In the biblical narrative, the serpent broaches the subject of the forbidden fruit and by shifts of accent and meaning makes the temptation thinkable. Still, it is the human decision to eat of the prohibited fruit that is at issue. Furthermore, it is a free and uncoerced act of disobedience. There is nothing here of the titanic defiance of the gods that we find in Greek myth and in nineteenth-century Romantic poetry. The Yahwist's descriptive account is straightforward, unsensational, and remarkably matter-of-fact: "So when the woman saw that it was good for food, and that it was a delight to the eyes, and that the fruit was to be desired to make one wise, she took of its fruit and ate; and she gave some to her husband, and he ate" (Genesis 3:6). Rather than finding in the episode anything heroic, the narrative emphasizes the scene's banality. Sensual pleasure ("good for food"), aesthetic enjoyment ("a delight to the eye"), and intellectual allure ("desired to make one wise") are allowed to supersede what the biblical writer would have thought of utmost importance, namely, the responsibility of choosing.

Here is no Prometheus of Greek myth, squared off against the great god Zeus. Here is no primal theft, a taking from God what by right or need is essential for human security or well-being or fulfillment. The bold deed of Prometheus in stealing fire from the gods for human use in forging—literally and figuratively—civilization was held to be heroic, Prometheus's punishment by Zeus peevish and unjust. The Yahwist's account of the fall, on the other hand, pictures the Creator's response as moderate and even caring, and Adam's violation as banal. Yet, however banal the motivation, the repercussion of violating the tabooed tree of knowledge is treated as profound—remedied, according to Christianity, only by Jesus' death on the cross.

Again, because Christianity is so diverse, there is a diversity of understanding among Christian traditions, if not about what happened, at least about the meaning of the fall. Orthodox Christianity regards sin and the price of sin in the context of the impermanence and transience of existence. The tragedy of the fall was not just that human life loses its footing in the being of God and teeters on the abyss of the nothingness from whence it came, but the whole of the created world shares in humankind's fated corruptibility. Roman Catholicism, on the other hand, emphasizes the fault. It thinks of sin as an affront to God's moral order. But, whatever differences, most Christian formulas for explaining sin and its consequence take the simple narrative drama of banishment and estrangement of Genesis 3–11 as their point of departure. There we read of Adam's accusation of Eve, of Cain's jealousy of Abel and the first fratricide, of Lamech's revenge boast, of the disorder among the heavenly beings, of Noah and the Flood, of Noah's sons, of the advent of civilization, and of the Tower of Babel. The narrative of these chapters is nothing short of a drama written on a cosmic scale of alienations and the breakup of human community, and of a history propelled by evil impulses that spoil God's creation without satisfying the human need for communion with God and community with the neighbor.

And the gravity with which Christianity regards sin is evident in Paul's classic formulation in Romans where he writes that "sin came into the world through one man and death through sin, and so death spread to all men because all men sinned" (Romans 5:12). It is apparent also in the theological doctrine of *original sin*. The poignancy of the condemnation, however, is nowhere better communicated than in the Yahwist's narrative. According to Genesis 6:5, "The Lord saw that the wickedness of man was great in the earth, and that every imagination of the thoughts of his heart was only evil continually." The "heart" here and elsewhere in the Old Testament is inclusive of intellect and will as well as emotions; nothing essentially human is untouched by sin's original taint nor, according to the New Testament, are any people exempt—"both Jews and Greeks are under the power of sin" (Romans 3:9). Yet, however unpromising is life in the world after the fall and whatever blight mars human existence as a result of what theologians call "original sin," the Christian understanding of sin and the human condition, like its view of creation, is arrived at retrospectively, beginning with the gospel of Christ. And the story of *Paradise Lost* and "the fruit/ Of that forbidden tree, whose mortal taste/ Brought death into the world, and all our woe," as seventeenth-century English poet John Milton put it, is a story of a *felix culpa*, a happy fault, recollected from the perspective of "paradise regained."

SUMMARY

One of the great questions confronting early Christianity was the relationship of Jesus Christ to the Creator of Genesis. Had Christianity decided against the identification of Jesus with the God of the Old Testament, as Marcion wished, Christianity would have been a very different religion. As it turned out, the early church rejected Gnostic and Marcionite versions of the world and salvation. Taking the central elements of its theology from the Old Testament, normative Christianity adopted Judaism's positive evaluation of material reality. Yet, in relation to time, nature is consigned a supporting role in the Christian drama of salvation. For Christianity, time—not nature—is the primary medium of revelation, and history is where God's creative power and sovereignty are most apparent. History is also the appropriate context for human life, for human fulfillment, and for the exercise of human freedom. But the story of salvation, as Christianity tells it, is one not only of freedom's use but of its abuse. As the fall narrative of Genesis makes plain, uncreative choices are evident in the breakdown of trust and communication and in the fragmenting of community. Within the horizon of the Christian world view, this rupturing of community is seen in social terms as the absence of justice and love and in theological terms as disobedience and infidelity. Finally, normative Christianity conceives the meaning of all these separate elements—nature, time, the self, the human condition—in relation to Jesus Christ. Here, it is held, creation converges and is restored. And here in the spontaneous obedient love of Jesus is the meaning of authentic human being.

REVIEW AND REFLECTION

1. What are the basic elements of a world view and what sources do we have for reflecting on the Christian world view?
2. Discuss normative Christianity's view of God and compare it with the theology of Gnosticism and Marcionism.
3. How is the Christian view of God related to its doctrine of creation?
4. In biblical religion nature is neither sacred nor is it hostile to human life. What then is its character as the Priestly Writer pictures it?
5. Christians look to time as the arena of human action and the context of the divine/human encounter. How does this view of time compare with other ancient Near Eastern views of time?
6. How do Christians understand the human self as created in God's image? What importance does this understanding have for their way of conceiving of God's dealing with human beings?
7. Every religion identifies a source or cause for the unsatisfactoriness of human existence. What is the biblical and the Christian understanding of that source or cause?

END NOTES

1. For one of the best discussions of the Christian view of time in relation to other ancient views, see the chapter "Creation and Time" in Langdon Gilkey's *Maker of Heaven and Earth: A Study of the Christian Doctrine of Creation* (Garden City, NY: Doubleday & Company, Inc., 1959).

2. For a full discussion of these ideas, see G. Ernest Wright and Reginald H. Fuller, *The Book of the Acts of God: Contemporary Scholarship Interprets the Bible* (Garden City, NY: Doubleday & Company, Inc., 1957), pp. 67–69. For an excellent presentation of the biblical view of history, see Wright's "Biblical Point of View" in the same volume.

3. For a discussion of gender in the Genesis creation accounts, see Phyllis Trible, "Eve and Adam: Genesis 2–3 Reread" in *Womanspirit Rising: A Feminist Reader in Religion*, eds. Carol P. Christ and Judith Plaskow (San Francisco: Harper & Row, Publishers, 1979).

4. For a discussion of evil and human accountability, see my article "Enchantment and the Banality of Evil," *Religion in Life*, 49, no. 1 (Spring, 1980), pp. 81–95.

SUGGESTED FURTHER READING

ALBRIGHT, WILLIAM FOXWELL. *From the Stone Age to Christianity: Monotheism and the Historical Process*. Garden City, NY: Doubleday & Company, 1957.

ANDERSON, BERNHARD. *Creation Versus Chaos: The Interpretation of Mythical Symbolism in the Bible*. Philadelphia: Fortress Press, 1987.

ANDERSON, BERNHARD W. *Understanding the Old Testament* (3rd ed.), Englewood Cliffs, NJ: Prentice-Hall, Inc., 1975.

BARRETT, CHARLES D. *Understanding the Christian Faith*. Englewood Cliffs, NJ: Prentice-Hall, Inc., 1980.

GILKEY, LANGDON. *Maker of Heaven and Earth*. Garden City, NY: Doubleday & Company, Inc., 1959.

MCFAGUE, SALLIE, *Models of God: Theology for an Ecological, Nuclear Age*. Philadelphia: Fortress Press, 1987.

PAGELS, ELAINE. *Adam, Eve, and the Serpent*. New York: Random House, 1988.

RAD, GERHARD VON. *Genesis: A Commentary*. Philadelphia: The Westminster Press, 1972.

SANDMEL, SAMUEL. *The Enjoyment of Scripture*. New York: Oxford University Press, 1972.

3 | Jesus and the New Testament

Introduction

Religious symbol, story, and ritual are the response to those formative disclosures of the holy known as *hierophanies*. And it is by symbol, story, and ritual that those disclosures are made present again to the believing community or, to put it another way, that the believing community is made contemporary with the sacred time of its beginnings. The evocation of sacred symbols, the recitation of sacred story, and the enactment of sacred ritual, in short, make possible access to the redemptive, emancipating, liberating persons, events, or revelations of its sacred past. Thus, for example, Jews recall and experience anew Exodus deliverance at Passover when Jewish families come together for a special meal, the seder, and hear once more of God's mighty acts in the reading of the Passover Haggadah. As the words recounting the events of Exodus are recited, the years that separate the present community from the time of its ancient Hebrew ancestors are bridged and the redemptive power of Exodus and God's mighty acts become a present reality. [1] Similarly, Christians recollect and ritually represent through proclamation and preaching and liturgy and sacrament the meaning of God's mighty act of deliverance in Jesus of Nazareth.

In its primitive form this Christian story speaks of Jesus of Nazareth, whose "mighty works and wonders and signs" and above all whose death and resurrection happen "according to the definite plan and foreknowledge of God" (Acts 2:22–28). As the words of this earliest preserved Chris-

The New Testament and its Background—
Key Dates

Dates	Persons and Events
150 B.C.E.	Pharisees and Sadduccees first mentioned
63 B.C.E.	Romans conquer Palestine and capture Jerusalem
31 B.C.E.–14 C.E.	Caesar Augustus, first Roman emperor
27 B.C.E.	Roman Empire is born
37 B.C.E.–4 C.E.	Herod the Great reigns as king of Judea
c. 4 B.C.E.	birth of Jesus in Palestine
4 C.E.–39 C.E.	reign of Herod Antipas, Tetrarch of Galilee and Perea
6 C.E.	direct Roman rule of Palestine
14 C.E.–37 C. E.	Tiberius, Roman emperor
26 C.E.–36 C.E.	Pontius Pilate, prefect of Judea, presided at the trial of Jesus
c. 27/28 C.E.–30 C.E.	Jesus' public ministry
c. 30 C.E.	death of Jesus of Nazareth
c. 35 C.E.	Paul's conversion to Christianity
50s C.E.	Paul's epistles
70–95 C.E.	the Gospels of the New Testament

tian sermon make clear, the Christian story gives an account of the history of a particular man, according to New Testament scholar Geza Vermes, an itinerant Jewish preacher and healer who resembles Jewish holy men. [2] It is the account of a spirit-filled, charismatic teacher and prophet who lived at the beginning of the first century of the common era, gathered around himself a following from the lower social classes of Galilee, taught that the awaited reign of God was dawning, and was crucified in Jerusalem at the hands of the Roman procurator, Pontius Pilate (26–36 C.E.). And so as we approach the Jesus story we need to look into the historical context and circumstances of its protagonist. We want to ask how Jesus' contemporaries might have viewed him, and how he might have appeared within the context of first-century Palestinian Judaism. Yet, New Testament scholars have found the quest for the historical Jesus not only an elusive but a secondary one. The Jesus of the Christian religion is finally the Jesus of ultimate concern. To understand Christianity in relation to this Jesus, we want to see then how the New Testament "sees" the historical Jesus and how its writers discern transhistorical significance in this historical life.

THE JEWISH CONTEXT

Though the meaning of the historical Buddha transcended the region of his birth in northern India, Gautama's teachings were very much rooted in the religious experience of the Hinduism of his day. So too do Christian roots reach down into a particular history and culture—the history and culture of first century C.E. Judaism. Before we turn to the New Testament, we will look at this Jewish context within which Jesus' ministry and message was formed. We begin with the Jewish Temple as Israel's unifying sacral institution. Next we examine the place of the *Torah* as the source and sanction for holiness of Israel's covenant with *Yahweh*. The third feature of Judaism important for our understanding of Jesus and the New Testament is Jewish *future hope*, conceived in the period after 200 B.C.E. as apocalyptic expectation of a divine or heavenly figure who restores the golden age of King David or inaugurates a new, paradisal age of peace, prosperity, and justice.

The Temple

A sacral institution of immense importance, the ancient Jewish Temple atop Jerusalem's Mount Zion functioned as both the religious and political center of the Jewish state. Today all that remains is the western wall of the Second Temple destroyed by the Romans in 70 C.E.. But, during the time of Jesus' historical ministry, Herod's Temple, as it was called, still stood and featured prominently in the events of Jesus' final days and in the life of the early Jerusalem church which continued to gather there. Like the temples of other ancient oriental religions, the Jewish Temple was first and foremost the abode of deity. It was here in the "House of Yahweh," as the Jerusalem Temple was also called, that the Holy One of Israel might be approached and that sacrifice might be offered. Here animal and cereal offerings were brought in thanksgiving; here too sacrificed animals became the basis of a divine/human communion. Above all, Temple sacrifice was offered for the atonement of personal and corporate sins on the Jewish Day of Atonement (Yom Kippur) when Israel's guilt was ritually transferred to a slaughtered bull.

Until its destruction in 70 C.E., the Temple was Judaism's principal sacral institution, and to it pilgrimage was made during the seasons of Israel's great pilgrim festivals—Passover, Weeks, and Booths. Two of those religious festivals—Passover (Pesach) and Weeks (Sukkoth or Pentecost)— in particular feature in the New Testament, the first in relation to the crucifixion, the second in connection with the advent of the Holy Spirit. Originally agricultural festivals, these festivals came to have significance in relation to Israel's sacred history. Passover commemorates the Exodus and the Hebrews' precipitous flight on the night that Yahweh visited death to the first-born of Egypt, the night the Lord passed over the households of the Hebrews where the blood of sacrificed lambs marked the door posts and lintels of their houses.

At the time reflected in the New Testament, the feast of Passover was preceded by the Day of Preparation and the ritual slaughtering of goats or lambs and the sprinkling of the Temple altar with the blood. Then, when the feast proper began, pilgrims who had come to Jerusalem retired to houses or apartments within the city wall to share a common meal of lamb, unleavened bread, and spices, foods symbolic of the events of Israel's last, hasty meal in Egypt. The feast of Weeks follows fifty days later (hence its name Pentecost) and calls to mind the Israelite arrival at Sinai, the Mosaic Covenant, and the sacred constitution of Israel as a chosen nation. On these and at other times in the cycle of Jewish holy seasons, Jews ritually commemorate and reenact—as the Christians would later do in connection with their own sacred past—the formative events of their sacred history and the conditions for Israel's being a chosen and holy nation.

The Role of the Torah

The Hebrew Bible is in a sense Judaism's religious charter. There is found the narrative of Israel's epic history. There we read of Israel's patriarchs, of slavery in Egypt and Exodus deliverance, of the Sinai covenant and the conquest of Canaan, the promised homeland of Abraham's descendants. There too, in what can only be described as a library of sacred writings, we hear of prophets and kings and royal courts, of shrines and Solomon's Temple, of prayers and rituals and revealed law. But of all these narratives, collected into a canon of twenty-four books, none is more sacred or central than the first five. Known as the Pentateuch or the Torah, these books set forth the terms of Israel's covenant with God and Israel's covenantal standard for ritual and ethical purity. At the heart of Torah, one finds a code for both ritual and ethical conduct—the Ten Commandments and the instructions for Israel's cultic life. In addition to this core of ritual and ethical prescriptions, the Torah contains instruction covering all the situations and circumstances of ordinary life, everything from prayer and the observance of Sabbath and holy days to dietary stipulations about pure and impure foods. Here is, in short, a comprehensive blueprint for ritualizing the whole of ordinary life which Judaism, from the time of Ezra in the sixth century before the common era, understood as an essential condition for covenant loyalty. But how the Torah was to be interpreted and how this divinely revealed outline for holiness was to be implemented was a matter hotly contested at the beginning of the common era's first century.

Particularly relevant as background for the New Testament was the diversity of Torah interpretation among Palestinian Jewish sects. Readers of the New Testament will be familiar with the Sadduccees. This conservative, largely aristocratic and priestly party was associated with the Temple and with the religious and administrative functions of the Temple cult. Politically, the Sadduccees were advocates of the status quo and sought good relations with the Romans. Religious conservatives as well, the Sadduccees conceived of the Torah in its narrowest sense. Torah was for them restricted to the written Scripture found in the Pentateuch. What was non-Pentateuchal, so the Sadduccees reasoned, was without the sanction of revealed authority and was not therefore to be accepted as doctrine.

Of a different persuasion were the Pharisees. Members of this sect were largely laypersons from the Jewish middle class who reflected the interests of their class. Torah for them meant something more like instruction than law and was thought to have application to every aspect of ordinary life. The written Torah, of course, was not in any way minimized or denied by this group, but Pharisees believed that the circumstances of life required the continual adaptation of this ancient text to changing times and conditions. The consequence was that alongside the written Torah there developed an inspired and authoritative tradition of interpretation created and presided over by lay religious scholars and teachers. These teachers or rabbis held that both written Scripture and the tradition of oral commentary (collated by the Pharisees' successors as the Mishnah) were both revelation and together contained authoritative instruction for a life of holiness in fulfillment of Israel's covenant with God. This Pharisaical program for a holiness of *ritual purity* and ethical obedience differed in important respects from the Christian view that salvation comes through a personal devotion to Jesus and the inner transformation of experience.

Mention should be made also of the Zealots and the Essenes. Like the Pharisees, these two Jewish sects held to a standard of ritual separation. But ritual separation and Torah loyalty had political as well as religious implications for the Zealots. They held that expulsion of the Romans was an essential condition for covenant observance and ritual purity. The Essenes—convinced of the ritual impurity also of the Jerusalem priesthood—formed autonomous, quasi-ascetic monastic communities in the desert where they believed God had called them, as Israel's holy remnant, to be recipients of a new covenant and to await the imminent end of the present evil age.

The Messiah and Future Hope in Israel

The Shema, Judaism's central declaration of faith, proclaims the oneness and uniqueness of God. God is a sovereign creator, a transcendent lord over the world and history; revealed at Sinai as Yahweh, this God also is pictured as One who initiates the covenant, reveals the Torah, requires obedience and sanctity, and guides Israel's destiny. Yet the centuries before the common era strained Israel's optimism about its historical destiny. The Babylonians overwhelmed the kingdom of Judah in 587 B.C.E., destroyed the Temple, and exiled the nation's leading citizens. The Jews were returned to their homeland by the Persians in 338 B.C.E. and were encouraged to rebuild the Temple, but an independent Jewish state was fated to be an elusive hope. The rise of Greek power and the hegemony of Hellenistic culture in Palestine followed in the fourth century. Then Palestine found itself conquered again in the first century B.C.E., this time by the Romans. Political frustration, powerlessness, and alienation were inevitable.

Still, Israel remembered God's eternal covenant with the royal house of David (2 Samuel 7:12–14; Psalms 89:3–4), and the divine promise kindled Israel's hope that God would send a royal *Messiah* ("the anointed") to overthrow foreign rule and establish "a son of David" again on Israel's throne. The form this future hope took within Judaism, however, varied. The Zealots expected that God would intervene in history, raise up a political Messiah and deliverer of Israel. The Romans may have thought Jesus just such a political Messiah. The New Testament, however, indicates the influence of another type of future hope, a transcendent hope for deliverance beyond history and the present age. This transcendent hope, formed in connection with Jewish apocalyptic literature in the period following 200

B.C.E., arose from a despair in the catastrophic course of history, a belief that this age is controlled by an evil force of mythic proportions, and a conviction that the wicked prosper and the good suffer.

Balanced by a radical future hope, a hope beyond history or history's horizon, apocalypticism offered a vision of reversal in which God or a divine agent would intervene, overthrow the present world order, judge evil, vindicate the innocent, and restore a paradisal or golden past age or establish a new age of righteousness, peace, and prosperity. Some *apocalypses* (a word meaning an "uncovering" or a "revelation") predicted a heavenly Messiah who would restore and rule over God's Kingdom. Others anticipated a preexistent heavenly redeemer, identified as "the Son of man." The Essenes taught the advent of two divinely sent figures, a priestly "anointed" of Aaron and a kingly "anointed" of Israel. Christians, on the other hand, recognized in the person of Jesus the anticipated Messiah (Greek, *christos*) and believed his words and deeds decisive for the dawning of the new age of God's rule.

JESUS OF HISTORY AND TRADITION

Life and Ministry

Apart from the *synoptic Gospels* (Mark, Matthew, Luke) and John, we know little about the historical Jesus. He does not appear in non-Christian literature until the end of the first century C.E. and then mention of him is incidental and vague. We are reasonably certain, however, that he was born at or shortly before 4 B.C.E. to Joseph, a carpenter of Nazareth, and Mary. His early years were lived amidst the rural village life of Galilee. His native tongue was Aramaic, the language of Palestine, and it is almost certain that he used Aramaic in his preaching and teaching. He may also have had a familiarity with Greek, the Roman world's international language of culture and commerce. More than this cannot be said with historical assurance of the early years of Jesus' life.

To the historical ministry, Matthew and Luke added birth narratives. In Matthew's account, the infancy of Jesus is surrounded by a mystery and majesty. An angel announces Mary's miraculous conception; Magi from the East, guided by a bright star, offer treasure of gold, frankincense, and myrrh to the infant Jesus; the holy family is delivered from Herod and escapes to Egypt; Herod, hoping to kill the prophesied future king, slaughters the innocent male children of Bethlehem. Luke completes the nativity scene. Though placing Jesus' birth in relation to the world political history (Matthew stresses Jesus' relation to prophecy and Old Testament history), Luke emphasizes the human dimension with reference to swaddling clothes, the manger, and shepherds by night. He also stresses the holy family's simple Jewish piety with episodes from Jesus' childhood—the circumcision, the presentation in the Temple and the revelation to Simeon, and Jesus' teaching in the Temple at the age of twelve.

It would appear that Jesus' public ministry, probably between 27 and 30 C.E., was linked with John the Baptist. John was an enigmatic, prophetic figure who had his own disciples and whose movement may even survive today in Iraq and Iran as a Gnostic sect, the Mandaeans. It would appear too that John baptized Jesus, though the reason Jesus submitted to John's *baptism* is unclear and their relationship is ambiguous. The late first-century Ignatius of Antioch believed that Jesus was baptized "to cleanse the water." For the Gospels, the baptism was a theophany, a disclosure of Jesus' identity as "beloved Son." The Gospel writers assign John the Baptist a derivative role as the one who comes before Jesus to prepare for the long expected Messiah (i.e. "the anointed of God"). That John's movement had its own separate identity and differed from Jesus' movement in important respects, however, is also indicated in the Gospels. "Why do we and the Pharisees fast," the disciples of John ask Jesus, "but your disciples do not fast?" (Matthew 9:14: also Mark 2:18 and Luke 5:33). Both were spirit filled, charismatic preachers, but John was an ascetic, world renouncing prophet. He lived apart in the wilderness of the Jordan steppe, dining on locusts and wild honey and clothed in a camel-hair cloak fastened at the waist with a leather belt. And, like the quasi-monastic Essenes with whom he has been associated, John proclaimed the end of the present age, a time of judgment, the need for repentance, and a final ritual purification, an eschatological baptism.

As a prophet, Jesus was very different from John, nor does he conform very well to the traditional Hebrew image of the prophet. There is no evidence of Jesus having visions, dreams, or other ecstatic experiences. There was apparently nothing distinctive about his dress. His sayings do not refer to a prophetic call or commission, and they are not prefaced by the customary prophetic formula, "thus says the Lord." Nevertheless, he exercised the commanding authority of a prophet. He healed the sick. He expelled demons and is said to have answered his critics that "if it is by the finger of God that I cast out demons, then the Kingdom of God has come upon you" (Luke 11:20). He preached, like the prophets of Israel, as one authorized to speak on behalf of another. Furthermore, his words correspond to "the outmoded and archaic ideals of the prophet and wisdom teacher" [3] even though the age of prophecy had long since passed from Israel. Yet Jesus' words distinguish as well as confirm his relation to the prophetic tradition. He preached not merely judgment, repentance, and the promised future age as John did. He announced the Kingdom's benefits as a present reality, manifest in his healing and exorcism and in the forgiveness of sin. Above all, he seemed to have thought of his own words and deeds as somehow connected to God's reign, as one visible sign of the future Kingdom dawning now "in the midst of you" (Luke 17:21).

This sense of the "already" in connection with the Kingdom may explain another important difference between Jesus and John. Whereas John was ascetically oriented, Jesus is frequently pictured as enjoying the pleasures of table fellowship. This, of course, is not remarkable in itself. Meals had a special importance in ancient Near Eastern culture and religion, where eating and drinking could symbolize friendship and mutual obligation. In the Old Testament, sacred meals signaled the ratification of covenants and a relationship of intimacy and trust between God and Israel. In Judaism, the Passover meal, which Christians associate with their own sacred meal, is the annual commemoration of the Exodus and God's great act of deliverance. A communal meal which began with the blessing of bread and wine had religious significance for the Essenes, perhaps as a ritual act anticipatory of the banquet of the new age.

Jesus' Palestinian ministry also indicates a religious significance of his table fellowship. Consistent with the picture of the Gospels, this eating and drinking with friends and disciples signified a foretaste of the great banquet or feast to be celebrated in God's presence in the Kingdom. One interpretation understands the Lord's Prayer (i.e. "Give us this day our daily bread") as itself a petition for future blessedness in the present age. Yet Jesus' custom of eating and drinking with "tax collectors and sinners," persons whose economic status or occupation prevented them from a strict observance of Jewish ritual regulations, set him apart from ritual rigorists like the Essenes and Pharisees. His sharing food and drink with such persons was in fact interpreted as a threat "to the central ordering principle of the Jewish social world: the division between purity and impurity, holy and not holy, righteous and wicked." [4] It threatened too the ritual order that many Jews thought to be an essential condition of Israel's loyalty to God.

Jesus' attitude toward women is of special interest for what it reveals about his attitude toward the prevailing religious and social attitudes of his day. According to conventional wisdom, the social world of women was an inferior and for the most part a segregated world. Women, for example, were not taught the Torah nor were they allowed to be teachers of the Torah. And in synagogue worship they were required to sit apart from the male congregation which recited at each service the prayer—"Blessed art thou, O Lord, who hast not made me a woman." Yet the picture that we have of Jesus turns the attitudes and practices of his contemporaries upside-down. He breaks with traditional Jewish prohibitions on men speaking to women in public places when he initiates a conversation with the Samaritan woman at the well. We know too that he welcomed women into his inner circle, a group of whom broke with traditional Jewish custom by leaving their homes and joining him in his itinerant travels. Some of these female disciples accompanied him to Jerusalem where they remained faithful to Jesus when his male companions deserted and fled. We know too that he instructed women in sacred things and that women were among those most receptive to his message. In the story of Mary and Martha (Luke 10:38–42), Jesus gives positive approval to Mary's assuming the traditional role of the male disciple who sits at the master's feet to receive instruction in sacred things. And, according to the Gospel accounts, the risen Jesus first appears to Mary Magdalene and other women who receive the first commission to witness the Resurrection.

The patriarchal perspective of the dominant culture reemerged as a prevailing point of view among the early Christian churches. As one New Testament scholar observed, "the radical attitude of the Jesus movement toward women was already modified within the church before the New Testament documents were even completed." [5] Yet, we have an image of the historical Jesus shattering social and religious convention. The Gospels picture him as a charismatic teacher and preacher whose movement and ministry had a radically inclusive character. "He promised God's Kingdom not to the rich, the established, and the pious, but to the poor, the destitute, and the prostitutes." [6]

It was, in short, Jesus' custom to associate with groups defined as marginal by the social and religious establishments of his day. As he traveled from village to village and town to town, it was his practice also to share table fellowship without regard for the ritual fellowship that united Israel in a covenant relationship with God. He performed miracles. Indeed, the image of Jesus as a spirit-filled miracle worker, perhaps in the magico-medical tradition of Jewish lore, may have been the popular impression of Jesus during the period of his historical ministry. As a healer and exorcist, he delivered those possessed from the power of demons, restored health to the diseased, and resuscitated the dead. As a wonderworker, he displayed a commanding power over nature. According to the synoptic Gospels, he multiplied loaves of bread and fishes to feed five thousand on one occasion, four thousand on another; he stilled a storm at sea; and he walked on water. Yet his mighty deeds, like his table fellowship, were described as visible signs of the already dawning reign of God. The reign of God was central as well to his teaching.

Teaching of the Kingdom

What was religiously significant about the historical Buddha was his teaching. For Buddhists, the teaching of the Buddha is of supreme importance in the attainment of nirvana and in cessation of suffering, the source of human unhappiness. The opposite is true of Christianity. Jesus—and not his teaching—is the content of the Christian teaching. Yet his teachings were a prominent part of his ministry, and the titles teacher and rabbi were used of him in the New Testament. But in what sense was Jesus a religious teacher and rabbi? Certainly not in the traditional sense that has come down to us through Rabbinic Judaism. He did not confine his teaching to the synagogue, appeal to the Torah for his authority, debate the fine points of Jewish law, or form a school. Like the rabbis, he taught in synagogues, but he preached also in open fields, on the sides of mountains, and beside the sea. He was surrounded by disciples and apparently taught them privately, yet he frequently addressed large crowds. And he seems to have used with greater frequency than others the parable. According to Luke, "he did not speak to them without a parable" (Luke 4:34). Indeed, of Jesus' words in the Gospels, more than one-third are in the parabolic form. He used single metaphors and similes: "Be wise as serpents and innocent as doves" (Matthew 10:16); vivid gnomic or proverbial sayings: "Do not give dogs what is holy; and do not throw pearls before swine, lest they trample them under foot and turn to attack you" (Matthew 7:6); and figurative stories like that of the prodigal son (Luke 15:11–32).

Though the parable was not original with Jesus, it would be accurate to say that he used it with a frequency and originality not evident anywhere else in the Bible. As a literary form, the parable deals with the familiar in life and experience. Jesus' parables tell of landowners and laborers, the rich and the poor, the righteous and sinners, wayward sons, unscrupulous stewards, good neighbors, farmers at harvest time, shepherds, little children, and feasts and weddings. As mirrors of everyday experience, parables were often used to instruct or illustrate. Jesus, however, used them to announce what his deeds also announced. By a paradoxical positioning of the familiar and the strange, the anticipated and the startling, Jesus' parables were a challenge to see and respond to the Kingdom or reign of God.

To be sure, not all of Jesus' teaching stress the paradoxical. The proverbial sayings represent conventional wisdom based on observations about the familiar world around. Who, for example, fails to recognize the rightness of Jesus' counsel "that whatever you wish that men would do to you, do so to them" (Matthew 7:12). Reflection on the fate of great reformers lends persuasive force to the saying that "a prophet is not without honor, except in his own country, and among his own kin, and in his own house" (Matthew 7:6). The frustration of sharing insight or advice with those unwilling or unable to receive it suggests the prudence of not throwing "pearls before swine" (Matthew 7:6). According to the wisdom tradition reflected in these sayings, this world is God's, and it is proper to order one's life according to the order of this world. Yet on balance Jesus' teaching gives most weight to discontinuity. Though Jesus was not an apocalypticist in the usual sense, his deeds and sayings dramatize a cosmic, eschatological struggle against the present evil age and, in the face of judgment, the urgent and unconditional requirement of a radical change of heart and mind.

Side by side with proverbial wisdom, we find sayings remarkable for their demand for a radically new, even shocking outlook on reality. To the person who would bury his father, Jesus says, "Leave the dead to bury their own dead" (Luke 9:60). To the one who wants to take leave of family, Jesus responds, "No one who puts his hand to the plow and looks back is fit for the kingdom of God" (Luke 9:62). These sayings signal a dramatic crossing over into a threshold world, a world between the old and the new, the world of the Kingdom already in the process of arriving. Not dissimilar to the ritual world described by anthropologist Victor Turner [7], the world of the parables is one of surprise, wonder, and joy. And, just as in his public ministry, Jesus' parables not only challenged the conventional social and religious wisdom of the day. His message—addressed to publicans and prostitutes and even to the despised Samaritans—entailed a shocking reversal of that wisdom. Accepted moral norms, social proscriptions, and even religious obligations are found not to apply. Relationships, conditions, and circumstances are reversed. Ordinary expectations and beliefs are suspended.

Buddhists have a saying that with earthly thoughts one cannot penetrate the mystery of nirvana. Jesus' way of expressing the inadequacy of worldly wisdom for understanding the Kingdom came in the form of a rebuke to his disciples who would have turned the children away. Those who inherit the Kingdom, Jesus said, must receive it like a child (Mark 10:15). Skill in reading apocalyptic signs is useless for predicting the time of the Kingdom's coming; human effort is powerless to bring the Kingdom to pass. The Kingdom, Jesus teaches, comes of God's sovereign act, and will be received by those who recognize it as something lost but found or something harvested though not planted.

The parables also portray a world turned topsy-turvy. Reminiscent of Jesus' own custom of eating with outcasts, those who are at the bottom of the social scale are given places of honor at the head of the table. Invited guests at a banquet are rejected and the host sends servants with the instruction, "Go out to the highways and hedges, and compel people to come in, that my house may be filled" (Luke 15:23; also Matthew 22:1-4). In such a world, places of precedence are taken from the wealthy and powerful and transferred to persons whose position in the present age is marginal. Among some groups like the Ndembu of Africa, this process of status reversal constitutes an important part in the conferring of tribal authority on their chiefs. Before authority is transferred to a chief, that person first must submit to a ritual humiliation by assuming the dress and demeanor of a suppliant and a beggar. In the Kingdom of Jesus' teaching, the reversal of status is even more dramatic. The poor in spirit, the meek, those who hunger for righteousness, the merciful, the pure in heart, the peacemakers, and the unjustly persecuted are singled out for privilege and blessing.

Finally, sayings and parables provoke a radical questioning of received values and norms. The Kingdom of heaven, we read in Matthew, is like an owner of a vineyard at harvest time who sends for field hands at staggered intervals throughout the day; he pays them all the same wage—those who worked through the day in the hot sun and those who were called at the eleventh hour (Matthew 20:1 ff.). If the justice of the Kingdom were distributive, Jesus proposes the unthinkable. But then the point of the parable is that God's Kingdom is not thinkable with ordinary thoughts nor is it to be measured by human standards.

Ethics of the Kingdom

Just as the parables and sayings call for a new way of seeing the world, so too do they set forth the need for a new and uncompromising ethics in response to God's coming reign. This can be seen especially in the Sermon on the Mount. There the so-called Antitheses have the effect of intensifying the obligation of the commandments, sometimes in ways that strain scrupulous observance, sometimes in ways that tax prudence and common sense. A sample from the Sermon on the Mount makes the point:

> You have heard that it was said to the men of old, "You shall not kill; and whoever kills shall be liable to judgment." But I say to you that every one who is angry with his brother shall be liable of judgment. . . .(Matthew 5:21–22)

> You have heard that it was said, "An eye for an eye and a tooth for a tooth." But I say to you, do not resist one who is evil. But if anyone strikes you on the right cheek, turn to him the other also; and if anyone would sue you and take your coat, let him have your cloak as well; and if any one forces you to go one mile, go with him two miles. (Matthew 5:38–42)

> You have heard that it was said, "You shall love your neighbor and hate your enemy." But I say to you, Love your enemy and pray for those who persecute you, so that you may be sons of your Father who is in heaven; for he makes his sun rise on the evil and on the good, and sends rain on the just and the unjust. (Matthew 5: 43–45)

It is evident that Jesus is not elaborating merely a new ethical system. What he proposes cannot be satisfied even by the most conscientious attention to external observance. As the rich young man who comes to him discovers, response to the Kingdom requires that nothing can be withheld; no rationalization or excuse or indecision is acceptable. To this otherwise morally upright person, Jesus says, "You lack one thing; go, sell what you have, and give to the poor, and you will have treasure in heaven; and come, follow me" (Mark 10:21). Discipleship demanded a personal loyalty to Jesus and an inner transformation of experience that transcends both ethical and ritual law.

Jesus even transformed Judaism's ancient declaration of faith by locating it in relation to the unconditional requirements of God's Kingdom. Thus, in answer to one who asked what must be done to inherit the Kingdom, he pointed first to the Shema: "Hear, O Israel: the Lord our God, the Lord is one; and you shall love the Lord your God with all your heart, and with all your soul, and with all your mind, and with all your strength" (Mark 12:29-30; Deuteronomy 6:4-5). To this, he added Leviticus 19:18, "You shall love your neighbor as yourself" (Mark 12:31). But Jesus, according to Luke, is pressed for further clarification—"And who is my neighbor?" What follows is a story familiar to most, the parable of the good Samaritan [8].

Jesus' telling of this story (see Luke 10:30-37) is significant in that he avoids making moral judgment. Had he been interested in relating an exemplary story about neighborliness, he might better have made the Samaritan the victim. As it stands, Jesus does not offer his Jewish audience an emblem of the good person. He confronts them rather with the good *Samaritan* and with a proposition that would have strained belief for Jews of Jesus' day who thought of Samaritans as despised foreigners. Yet unexpectedly, Jesus allows this deed to represent the meaning of love in the face of God's Kingdom. The parable's point is that the despised Samaritan does the good deed, and does it simply and spontaneously with thought only for what circumstance and need require. No evasion compromises the act; no thought is given to the merit of the deed. In the spirit of the great Commandment, charity is offered with a purity of heart, mind, and soul.

JESUS' FINAL DAYS

Jerusalem at Passover

Central to the story of Jesus was his decision to journey to Jerusalem at the time of Passover, Judaism's great festival of freedom and hope. It was during this religious season that Jews from all over the world assembled in the city of David to commemorate Israel's deliverance from physical and spiritual oppression. The presence of Romans, whose procurator Pontius Pilate had come down from the coastal city of Caesarea to keep order, could only have amplified Passover meaning. One can well imagine too how the appearance of the Galilean prophet of the Kingdom and his demonstrative entry might have kindled, if only for a brief time, hope among the Passover pilgrims gathered in the city. As the Gospels relate the event, Jesus came through the streets as the Messiah prophesied by Zechariah, "humble and riding on an ass, on a colt the foal of an ass" (9:9) and was greeted by the crowd, "Blessed is he who comes in the name of the Lord!" (Mark 11:9)

Seen from the earliest Christian witness, here was the fulfillment of God's redemptive plan. Here was the bringer of God's promised reign. Here was the deliverer whose violent death would atone for the sins of many. That Jesus presented himself thus in messianic terms is doubtful. His ministry had been to call Israel to decision in the face of God's impending reign. And the prediction that "the Son of man must suffer many things, and be rejected by the elders and the chief priests and the scribes, and be killed, and after three days rise again" (Mark 8:31: see also Mark 9:31; 10:32 ff.) reflects the witness of the church and its Easter experience. That, however, Jesus anticipated his suffering and death and understood his fated ordeal as instrumental in the coming of God's reign is probable.

The very real and menacing shadow of opposition had already darkened his ministry in Galilee. Though the Pharisees were not to play a role in his arrest, these Torah loyalists had been offended by Jesus' disregard of Torah observance. Herod Antipas of Galilee had demonstrated his disposition when he had John the Baptist beheaded; Luke reports that Jesus knew of Herod's plans to kill him as well (Luke 13:31). And Jesus' connection with Galilee, hotbed for anti-Roman feeling and stronghold of the Zealots, would have aroused suspicion among the pro-Roman Sudduccean party even if Jesus had not publicly challenged their religious and economic authority in the cleansing of the Temple (Mark 12:15 ff.). We are given to believe that only Jesus' popularity among the people, many of whom had arrived in Jerusalem from his native Galilee, made the Jewish authorities wait for the right time to arrest him, sometime before the beginning of the Passover feast (Mark 14:2).

In spite of the danger, Jesus spent the final days before his arrest teaching in the Temple precincts and his nights in Bethany east of the Mount of Olives. Then, according to the Gospels, he sent his disciples into Jerusalem to prepare a large upper room for a meal that came to be known as the *Last Supper*. The words *after supper* that Paul knows from tradition indicate a complete meal. There would have been a blessing and the breaking and distribution of bread; then at meal's end a blessing and passing of a cup of wine. At one level, this farewell meal must have been very much like other meals that Jesus customarily shared with his disciples during the travels of his ministry around the northern shore of the Sea of Galilee. It is likely too that his confrontation with the Jerusalem authorities and the very real threat to his own person must have intensified the customary meaning of the fellowship meal. Yet the Gospels see much more in this scene. Foreseeing his own imminent death, we are told, Jesus tells the disciples that he next will eat and drink in God's Kingdom (Mark 14:25; Matthew 26:29). And in the context of this eschatological saying he instructs them in the meaning of his death which reads in the earliest received tradition:

> "This is my body which is for you. Do this in remembrance of me." In the same way also the cup, after supper, saying, "This cup is the new covenant in my blood. Do this in remembrance of me." (1 Corinthians 11:24–25).

The Gospels give conflicting accounts of the day Jesus was to have uttered these words, though Christians assign the observance to Holy Thursday. The synoptics think of the meal as a Passover, whereas John's Gospel has Jesus crucified on the day before Passover at the hour the Passover lambs were sacrificed. The New Testament also offers different perspectives on the event in an attempt to comprehend and communicate its power and its meaning for Christian worship. Paul conceives of it as a new covenant and as a bond of Christian fellowship in the one body of Christ; though more elusive, John sees in the bread and wine a sacrament of sacred food and drink; Matthew finds here sin's forgiveness; and Mark discerns in this last meal the atoning efficacy of Jesus' death.

Arrest, Trial, and Crucifixion

The anticipated confrontation with Jewish authorities materialized in the events following the fellowship meal in the upper room. Jesus is said to have predicted his betrayal and Peter's denial before withdrawing to the garden of Gethsemane across the Kidron Valley east of Jerusalem. It was to this garden retreat on the west slope of the Mount of Olives that the betrayer Judas Iscariot guided an armed band from the chief priest's household. The sign of identification was to be the customary greeting that passed between pupil and teacher; Judas hailed Jesus, "'Master,' and he kissed him" (Mark 14:45). Resistance among the Galileans was quickly broken; the disciples were dispersed, though Peter followed the arresting party at a distance; and Jesus was led off to what Mark and Matthew describe as a special session of the Sanhedrin, the council of chief priests and elders in Jerusalem.

Although the historical trial is impossible to reconstruct, Mark represents it as a night trial close on the heels of the arrest. The council hears conflicting testimony of Jesus' guilt. The high priest Caiaphas then questions Jesus about the saying that he would destroy the Temple, and he exacts from Jesus an affirmative to the inquiry, "Are you the Christ, the Son of the Blessed?" (14:612). This is taken to be blasphemy (punishable in Jewish law by stoning); the council calls for Jesus' execution; and Jesus is carried before the Roman procurator. The story of Jesus' final hours now moves quickly to its conclusion. Pilate inquires of Jesus, "Are you the King of the Jews?" (15:2), to which Jesus gives an evasive answer. Though Pilate is known from external sources to have been brutal, indifferent to Jewish wishes, and insensitive to Jewish religious scruples, he is said here to appeal to the crowd on Jesus' behalf, is frustrated in his appeal, yields to the accusers, and sentences Jesus to crucifixion, a punishment reserved for criminals of the lowest classes and the most heinous crimes—not for blasphemy. To this story Matthew adds the suicide of Judas, the dream of Pilate's wife, and Pilate's hand washing. In Luke's narrative, Pilate declares Jesus innocent and sends him to Herod Antipas for further questioning.

The Roman procurator's conduct in these accounts is uncharacteristic and his innocence of Jesus' death is unlikely and probably reflects early Christian apologetic interest. That the pro-Roman priestly and Sadduccean members of the Sanhedrin had Jesus arrested, informally interrogated, and transferred to Pilate is probable. That Jesus was thought to be politically dangerous and tried for sedition (not blasphemy) against the Roman state, however, is indicated by crucifixion and the placard placed over Jesus, "King of the Jews."

For Mark this is but another failure to understand Jesus' mission and message. Redemption comes not through political insurrection but rather through the humiliation of one, who like the suffering servant of Isaiah, innocently suffers for others (see Isaiah 53). Nevertheless, the circumstances of Jesus' death indicate that he received a punishment often reserved by the Romans for provincial insurgents. According to Roman custom in such cases, Jesus was flogged and, assisted by Simon of Cyrene, forced to carry a part of the cross to the place of execution, a small skull-shaped hill known as Golgotha just outside the north gate of the city. At this place, Jesus was stripped and nailed to the upright pole and crossbar. A placard announcing his crime was affixed above his head. And there he faced a death that came quickly by usual standards. Often the victim of crucifixion lingered several days only to die of hunger, thirst, exposure, and the trauma of scourging. By the ninth hour of the day and after only six hours, Jesus is said to have breathed his last, and his body, according to Jewish law, was taken from the cross and placed in the rock tomb of a Jerusalem disciple, Joseph of Arimathea.

Little wonder that the ancient Jewish historian Josephus called the crucifixion "the most wretched of deaths" and that the ancient Hebrews thought its victims "accursed by God" (Deuteronomy 21:22–23). Yet Christians speak of the day of the crucifixion as Good Friday and take the cross to be a sign not of shame and ignominy but of victory and exaltation, a transformation of meaning already apparent in Paul's writings. Paul wrote his missionary congregation—many of whom may have had difficulties understanding or accepting this symbol—that "the crucifixion, a stumbling block to Jews and folly to Gentiles" (1 Corinthians 1:23) is in reality a display of divine wisdom and power.

In Mark's account of Jesus' suffering (known among Christians as Christ's Passion), even minor details speak of God's providence. To fulfill the Scripture, Jesus is offered wine mixed with myrrh (see Psalm 69:21); his garments are divided among the soldiers who cast lots for his seamless robe (see Psalm 22:18); he is mocked by passers-by who wag their heads (see Psalm 22:7)—all according to inspired prophecy. And the cry of dereliction, the last uttered words from the cross, does not signify defeat; rather it echoes the Psalmist's confidence in God's deliverance. Mark knows very well that this image of Jesus does not conform to the picture of Jesus as a worker of miracles. Though Mark speaks of a darkening of the sky and the tearing of the Temple veil, Jesus here offers no miracle to stay his suffering or death. The one who exorcised demons, healed the sick, and quieted the storm at sea now takes no action on his own behalf and offers no sign to the crowds. But that is Mark's point. The sign that counts is the sign of obedient love; the imitable pattern—reenacted ritually at Christian baptism—has become the pattern of the cross (8:34). And yet, reminiscent of Taoist wisdom, the wisdom of the cross in Christian interpretation discloses the paradoxical conjunction of acting by not acting (*wu wei*). It reveals the power that lies hidden in the gesture of self-emptying.

THE RESURRECTION

Accounts of the Resurrection

The force of personality and originality of teaching would otherwise distinguish Jesus as a religious figure of importance in the history of religion. And these were remembered and preserved, first in the oral tradition of the church and then authoritatively in the New Testament Gospels. Yet the Easter experience alone accounts for the transformation of the Jesus movement and the emergence of the Christian religion. As Catholic theologian Hans Kung phrased it, "Jesus the preacher becomes Jesus the preached," [9] preached above all as one "raised from the dead" (Romans 10:9). According to the church's most primitive proclamation or *kerygma*, Jesus was much more than a teacher or prophet, more even than the herald of God's coming Kingdom. Jesus of Nazareth, who suffered, was crucified and buried, was brought back to life, though not as a one merely resuscitated or revived. Experienced by the disciples as alive again, Jesus' resurrection from the dead signaled the beginning of a new eschatological age, the first fruit of God's universal reign.

In the New Testament Gospels the visit to the tomb at dawn on that first Sunday after the crucifixion served to announce this momentous event, and Christians over the centuries have followed the Gospel stories in giving prominence to the empty tomb in commemorating the Easter faith. Thus, fittingly, every Easter, just before dawn, Jerusalem's Greek Orthodox patriarch descends to the Holy Sepulchre where Jesus is believed to have been buried and from the dark interior carries the holy fire, proclaiming anew the resurrection.

Yet, if the empty tomb was a vehicle for proclaiming the resurrection, it was the resurrection appearances to which the New Testament points as confirmation of the disciple's faith and the church's hope. Paul, who apparently did not know the tradition of the empty tomb, knows of the witnesses to the resurrection, among whom he numbers himself. In 1 Corinthians 15, where he speaks at length of this, he writes that the risen Jesus "appeared to Cephas, then to the twelve. Then he appeared to more than five hundred brethren at one time, most of whom are still alive, though some have fallen asleep. Then he appeared to James, then to the apostles. Last of all, as to one untimely born, he appeared also to me" (15:3–8). Here is the tradition Paul received, perhaps at the time of his conversion (ca. 35 C.E.); the same tradition he delivered to the congregation at Corinth as a teaching of first importance.

The Gospel writers know also of this appearance tradition, though Mark ends with only the prediction that Jesus will meet his disciples in Galilee. We should note in particular that the Gospels identify the women who followed Jesus as the first witnesses to the resurrection. Though Paul does not mention Jesus' female disciples in this connection, the fact that Gospels not only know of the appearances to the women but identify them by name suggests the certainty of this tradition. As one New Testament scholar has observed, "the women were the primary apostolic witnesses for the fundamental events of the early Christian preaching: they were witnesses of Jesus' ministry, his suffering and death, his burial and his Ressurrection. They were moreover sent to proclaim the message of the Resurrection." [10] The Gospels do however differ in respect to detail. Matthew writes of a first appearance to the women in the garden and then of Jesus' mountaintop commission in Galilee, where he instructs the disciples to baptize and teach. Luke and John testify to an incorporeal presence who mysteriously and inexplicably materializes and disappears. And yet they too see in this risen Jesus one whom they knew in Galilee. Though a numinous person, the resurrected Jesus walks and talks with the disciples, eats with them, on one occasion in Jerusalem, on another in Galilee, and presents his wounds to Thomas's touch.

As the Christian mission pushed beyond the Jewish environment of its beginnings, it fell to Christian Apologists to interpret resurrection meaning to gentile converts for whom the Hebrew conception of the person as a living body, animated by the breath of God (see Genesis 2:7) was alien. The conception of an immortal soul would have been familiar to Hellenized converts. Their thought had been tutored by Plato and other philosophers who taught that the body is but the soul's tomb and that at life's end a deathless, bodiless afterlife awaits. Even the pattern of salvation through identification with the dying and rising god of the Greek mystery cult would have made sense. But it took the persuasive force of Christianity's first great interpreter to communicate the meaning and power of the resurrection faith. According to Paul, had Jesus not risen from the dead there would have been no reversal of Adam's fall, no victory over death, and no warrant for Christian hope. Against those who look for a present transformation, as apparently members of the Corinthian church did, Paul holds (see 1 Corinthians 15) that the final defeat of death for believers is a future event. Though believers participate through baptism in the benefits of Christ's resurrection, a general bodily resurrection awaits the Parousia, the coming of Christ a second time.

Paul was aware too that the Parousia had been delayed and that "some [who expected to see its arrival] have already fallen asleep" (15:6). Nevertheless, he takes Christ's resurrection as a pledge of that apocalyptic hope, as "the first fruits of those who have fallen asleep" (15:32). As to the Corinthians' concern about the corruptible bodies of departed believers, Paul assures them that on the day of the general resurrection the perishable body will be exchanged for an imperishable, spiritual one. And this he describes in ecstatic, visionary terms as happening "in a moment, in a twinkling of an eye. For the trumpet will sound, and the dead will be raised imperishable and shall be changed" (15:52). As for those who die before the *eschaton*, Paul elsewhere implies some kind of existence in the interim between death and Christ's Second Coming. This conviction was developed later in the Roman Catholic teaching that saved souls at death go immediately to heaven or to an intermediate penitential state known as purgatory. Among Christians in general, the idea of a disembodied soul, reembodied on the day of the general resurrection, gained early popularity and is widely held by Christians to the present day.

Coming of the Spirit

The story of Jesus' last days in Jerusalem is also the story of the Christian churches, ritually reenacted each year during Holy Week. Using traditional rites, some of which originated in the fourth century, others elaborated during the Middle Ages, Christians celebrate Palm Sunday and Jesus' entry through the gates of Jerusalem. With the blessing and carrying of palms or olive branches in procession and the singing of hymns, often the hymn of the Carolingian bishop of Orleans, "All glory, laud and honor to thee Redeemer, King," the week of Christ's Passion begins triumphantly. A more solemn mood accompanies the commemoration of the Last Supper, the crucifixion, and Christ's entombment. As Christ knelt to wash his disciples' feet, so Christians ritually perform feet washing on Holy Thursday. On Good Friday, they trace Christ's steps through the stations of the cross or kneel in veneration before the cross. On the evening of Holy Saturday, the day of Christ's entombment, the Paschal Candle—a sign of the Light of Christ—is carried through the dark of the church and its fire is passed from candle to candle until all the worshippers hold kindled tapers. Then, often at dawn on Sunday, Christians joyously celebrate the oldest and most important of the Christian festivals, "the feast of feasts," as Pope Leo the Great called it in the fifth century. This Feast of the Resurrection, known popularly as Easter, proclaims Christ's rising from the dead and inaugurates the ecclesiastical season of Eastertide (also Paschaltide) that extends to Pentecost fifty days later.

Through the cycle of feast days culminating with Easter, Christianity traces the events in the life of Jesus central to salvation. The last great religious festival of the Christian year, the feast of Pentecost, however, features the Holy Spirit and the Christian community that the Spirit empowers in its baptism, prayer, worship, and preaching. Pentecost thus signals a transition from what New Testament scholar Norman Perrin speaks of as "the time of Jesus" to "the time of the church." [11] It is clear too from the perspective of the New Testament that the coming of the Spirit is conceived as the dawning of a new age in fulfillment of Hebrew prophecy (Joel 2:8-32) which the church was to speak of in its preaching.

This event, which took place during the Jewish festival of Weeks, a festival that commemorates Israel's formative wilderness experience, is thought also to commemorate the birth of the Christian church. Of this event the Acts of the Apostles says that after Jesus' ascension into heaven, when the apostles and others were gathered in Jerusalem, "a sound came from heaven like the rush of a mighty wind, and it filled all the house where [the apostles] were sitting. And there appeared to them tongues as of fire, distributed and resting on each one of them. And they were filled with the Holy Spirit and began to speak in other tongues, as the Spirit gave them utterance" (2:2-4).

The descent of the Spirit and the tongues of fire have been given various meanings by Christians. Paul associates the Spirit and the manifest sign of ecstatic speech as evidence of divine power communicated at baptism. Twentieth century Pentecostal Christians expect a charismatic baptism of fire and regard it as an essential, authenticating mark of Christian experience. Christians of the Orthodox world understand the Holy Spirit of Pentecost as a summons to human unity and the restoration of the creation. At the end, as in the beginning, so it is believed, the Spirit hovers over creation or dovelike broods over it, in the words of Jesuit poet Gerard Manley Hopkins, "with warm breast and with ah! bright wings." Yet, in Acts the immediate context of Pentecost is Christianity's worldwide mission, symbolized by the gift of tongues, to preach the gospel of Jesus first "in Jerusalem and then in all Judea and Samaria and then to the end of the earth" (Acts 1:8). This insured that Christianity would be a missionary religion. It also meant that the early Christian movement, committed to geographic expansion, would face the task of institutionalization and tradition formation incumbent on all emergent religions.

SUMMARY

Christianity, like Judaism, is based on the belief that God's redemptive activity is revealed in human history. God's eternal purpose, so Christians affirm, is disclosed decisively in the ministry, the passion and crucifixion, and above all the Resurrection of a particular man, Jesus of Nazareth. And so the Jesus story that is central to Christianity is fundamentally a historical one. As recent New Testament scholarship has reconstructed it, it is the story of a Jewish preacher, healer, and exorcist. It is the story of a prophet who announces the imminent arrival of God's expected reign and who regards his own mighty deeds as somehow instrumental in the overthrow of Satan's dominion and the coming of a new age of peace and justice. As his teaching reveals, however, this eschatological age represented something radically new and discontinuous. By contrast to traditional standards of Jewish holiness based on Torah loyalty, the holiness of the Kingdom was the fruit of an inner transformation of experience expressed in a life of spontaneous love.

Yet, the Christian story is much more than a story of a Jewish holy man, more than a sacred narrative of an exemplary life, more than the account of an inspired teacher. The Jesus story of Christian faith and tradition is the recollection of a divine redeemer whose true identity was revealed to an inner circle through the Resurrection appearances. It is the story of an atoning, sacrificial death; it is a messianic story of the new age; it is a missionary story of the apostles and the church. What we will find in the next chapter is that this master story was also instrumental in the formation of Christian tradition.

REVIEW AND REFLECTION

1. The context of Jesus' historical ministry was Judaism of the first century of the common era. What were the three main features of Judaism at that time?
2. What were the important religious groups active in Palestine at the time of Jesus? What did they have in common? What were their major differences?
3. How does this Jewish background help us better understand the historical Jesus?
4. Biblical scholars agree today that it is possible to sketch a tentative picture of the historical Jesus. What kind of religious figure does he seem to have been?
5. What is a parable and what did Jesus seek to communicate in his parables? What image of the Kingdom of God emerges from the parables?
6. Describe the events of Jesus' last trip to Jerusalem. What can we infer about his purpose from those events?
7. What special importance did the Resurrection hold for the followers of Jesus and what problems did the idea of the Resurrection make for missionaries to non-Jews like Paul?
8. What was the original Pentecost and how is the miracle of Pentecost related to the church?

END NOTES

1. For a helpful anthology of readings on all aspects of Jewish religious experience, see Jacob Neusner. ed., *The Life of Torah: Readings in the Jewish Religious Experience* (Encino and Belmont, CA: Dickenson Publishing Company, Inc., 1974).

2. Geza Vermes, *Jesus the Jew* (New York: Macmillan, 1973) discusses Jesus in relation to this Jewish charismatic tradition.

3. Helmut Koester, *Introduction to the New Testament, Volume II: History and Literature of Early Christianity* (New York and Berlin: Walter de Gruyter, 1980), p. 78.

4. Marcus J. Borg, *Jesus A New Vision: Spirit, Culture, and the Life of Discipleship* (San Francisco: Harper & Row, Publishers, 1987), p. 132.

5. Marcus J. Borg, *Jesus A New Vision*, p. 135.

6. Elisabeth Schussler Fiorenza, "Women in the Early Christian Movement" in *Womenspirit Rising: A Feminist Reader in Religion* (San Francisco: Harper & Row, Publishers, 1979), p. 88.

7. I am dependent on Victor Turner, *Ritual Process: Structure and Anti-Structure* ((Ithaca, NY: Cornell University Press, 1969) for the description of ritual as threshold experience.

8. My discussion of the parable of the good Samaritan is indebted to Norman Perrin and Denis Duling, *The New Testament: An Introduction*, 2nd ed. (New York: Harcourt, Brace, Javanovich, Publishers, 1982), pp. 416–417.

9. Hans Kung, *The Church*, trans. Ray and Rosaleen Ockenden (New York: Sheed and Ward, 1967), p. 80.

10. Elizabeth Fiorenza, "Women in the Early Christian Movement," in *Womanspirit Rising*, p. 90.

11. Norman Perrin and Denis Duling, *The New Testament: An Introduction*, p. 307.

SUGGESTED FURTHER READING

BORNKAMM, GUNTHER. *Jesus of Nazareth*. trans. Irene and Fraser MCLUSKEY with JAMES M. ROBINSON. New York: Harper & Row, Publishers, 1959.

BORG, MARCUS J. *Jesus: A New Vision: Spirit, Culture, and the Life of Discipleship*. San Francisco: Harper & Row Publishers, 1987.

CONZELMANN, HANS. *Jesus*. ed. John Reumann and trans. J. Raymond Lord. Philadelphia: Fortress Press, 1973

C. H. DODD. *The Founder of Christianity*. New York: The Macmillan Publishing Company, 1970.

FISHBANE, MICHAEL. *Judaism: Revelation and Traditions*. San Francisco, CA: Harper & Row, Publishers, 1987.

KEE. HOWARD CLARK. *Jesus in History*. 2nd ed. New York: Harcourt, Brace, Jovanovich, Publishers, 1977.

KOESTER, HELMUT. *Introduction to the New Testament*. Vol. 2: *History and Literature of Early Christianity*. New York and Berlin: Walter de Gruyter, 1980.

PERRIN, NORMAN and DENIS C. DULING. *The New Testament: An Introduction*. 2nd ed. New York: Harcourt, Brace, Jovanovich, 1982.

4 | The Formation of Christian Tradition

INTRODUCTION

From an early period the Christian community believed itself to be divinely constituted. Not only had the apostles been witnesses to the Resurrection appearances and commissioned by the risen Lord to baptize others in his name, but the Holy Spirit at Pentecost had come upon the Christian assembly in Jerusalem as a sign of Christ's living presence among them. At the beginning of the third century, the church was even included among the articles of belief that candidates for baptism affirmed. According to *The Apostolic Tradition* (c. 215 C.E.) of Hippolytus of Rome, those desiring admission to the church were asked: "Do you also believe in the Holy Spirit in the holy church for the resurrection of the body?"

The image that emerges is that of a holy community with a sacred charge to preach and baptize. And yet the character of the church and the content of its preaching were still fluid during the first several centuries of its history. Christians were conscious of being recipients of a divine revelation; they understood themselves to be charged with witnessing a sacred event. Yet external and internal circumstances forced the early church to clarify both its teaching and its authority to teach. The result was an *orthodox* (normative or standard) view of the character of Christian ministry, Scripture, and creed. The process whereby these elements of Christian tradition came into being during the church's formative period is the subject of this chapter.

Christian Beginnings—Key Dates

DATES	PERSONS AND EVENTS
64 C.E.	Neronian persecution; the death of Peter in Rome by crucifixion
c. 35–107 C.E.	Ignatius of Antioch whose letters speak of the bishop as a symbol of Christian unity
end of 2nd century C.E.	the Old Roman Symbol, the official baptismal confession of the Roman church; also an early version of the Apostles' Creed
d. c. 160 C.E.	Marcion, a heretical Christian who rejected Jewish Scripture and prepared an early Christian canon
c. 170 C.E.	Muratorian Canon, the oldest extant list of New Testament writings
c. 130–c. 200 C.E.	Irenaeus, the first great Catholic theologian and advocate of apostolic succession
c. 160–c. 220 C.E.	Tertullian, an influential North African Christian theologian who first used the term New Testament
c. 170–236 C.E.	Hippolytus, whose *Apostolic Tradition* contains the first full text of the Eucharist
313 C.E.	Edict of Milan, ends persecution and grants legal status to Christians
325 C.E.	Council of Nicaea, the first universal convocation of Christian bishops; dealt with the divinity of Jesus; Athanasius (296–373) was its leading theologian
367 C.E.	Athanasius circulates a letter to his churches containing the first complete list of undisputed New Testament books
451 C.E.	Council of Chalcedon, the fourth ecumenical council of the church; dealt with the humanity of Jesus

THE MEANING OF TRADITION

The Idea of Tradition

Church historian Jaroslav Pelikan makes an important contribution to the study of religion when he contrasts tradition with traditionalism. Tradition, he writes, is "the living faith of the dead"; traditionalism is "the dead faith of the living." [1] Most of us have some firsthand experience with what Pelikan is talking about. We have encountered empty forms—gestures, customs, verbal expressions, ceremonies—which may once have had expressive power but no longer do. This is what is meant by traditionalism. But, when the received past commands allegiance and shapes contemporary existence, we are talking about tradition. When transformative insight, revealed teaching, or memory of a sacred event is transmitted, we are reflecting on *religious tradition*.

For the purposes of religious studies, then, tradition is not something peripheral but fundamental to living religion. Rather than obscuring, the study of tradition allows us to isolate what a religious community deems essential for enlightenment or salvation. It permits us to identify the indispensable deposit of religious insight or faith. Of equal importance, tradition lays bare the way a religious community evolves the standard or orthodox form of its teaching and canonical Scripture, and distributes religious authority to those who are its accredited tradition bearers. By this means, religions ensure that their originating insights, revelations, and formative experiences are preserved and given stable, transmittable form apart from which they would cease to exist. To put it another way, insight, revelation, and memory of a sacred event are recoverable because they were submitted to tradition at a critical point in the history of the religious group, usually at a point when the *deposit of faith* was in danger of being lost or radically revised.

Tradition in our discussion of Christianity also has this twofold sense and refers at once to a sacred content that is "handed over" and to a process of transmission, to the "handing over" (Latin *traditio*) that is its sacred context. Furthermore, tradition making, as an act of transmitting sacred content, tends not to be a late development or a dispensable accretion. Biblical scholars tell us, for example, that the New Testament itself reflects—and itself is the product of—the process we are describing. Thus, for example, Paul in his First Letter to the Corinthians was as careful to specify the dynamics of transmitting the gospel as he was to identify its content. At issue, as this letter shows, was the integrity of the Christian message Paul taught.

For I *delivered* [my emphasis] to you as of first importance what I also *received* [my emphasis], that Christ died for our sins in accordance with the scriptures, that he was buried, that he was raised on the third day in accordance with the scriptures, and that he appeared to Cephas, then to the twelve. (1 Corinthians 15:3b–5)

In Paul's statement here and again in 1 Corinthians 11:23–25 where he speaks of the Lord's Supper, we see the formation of tradition from the fluid contemporary perspective of first-century Christianity and one of its most creative originators. There are a number of things to notice about tradition in this early Christian context. Notice first the technical meaning given tradition as the "handing over" or the "delivering up." Notice too that Paul's understanding of tradition assumes a sacred context for the receiving and the transmitting of its sacred content. Paul no doubt came to possess the gospel he preached from other Christians after his conversion (c. 35 C.E.), perhaps during his three years with the congregation at Damascus, his visit to Peter and James in Jerusalem, and his sojourn in the regions of Syria and Cilicia. Finally, Paul's writings clarify the question about who is authorized to witness to the gospel. A sacred trust not to be left to chance or historical accident, we learn that the making of tradition is the special responsibility of accredited tradition bearers, among whom Paul numbers himself as a witness to the Resurrection.

The Heart of the Christian Tradition

No one word expresses the core of Christian teaching as well perhaps as the word *gospel*. An English word that translates *euangelion*, gospel means "good tiding" and was used in that sense in the ancient Greek world. It was thus that the calendar inscription from Priene announced the birthday of the god, an occasion for "the glad tidings" (Greek, *euangelion*). It was also as "good news" that the birthday of the Roman emperor Augustus Caesar was proclaimed. The term is found too in Hebrew Scripture to express the good news or glad tidings of Israel's redemption at God's hand. And in the New Testament Jesus uses *euangelion* of his mission ("to preach good news to the poor") and his Messiahship. The writer of Mark was the first to use the word in reference to the literary form of his writing. And it was Paul—the writer in the New Testament who used the word *gospel* with the greatest frequency—who spoke of the gospel of God's redemptive activity as revealed in the life, death, and Resurrection of Jesus Christ.

In the form of Christian preaching, this gospel was known also by the name *kerygma*, a word that means proclamation and the content of proclamation. As a kind of plot summary of salvation history, the kerygma rehearses God's redemptive plan for creation. It announces that Jesus was the Messiah promised by the Hebrew prophets, a figure whose existence and destiny are deeply rooted in human history and above all the history of Israel. He is thus preached as one born of David's seed and who died as Scripture foretold and was buried. Crucified, the kerygma affirms, he was raised from the dead to the right hand of God the Father and will return again as judge and savior of humankind.

The same themes similarly recur in Christian worship. The central prayer found in the earliest full text of the *Eucharist* (Greek meaning "thanksgiving") rehearses the basic themes of salvation history. After receiving the offering of bread and wine from the deacon, the bishop says:

> We give you thanks, O God, through your beloved Servant Jesus, whom at the end of time you sent to us as Savior and Redeemer and the Messenger of your counsel. Who is your Word, inseparable from you; through whom you did make all things and in whom you are well pleased. Whom you did send from heaven into the womb of the Virgin. Who, fulfilling your will, and winning for himself a holy people, spread out his hands when he came to suffer, that by his death he might set free those who believed in you. Who, when he was betrayed to his willing death, that he might bring to nought death, and break the bonds of the devil, and tread hell under foot, and give light to the righteous, and set up a boundary post, and manifest his resurrection, taking bread and giving thanks to you said: Take, eat: This is my body, which is broken for you. And likewise also the cup, saying: This is my blood, which is shed for you. As often as you perform this, perform my memorial. [2]

Here too we find a summary of the Christian drama, the shape of Christian story, the summary of God's revelation delivered through the prophets and the apostles, preached as gospel and celebrated in worship. Thanksgiving is offered for creation and redemption and what God accomplished through Jesus Christ is commemorated.

Turning to the *Christological* hymns of early Christian worship, we see that these themes once more become a recitation of affirmation and praise, though the emphasis here is on the cosmic character of the Jesus story. Originally, hymns of Christian worship, recited as Roman historian Pliny the Younger wrote "to Christ, as to a god," these early liturgical accretions of Christian tradition picture Jesus as a heavenly being like the descending/ascending redeemer of Gnosticism. He is said to exist before the Incarnation, a preexistent being with equality to God, who acted as God's agent in creation, and with God preserves and sustains the world. And, having been raised from the dead, he is exalted and enthroned in the heavenly realm where all cosmic powers are subject to him. Nevertheless, what distinguishes the Christian redeemer is that the hymns are finally anchored in the *kerygma* and attest to the Incarnation. Though the hymns enlarge on the historical perspective of the *kerygma* and locate Christianity's master story within a cosmic frame, they retain its fundamental traditionary belief that the divine Word, God's eternal *Logos*, descends from the heavenly to the earthly realm to suffer death on the cross. On this belief—that history is the locus of meaning and revelation—subsequent Christian tradition was to be unswerving.

THE TRADITION OF RELIGIOUS AUTHORITY

Apostolic Authority

Religious communities never seem to resolve definitively the question of religious authority. Today's Christians, for example, appear no closer to agreement about the status of the person or persons who exercise authority in matters of sacred obligation or who preside at worship than at any other period in their history. Yet the decision about the character and office of the religious specialist (e.g. shaman, priest, minister) is a matter of utmost importance for religious traditions. Of course, religious groups develop often elaborate organizational structures requiring persons of character and talent capable of managing complex institutional machinery. Not infrequently, the organizational needs of religious institutions are influential in the evolution of religious authority or at least the traits of those who hold authority. But authority within a religious community is also, even essentially, a sacred authority and is exercised on behalf of the integrity, preservation, and transmission of the religious community's originating revelation, formative symbols, and normative rituals and practices.

In many religious traditions, sacred authority originates with the religious founder and is then transferred to the founder's inner circle of disciples who are in a unique position to authenticate the founder's teaching and instructions. In Christianity this work fell to Jesus' inner circle and, according to early tradition, to the Twelve among whom Peter enjoyed special preeminence. It was to this group of followers—whose number included Mary Magdalene and other women (see Mark 15:40 ff.)—who had attended Jesus during his public ministry, received instruction in his message, accompanied him from Galilee to Jerusalem, and received a commission from the risen Lord to witness to the Resurrection. And it was to this inner circle of disciples that the first Christian missionaries (called *apostles*) were recruited. These missionaries were sent forth to preach and baptize. Others who were not of Jesus' immediate circle were also called to found churches and exercise apostolic authority. The most notable among them was Paul. Known as the Apostle to the Gentiles, Paul claimed special apostolic authority on the basis of a theophany, a vision or appearance of the risen Lord while he traveled on the road to Damascus.

Forms of First-Century Ministry

It is from Paul's writings that we get our earliest glimpse of the hierarchy of authority within the Christian movement. To the office of apostle Paul assigns priority. Next in dignity in his hierarchy of spiritual ministries were inspired preachers and interpreters known as prophets and teachers, followed by workers of miracles, healers, helpers, and administrators. It seems clear too that the church's earliest ministry was nonpatriarchal and inclusive. An eschatological community empowered by the Holy Spirit, the "status distinctions were abolished, and neither fixed structures nor institutionalized leadership was present." [3] A parity existed among Christian women and men not found in the prevailing social world of Christianity's beginnings. We know, for example, of famous Christian missionary couples—Junia and Andronicus and Prisca and Aquila. We know that women were leaders in house churches; in the case of churches like the one at Philippi, some house churches owed their beginning to the conversion of prominent and influential women. Women were also the recipients of the spiritual gift of prophecy, an office in the early church second only to that of the apostle.

Along with this itinerant, charismatic (i.e. spirit-filled) ministry, there existed as well a local, stationary pastoral ministry. We can infer too from the Christian literature of the period that the local ministry in the beginning was subordinate to the apostles and inferior in dignity to the prophets and teachers. In form this pastoral ministry was two tiered. It consisted of presbyters (also elder and later "priest") or bishops and deacons whose authority was restricted to local congregations. The apostles, prophets, and teachers of whom Paul wrote had a general ministry to the whole church. In some instances inspired utterance akin to that of the spirit-filled itinerants may have been expected of the regular, local ministry. For the most part, however, these ministers were charged with the administration of the local congregation's affairs and with the church's liturgical ministry. Presbyters and bishops—the terms were used interchangeably of the same person—were celebrants at the Eucharist; deacons assisted in the liturgy, and were charged with the church property and the administration of its charities.

It seems too that the local ministry was collegial and probably reflects the Jewish synagogue system of a council of elders. Thus Paul directs his letter to the "bishops and deacons" of the church at Philippi, the Acts of

The Christian bishop emerged in the second century as a symbol of
Christian unity and orthodox belief.

the Apostles and the Letter of Paul to Titus speak of presbyters and bishops (interchangeably), and the First Epistle of Clement of Rome (c. 95) indicates that a system of shared oversight existed also in the Roman church. Elsewhere at Jerusalem and Antioch the monarchical episcopate appeared as an early organizational pattern of ministry and may have encouraged the development of the hierarchical conception of bishop as chief administrator, liturgist, and pastor. The monarchical bishop also became important as a defender of Christian teaching and unity. Bishop Ignatius of Antioch, for example, advised the churches of Ephesus, Magnesia, Tralles, Philadelphia, and Smyrna to shun heresy and division and "follow the bishop as Jesus Christ followed the Father, and follow the presbytery as the Apostles; and respect the deacons as the commandment of God." It is clear from this that a threefold ministry with a subordination of function had already emerged in some churches at a very early date.

A fluid arrangement that allowed for the coexistence of several patterns of ministry and church order persisted until the apostles, through dispersal or death, began to disappear, and then the question of authorized tradition bearers arose with a new urgency. While the apostles lived, they instructed new converts, settled controversies, and guided the churches in doctrine and practice. But in their absence who would be responsible for the congregations dispersed over the length of the Roman Empire, and who would transmit the churches' received traditions? In spite of the dignity of the wandering prophets, prophecy was not without its problems. Among other things, charism, or the gift of the spirit, was unpredictable and often idiosyncratic; and the task of evaluating charism was understandably a perplexing one. To complicate matters further, the character of the Christian movement was altering. Starting as a "spirit-guided," eschatological sect under the umbrella of Judaism, Christianity by the end of the first century had become a geographically dispersed network of consolidated congregations coming to terms with the delay of the Parousia and the indeterminacy of its own historical existence. This is evident, for example, in the grammar of conventional morality that creeps into Christian literature and the intercessory prayers that the church offers now for temporal rulers. It becomes evident too in the subordination of women reflected in pronouncements like the one found in the *Apostolic Constitutions* of the fourth century. There we read that, "We do not permit our women to teach in Church, but only to pray and hear those that teach." [4]

The altered condition of the church becomes evident too in the growing importance and prestige of the regular pastoral ministry. A Christian manual of the period, known as *The Teaching of the Twelve Apostles* or *Didache*, for example, advised that only individuals of known probity be appointed to the offices of bishop and deacon. A similar emphasis surfaces

in 1 and 2 Timothy and Titus, New Testament writings appropriately designated the pastoral Epistles. Here the title presbyter and bishop have reference, as they do not for Paul, to special church offices, and the test for
candidacy has become character and morality rather than spiritual endow-
ment. The bishop as God's steward, we learn, ought not to be "arrogant
or quick-tempered or a drunkard or violent or greedy for gain, but hospita-
ble, a lover of goodness, master of himself, upright, holy, and self-
controlled" (Titus 1:7–8). The other emphasis we notice in the Christian
literature of this period is what has been called "a pattern of sound
words," that is, the received teachings of the apostles. Touchstone of faith
and doctrine, this teaching becomes the special responsibility of the church's
permanent clergy.

Apostolic Succession

The idea that the ministry of bishops and presbyters derived from the
apostles was, however, first offered by Clement of Rome as justification
for their rightful authority. In this letter, Clement, probably the preeminent
presbyter or bishop of the Roman church, urged a rebellious faction in the
Corinthian church to restore certain presbyters who had been expelled. He
reasoned that in God's wisdom nothing is without order or by chance and
reminded the Corinthians that God appointed times and seasons and
places for worship and service. He also appointed ministers. "The Apostles for our sake received the gospel from the Lord Jesus Christ," Clement
writes. "Jesus Christ was sent from God. Christ then is from God, and the
Apostles from Christ." He then concludes that after the death of the apostles provision was made that "other approved men" might succeed to
their ministry, and these persons were those who had been duly appointed
by the church.

Apostolic succession prepared for the transition from the immediate
authority of inspiration to the "official" and mediated authority of bishops. Irenaeus, second century bishop of Lyon, also found the principle
of value in combating heretical interpretations of Christian teaching. Like
Clement, Irenaeus assumed that the apostles were the authorized witnesses of Jesus' message and custodians of his mission. And in his controversy with Gnostic Christianity, he rested his defense of orthodox Christian belief on the apostolic character of the church's teaching.

To make good his claim, Irenaeus had to answer the Gnostic claim
that the revelation they possessed was a special, superior revelation entrusted by Jesus to his intimate followers and transmitted orally to a spiritual gnostic elite. His approach was simple and direct. Irenaeus answered

that the apostles' preaching was recorded in the Gospels—Matthew and John having been written by those apostles, Mark and Luke reproducing the message respectively of Peter and Paul. The claim that private teachings beyond what is taught openly in the written Gospels was, Irenaeus averred, without warrant. Had the apostles received additional instruction from Jesus, they would certainly have handed them over to their successors in the governance of the churches. But there was no authentic oral tradition among the Gnostics. Only the churches of apostolic foundation fully preserved apostolic tradition, and an orderly succession of ministers in those churches was guarantee of the faithful transmission of the tradition. Irenaeus concludes that he could enumerate the continuity of bishops in all the churches, but writes that mention of the Roman church is enough. Since the Roman church received its faith from the apostles Peter and Paul through a line of venerable bishops, harmony with that church is sufficient in itself to certify correct or orthodox belief.

Institutional Developments
to the Third Century

Irenaeus demonstrates how far the process of institutionalizing sacred power had progressed by the end of the second century. In little more than a century, the church had weathered the crisis that accompanied the disappearance of its original leadership. The immediate authority of the itinerant charismatics had been replaced by the mediated sacral ministry of bishops, presbyters, and deacons. This threefold hierarchical ministry emerged from the informal, fluid circumstances of the first century churches.

The principle of apostolic succession was joined to the idea of a hierarchical ministry. And this principle gave further legitimacy to episcopal authority and more generally to the church's quest for unity and stability in the areas of church order and faith. The assertion that the Christian ministry rested on the authority of the apostles had the additional consequence of enhancing the dignity of the church in Rome. The adoption in the third century of the secular provincial system of the Roman Empire meant that the church also would have a formal institutional structure expressive of its ecumenical (general or universal) mission and character. At the church's first ecumenical council at the resort city of Nicaea (325), this interdependent network of local churches organized regionally under the bishops of the imperial provincial capitol cities was formally ratified, the honor of preeminent jurisdictional authority going to the churches of the empire's three greatest cities—Rome, Alexandria, and Antioch.

THE FORMATION
OF A CHRISTIAN SCRIPTURE

Scripture and Canon

The term "scripture" comes from the Latin *scriptura*, which refers to the act of writing or to the product of writing. More commonly, however, scripture refers to the sacred texts—or, what is called the foundational literature of the world religions. When we speak today of scripture, we usually have in mind sacred books like the Vedas of Hinduism, the Tripitaka of Buddhism, the Avestas of Zoroastrianism, the Qur'an of Islam, and the Jewish Bible. These sacred books—each of which is in fact a collection of writings—are regarded by the religious communities that hold them sacred as timeless revelations of ultimate mystery. They are timeless in the sense that they manifest reality that transcends ordinary temporal or spatial categories. The words of scripture are not merely human words expressing human desires and intentions. Hindus believe that the Veda was revealed to primal sages at creation. That portion of the Avestas known as the Gathas is thought to be the revelation of the god Ahura Mazda to the prophet Zarathustra. The Torah is held to be the disclosure of Yahweh's unchanging purpose to Moses at Sinai. Moslems believe the Qur'an to be the uncreated word of Allah. Likewise, religious communities believe that the record of events, rituals, sacred stories, laws, and codes of conduct found in scripture are foundational in character, charters for worship and life.

Sacred scripture is sacred because it manifests the holy, is mediated through inspired human agents, communicates revealed truths, and discloses timeless patterns of thought and action. Yet we know too that scriptures—though they are thought to have a precedence of being—do not have a chronological priority to religious community and are often the product of a process of canonization. Briefly stated, *canonization* is the process whereby religious communities identify those writings that are approved for reading at services of worship, exposition or preaching, and determining moral and doctrinal norms. The end result of the process is usually an authoritative list of religious writings called a *canon* (from the Greek meaning "rule" or "standard"). And more often than not, canonical scriptures evolve over long periods of time in concert with standards for worship and practice. The Jewish Bible is an excellent case in point. Though Israel came into existence at the time of the Exodus (c. 1290 B.C.E.), it was not until the seventh century before the common era that the first step toward canonization was taken. According to Jewish tradition, the book of Deuteronomy was discovered during the reign of King Josiah, when it was accepted as revelation. Not until roughly 400 B.C.E. was the Torah, with Deuteronomy as its nucleus, fully formed. By 180 B.C.E. we know that the canon of the Prophets had attained a status second to the

Torah as the Scripture of Judaism. Later still, sometime in the first century
C.E., a third canon known simply as the Writings attained official status
and together with the Torah and the Prophets was officially and definitively recognized as the Hebrew Bible by the rabbinic courts of Jamnia in
90 C.E..

The First Christian Scripture

Christianity inherited Judaism's Scriptures, reinterpreting their
meaning and eventually renaming them the Old Testament. Yet, just which
collection of Jewish Scripture Christians ought to use is disputed. Roman
Catholics, for example, adhere to the Greek canon (the Septuagint) of Hellenistic Judaism, a fluid, more expansive canon that includes books rejected by the rabbis of Jamnia and excluded from the Hebrew canon. These
books, termed deutero-canonical (secondary) writings by Catholics and the
Apocrypha (Greek meaning hidden things) by Protestants, together with
the Hebrew canon, constitute the Old Testament for Catholic Christians.
At the time of the Protestant Reformation, Luther decided in favor of the
Jamnian canon and in his 1534 German translation of the Bible placed the
Apocrypha in a separate section at the end of the Old Testament. For Lu-
ther and Protestantism, the Apocrypha is not equal to Scripture and in fact
is absent from the popular Protestant translations, the Revised Standard
Version and the New English Bible.

Though Christians disagree about the shape of the Old Testament,
they do not, however, doubt that the Jewish Bible is a Christian Scripture.
And, of course, the first generation of Christians knew no other Bible.
When they spoke of Scripture, it was to Judaism's Bible that they referred.
Furthermore, the sacred writings of Judaism were Scripture for Jesus and
had both the implicit and explicit sanction of his teachings. During his public ministry, he is portrayed as one who frequently cites Scripture, affirms
the authority of "the law and the prophets" (Matthew 5:17), and speaks
of fulfillment of "the law of Moses [i.e. the Torah] and the prophets and
the psalms [i.e. the Writings]" (Luke 24:46).

It was a natural development for Christians to adopt Israel's sacred
writings as the first Christian Scripture, but in the beginning the Christian
canon was open. First-century Christianity supplemented Jewish Scripture
with an oral tradition of the words and deeds of Jesus, transmitted under
the authority of the "Lord." In the period from approximately 33 to 70
C.E., the church assembled Jesus' sayings, parables, miracles, and passion
narrative, employed them in worship, in the instruction of initiates (i.e.
catechesis), and in its preaching and its missionary endeavors. And from
roughly 70 to 95 C.E. the Evangelists drew this oral material together in the
form of Gospels.

Even three decades into the second century, this oral "scripture," described by the Christian bishop of Hierapolis as "the words of a living and surviving voice," was preferred above the church's emerging literary culture. Nevertheless, the books that are now in the New Testament had been prepared, circulated, and were in the process of attaining scriptural status when Papias—this early second-century Christian bishop—expressed his preference. The Pauline epistles by the end of the first century were collected and in circulation. Toward the middle of the century, the epistles were described as Scripture. And the four Gospels, which Christian apologist Justin Martyr characterized as the work "of the apostles and those who followed them," were being used alongside the Old Testament in Christian worship.

Step Toward Canonization

Christian literature by the second century rivaled the oral tradition as a vehicle for transmitting the Jesus tradition. Paul had also demonstrated the value of the letter for instruction and ecclesiastical policy, and others followed him in the use of this literary device for the building up of the churches. An important stimulus for the development of a canon of sacred writings, however, arose in connection with Christian doctrine. There was, for example, a subgroup of Jewish Christians who thought that Jesus was a human who perfectly fulfilled the Law and whose mission had been the reform of Judaism. Known as Ebionites, this strain of Jewish Christianity adhered to the Mosaic Law, used Hebrew in worship, accepted only one Gospel, and rejected the Pauline tradition.

A greater stimulus to developing an orthodox Christian canon came from Gnostic Christians. We saw in an earlier chapter that the Christian version of Gnosticism dismissed the kerygma of Jesus' crucifixion and resurrection and taught that Jesus was rather a heavenly revealer of a perfect wisdom, a perfect *gnosis* as that wisdom was called. They also held that not everyone was equally suited to receive this saving *gnosis* and that Jesus secretly communicated his teachings to the apostles, who in turn instructed a spiritual elite in this hidden tradition of revelation. Thus, while the orthodox churches possessed Jesus' public message, Gnostics possessed an open-ended canon of writings which, like the Gospel of Thomas, claimed to preserve "the secret words which the living Jesus spoke."

Here then were Christians transmitting a rival Jesus tradition under the authority of the apostles in a canon that at least theoretically was impossible to limit. The Roman Christian Marcion represented a very different challenge for the orthodox churches. Study of the Jewish Scripture convinced him that the god of the Jews, the god of Genesis and Exodus, was not the supreme God, the God revealed by Jesus. The god of Hebrew

Scripture was, Marcion believed, an inferior creator, a demiurge, whose rule extended over human beings through harsh, exacting, and ultimately arbitrary commandments and laws. The God whom Jesus revealed and preached, by contrast, was a God of infinite love and mercy. Not having been inspired by the true God and Father of Jesus Christ, Jewish Scripture (called for the first time the Old Testament) was thus rejected as incompatible with Jesus' gospel of love. Marcion was conscious too of the extensive influence of Jewish thought and theology on the apostles, whose writings he also dismissed as a corruption of the Christian witness. Only the apostles Paul and Luke reflected a Christian gospel of grace and love. And so deviating from the church's practice of simply adding Christian writings to the Hebrew Bible, Marcion took the radical step of disavowing Jewish Scripture and creating an entirely separate list of authoritative Christian books, comprised of ten letters of Paul and an edited version of Luke's Gospel.

A Normative Christian Canon

Marcion was the first to suggest the Christian canon consisted of two parts, Gospels and epistles; his separation of the Testaments also influenced the subsequent development of the orthodox canon, although it was the North African theologian Tertullian who first spoke of a *Novum Testamentum*, a New Testament. But perhaps Marcion's most significant influence on the orthodox canon was the reaction his own canon prompted among the churches. By the end of the century, the Roman church had formulated not only a list of approved Christian books but had developed criteria for approval. In a document known as the Muratorian fragment, a writing notable for its anti-Marcion tone, we can see that the Roman church was already advanced in the process of canonization. Some writings, the fragment noted, were approved for reading in services of worship; some were valued as edifying, though not to be enrolled as Scripture along with the prophets (i.e. the Old Testament) and the apostles; some books were to be repudiated. The fragment's New Testament canon includes four Gospels, Acts, thirteen letters of Paul, Jude, first and second John, a work attributed to Peter, the Wisdom of Solomon, two apocalypses, and the Revelations of John and Peter. A glance at today's New Testament indicates that the Muratorian "canon" omits some books that were eventually approved and includes two books that were ultimately rejected. Nevertheless, the fragment shows how far the process of formalizing a Christian Scripture had advanced. It shows too that appropriateness for worship and use in the building up of churches were important criteria for collecting and approving an authorized list of Christian writings. Controversy with the Marcionites and Gnostics, however, gave doctrine a prominence in sifting out "fakes," books that pass under the name of an apostle but "cannot be received in the catholic church."

A view as to the approved or acknowledged books formed at an early date among the churches, yet a catholic (i.e. universal) consensus was still to be realized. On the report of the famous theologian Origin of Alexandria, all twenty-seven books that now form the New Testament were known and in circulation among the churches, but not all were everywhere accepted. The standing of James, Jude, second Peter, and second and third John had still to be settled. To further complicate things, the Greek-speaking churches of the East were reluctant to acknowledge the Revelation of John, and the Latin churches of the West harbored a similar reluctance about the letter to the Hebrews. And then there were writings on the margin of the canon, writings that came to be known as the Apostolic Fathers, writings such as the Shepherd of Hermas, the epistle of Barnabas, the Didache, and first and second Clement. As late as the fifth century, for example, first and second Clement were found in a Greek manuscript of the New Testament.

The picture that emerges from this history of canonization is one of winnowing wheat from the chaff, and it was not until Athanasius, bishop of Alexandria, circulated an Easter letter among his churches in the year 367 that we hear of the "books that are canonical and handed down to us and believed as divine." Athanasius's list included all the books that Jerome was to include in the Vulgate, the Latin translation of the Bible that became the standard in the West until the Protestant Reformation. Henceforth, the Christian New Testament would contain four Gospels, Acts of the Apostles, seven so-called pastoral Epistles, fourteen epistles of Paul, and the Revelation of John.

THE TRADITION OF CHRISTIAN BELIEF

The Idea of Religious Belief

The Buddhist initiate declares a resolve to follow the Eightfold Path by reciting what is called the Triple Jewel. The initiate's commitment to the Path commences, it might be said, with the resolve to take refuge in the Buddha, the teaching of the Buddha, and the community of monks who live by Buddha's teaching. And when a student of Buddhism told me that the Triple Jewel is the closest thing to a creed in Buddhism, I thought his use of the word strange. As Christians use the word creed, a word from the Latin credo meaning "I believe," the reference is to formal statements which detail and define religious belief. I wondered what, for example, the

Nicene Creed might have in common with the Triple Jewel and in what sense the Buddhist affirmation was also an expression of a religious belief? The most obvious point of similarity is that both forms of affirmation are used in the context of initiation. Both are associated with initiatory rites and regulate entrance into the religious community. But what does it signify to make an affirmation of belief set within the initiatory rite?

The one thing we can say about religious belief with confidence is that it is experiential in nature. It is belief arising in conjunction with a community's deepest affirmations and loyalties. At some level religious belief may take on the character of intellectual assent, but even in those cases it is not an assent to abstract propositions. Religious belief arises rather in relation to a religious community's formative symbols and its central stories and rituals. The Triple Jewel of Buddhism thus indicates a dependency and trust with respect to the sources held indispensable for enlightenment; the Nicene Creed does the same with respect to the sources of Christian salvation. Both represent that "practical trusting in, reliance on, counting upon something" [5] that American theologian H. Richard Niebuhr writes of when he speaks of faith.

In connection with initiation and worship, we may conclude then that at a basic level religious belief represents a declaration of a fundamental trust or an abiding loyalty to a religious community, its sacred stories, and its way of life. And for that reason our discussion of Christian creed begins with early baptismal confessions and with prebaptismal instruction (i.e. catechesis). Yet, religious belief, especially in the form of its creedal affirmations, also defines the conditions for the community's existence. Often forged in the heat of controversy, statements of belief define what is consistent with the integrity of the community's understanding of its foundational experiences and stories, determine its normative forms of worship and practice, and establish the terms on which it appropriates ideas and values from its social and cultural environment.

The Baptismal Confession

Baptism is an early Christian rite of initiation, practiced among the churches from the beginning and believed to have been instituted by Jesus. Its earliest form, however, can only be imperfectly reconstructed, yet from what can be inferred from Christian writings of the period, the rite involved an anointing with oil, a laying on of hands, prayers for the gift of the Holy Spirit, the symbols of milk and honey signifying entrance into the promised land, and a ritual washing in a river or lake or baptismal font in a house church. Preparation for the rite was marked by a period of fasting, by the renunciation of the devil and his works, and by a confession of faith. The confessions were at first a simple, unembellished Christological affirmation—"Jesus is Lord." Baptismal formulas might also express the Trinitarian content of the faith reflected in the last chapter of the Gospel of Matthew—"Go therefore and make disciples of all nations, baptizing them in the name of the Father, of the Son, and of the Holy Spirit" (28:19). According to this formula, candidates would receive baptism at the hand of the bishop by immersion or infusion (a pouring of water over the head) at the affirmation of each article.

The need to defend normative Christian belief and practice, especially against the Marcionites and the Gnostics, led to a further development of the second-century baptismal interrogations. In the Roman church, for example, candidates were required to answer in the affirmative to a more fully detailed interrogation known from *The Apostolic Tradition* of Hippolytus.

> Dost thou believe in God the Father almighty? Dost thou believe in Christ Jesus, the Son of God, Who was born by the Holy Spirit from the Virgin Mary, Who was crucified under Pontius Pilate, and died and rose again on the third day living from the dead, and ascended into the heavens, and sat down at the right hand of the Father, and will come to judge the living and the dead? Dost thou believe in the Holy Spirit, in the holy Church, and in the resurrection of the flesh?

Three developments are to be noted in this interrogatory baptismal formula. It continues the Trinitarian pattern, but now the Christological core is enlarged to express the church's kerygmatic faith. It excludes rival versions of the Christian drama of salvation. Against the Marcionites, the confession affirms the sovereignty of God over creation and all creatures in its use of the word *pantokator*, a word translated above as "almighty" but perhaps better rendered "all ruling." Against the Gnostics, it affirms the humanity and historical reality of Jesus. Third, the formula asserts the authority of the church which is now listed among the affirmations of the faith. In a further development, the baptismal confession assumed a declaratory form. No longer expressed as answers to questions, these proto-creedal affirmations were used by the bishop in prebaptismal instruction and repeated as direct declarations by the initiates as a sign of membership and a symbol (i.e. a password or token) of orthodoxy. The most famous example of this kind of affirmation is the Roman Symbol, a fourth-century declaratory baptismal statement of the Roman church that became the basis of the Apostles'Creed.

The Rule of Faith

The Apostles' Creed, according to tradition, was a short summary of apostolic teaching drafted by the apostles themselves shortly after Pentecost as a guarantee of doctrinal continuity and unity. In fact, the creed in its present form is from a period not earlier than the sixth century. Yet the legend sheds light on the early development of doctrine among the churches. We have seen already that the baptismal confessions were important instruments in the formation of doctrine. We need to keep in mind that these early confessions had a ritual context and were transmitted in oral form within the setting of local churches. That meant, of course, that local usage determined the nature of the confessions; it meant also that there did not exist a uniform statement of belief, written down and subscribed to by all the churches.

The task of preparing universally accepted creeds fell to the great ecumenical councils beginning in the fourth century. Nevertheless, already in the second century, we know of a pattern of Christian teaching that made explicit the cardinal truths of Christian revelation. And, while not a formal creed, this pattern, called variously the "canon [rule] of truth" and the "rule of faith," enjoyed widespread acceptance among Christian churches as genuinely apostolic. Like the baptismal confessions of the churches, this rule of faith was an essentially oral tradition. Like the Apostles' Creed of Christian tradition, the rule functioned as a summary of the church's faith. And, like the church's creedal formulas, the rule's authority derived from two assurances. It bore the stamp of apostolicity and had the certification of inspiration, what Irenaeus called "an infallible charism of truth."

Councils and Creeds

Official recognition of Christianity by the Emperor Constantine in the fourth century marked the beginning of a great age of church councils, sometimes called the conciliar age. It was the charge of these assemblies of Christian bishops and religious leaders, gathered at Nicaea (325), Constantinople (381), Ephesus (431), and Chalcedon (451), to settle disputes and make official pronouncements on doctrine, worship, and church order. It fell also to these first councils to perform the task of translating Christianity's revelation into the conceptual language of theology and creed.

In part this task was possible because by the fourth century the church had begun to think in Greek philosophical terms about the mysteries of the Christian faith. The second-century apologist Justin Martyr, for example, wrote that, since Christ is Logos or the Reason of God imprinted in the mind of humanity, "whatever has been uttered aright by any men in any place belongs to us Christians." In part the work of formalizing Christian creeds arose from necessity. Controversy over belief again threatened orthodox teaching and Christian unity. Appeal to Scripture and the rule of faith, which the church had used successfully in the second century, proved inadequate at this time, however, for the controversy was among competing versions of orthodox belief. What was to be done when rival factions of normative Christianity appealed to Scripture for justification of their views? What instrument could be used to arbitrate among the variant interpretations of the ultimate Christian mysteries? At the urging of his chaplain, Constantine gave his answer by inviting Christian bishops to the resort town of Nicaea on the Bosphorus for what became the first general or *ecumenical council* of the church.

The theological issue that perplexed and divided Christian bishops leading up to Nicaea was the mystery of the Trinity. What, the bishops were forced to ask, was the relation of Jesus to God, of the Son of God to the eternal Father? A presbyter in the church of Alexandria named Arius argued Jesus was less than God. Although a heavenly being above the angels, and God's agent in creation, Jesus, so Arius held, was essentially a created being who lacked the true nature of divinity. Since Arius could debate with his opponents on biblical grounds, matching them text for text, the anti-Arian party meeting at Nicaea under Athanasius, another Alexandrian, formulated their defense of the full divinity of the Son on extrabiblical grounds. Using a Greek concept, they held that Jesus was "of the substance [*ousia*] of the Father" and "of one substance [*homoousios*] with the Father." These abstract words, along with other clarifying phrases, were added to the baptismal confession of Caesarea to make the Creed of Nicaea. Revised again at Constantinople, this first universal creed became the Nicene Creed, still used by Roman Catholics, Orthodox Christians, Anglicans, and some Protestants as a common expression of belief and an instrument of worship.

Having asserted Christ's divinity, it was next the church's business to find a way to express the belief that the divine was fully revealed in the undiminished humanity of the person of Jesus Christ. Once again, the failure of certain thinkers to adequately express the sense of Christian mystery was the cause for the convocations at Ephesus and Chalcedon. The pious bishop Apollinaris of Laodicea, for example, reasoned that the eternal Logos of God displaced the human reason of Christ when at the time of the Incarnation it was united with the human body and spirit. It was objected, however, that the whole of human nature required redemption. Another quite different account of this Christian paradox was offered by Nestorius. He taught that the two natures of Christ—the human and the divine—remained separate and distinct at the time of the Incarnation. He also rejected the title *theotokos*, "mother of God," in favor of *Christotokos*, "mother of Christ," for the Virgin Mary. The Christian monk Eutyches objected and argued that after the Incarnation there remained only one nature, the human having been absorbed by the divine.

The teaching of both Nestorius and Eutyches were rejected by the orthodox councils. But they also had their supporters who separated from the orthodox form of Christianity to constitute separate churches, churches that survive still today. For the orthodox party, however, each of these theologians presented a serious threat to Christian teaching. Nestorius, it was held, failed to do full justice to the unity of the divine and the human in the person of Christ; Eutyches failed to appreciate fully Christ's humanity. It fell to Pope Leo I to express the opinion of the majority of Christian bishops concerning the union of divinity and humanity in the person of Jesus. In his famous letter, Leo wrote to the council fathers assembled at Chalcedon:

> . . . thus the properties of each nature and substance were preserved entire, and came together to form one person. Humility was assumed by majesty, weakness by strength, mortality by eternity; and to pay the debt that we incurred, an inviolable nature was united to a nature that can suffer.

Building on the *Tome* of Pope Leo I and using the Greek terminology for substance (*hypostasis*) and person (*prosopon*) to speak of the unity of Christ's person, the Definition of Chalcedon asserted that Christ is to be recognized "In two natures, without confusion, without change, without division, without separation" and that Mary his mother is to be known as "God bearer" (*theotokos*).

The Achievement and Failure of the Councils

The canons or rules regulating church administration and discipline were drafted by the councils, and the Council of Chalcedon elevated the church of Constantinople to patriarchal status, a dignity it shared only with the ancient Christian churches of Jerusalem, Antioch, Alexandria, and Rome. Yet the precision the creeds gave to the language of faith—developed earlier principally in the context of preaching, liturgy, instruction and apologetics—proved the most notable achievement of the conciliar age. Not that the great historical formulas purported in the words of theologian Alan Richardson "to solve the riddles of metaphysics." [6] One is struck in fact by how practical and situational they were, by how much compromise and consensus went into their making. The Creed of Nicaea and the Definition of Chalcedon, to take the most obvious examples, do not set out to explain the mystery of the Trinity and the Incarnation. They rather build protective hedges around the faith's great mysteries—proscribing heretical teaching on the one hand, specifying on the other hand the appropriate limits of orthodox belief and expression. To put it another way, the creeds functioned as interpretative blueprints, not exhaustively detailing belief but indicating uniform rules for the Christian understanding of its own apostolic traditions.

Yet, the church's goal of uniformity was realized only imperfectly. Though the councils sought Christian unity, they also sowed the seeds of Christian division. The Nestorian church, which today numbers no more than two hundred thousand and is found mainly in Iraq, Iran, India, and the United States, rejected the Council of Ephesus, the council's condemnation of Nestorius, and its use of the title *theotokos* of the Virgin Mary. The non-Chalcedonian or "Monophysite" churches, now found largely in Syria, Lebanon, India, Armenia, Egypt, and Ethiopia, divided from normative Christianity over the Chalcedonian formula that ascribed two natures—not one as they believe—to Christ. Even the canons making Constantinople a patriarchate of dignity and authority comparable to Rome prepared the way for conflict and eventually the Great Schism of 1054 that divided the Greek-speaking churches of the East and the Latin church of the West into two separate traditions—Roman Catholicism and Eastern Orthodoxy.

SUMMARY

We began by saying that religious tradition is living, dynamic, and progressive. It mediates the experiences of the religious past and makes their meaning and transformative power contemporary and accessible. We have seen that those foundational experiences are also formed by religious tradition and are susceptible of further formation and even re-formation as times change and cultural circumstances alter. But our objective in this chapter was limited to the first Christian centuries, to the time when the Christian ministry, Scripture, and creed initially took shape.

The making of tradition, we observed, was in part the self-conscious work of special religious figures whom we called tradition bearers. As often as not, however, tradition developed in relation to an emerging consensus of the geographically dispersed Christian communities. Like the creative process described by the playwright Luigi Pirandello in *Six Characters in Search of an Author*, tradition as we have watched it unfold seemed almost to "write itself" according to an internal logic. We saw, for example, that into the second century the elements of Christian tradition were fluid and largely local. Yet the contours of normative Christian tradition were already clear, the principle of apostolicity for ministry, Scripture, and creed already in place. All that was required was an official and universally agreed upon authorization, and this the conciliar age provided. The age of the great ecumenical councils began another important process as well. It assumed responsibility—carried further during the next period of Christian history—for bringing Christianity into creative contact with its culture.

REVIEW AND REFLECTION

1. What is the meaning and importance of religious tradition?
2. What is the content of the Christian tradition and what are the means Christians developed to preserve and transmit that content?
3. Describe the forms and function of ministry in first-century Christianity.
4. How did we account for the change from the charismatic ministry of the first century to the threefold pastoral ministry of the second century?
5. Explain the meaning of canonization and show how the Jewish Bible came to be canonized.
6. What prompted the early Christian churches to collect the sacred writings that became the New Testament?
7. Religious belief entails more than intellectual assent. What more is involved in religious affirmations of belief?
8. How did simple affirmations of belief in Jesus become the sophisticated creed of the ecumenical councils?
9. List the achievements of the first four ecumenical councils of the church.

END NOTES

1. Jaroslav Pelikan, *The Vindication of Tradition* (New Haven and London: Yale University Press, 1984), p. 65.

2. Henry Bettenson, ed., *Documents of the Christian Church*, 2nd ed. (London, Oxford, New York: Oxford University Press, 1974), pp. 75–76.

3. Elizabeth Fiorenza, "Women in the Early Christian Movement," in Carol P. Christ and Judith Plaskow, eds. *Womenspirit Rising: A Feminist Reader in Religion* (San Francisco: Harper & Row, Publishers, 1979), p. 88.

4. Quoted in Elizabeth Schussler Fiorenza, "Word, Spirit and Power: Women in Early Christian Communities," in Rosemary Ruether and Eleanor McLaughlin, *Women of Spirit: Female Leadership in the Jewish and Christian Traditions* (New York: Simon and Schuster, 1979), p. 43.

5. H. Richard Niehubr, *Radical Monotheism and Western Culture* (New York: Harper & Row, Publishers, 1970), pp. 116–117.

6. Alan Richardson, *Creeds in the Making: A Short Introduction to the History of Christian Doctrine*, 2nd ed. (New York: The Macmillan Company, 1969), p. 65.

SUGGESTED FURTHER READING

BENKO, STEPHEN. *Pagan Rome and the Early Christians*. Bloomington: Indiana University Press, 1986.

BULTMANN, RUDOLPH. *The Theology of the New Testament*. Vol. 2. London: SCM Press, 1965.

CHADWICH, OWEN. *The Early Church*. New York: Penguin Books, 1967.

FOX, ROBIN LANE. *Pagans and Christians*. New York: Alfred A. Knoft, 1987.

GAGER, JOHN G. *Kingdom and Community: The Social World of Early Christianity*. Studies in Religion Series. Englewood Cliffs, NJ: Prentice-Hall, Inc., 1975.

GOODSPEED, EDGAR J. *A History of Early Christian Literature*. rev. ed. by Robert M. Grant. Chicago: The University of Chicago Press, 1966.

KUNG, HANS. *The Church*. New York: Sheed and Ward, 1967.

MEEKS, WAYNE. *The Moral World of the First Christians*. Philadelphia: The Westminister Press, 1986.

PAGELS, ELAINE. *The Gnostic Gospels*. New York: Random House, 1979.

OUTLER, ALBERT C. "The Sense of Tradition in the Ante-Nicene Church," in *The Heritage of Christian Thought*. Eds. Robert E. Cushman and Egil Grislis. New York, Evanston, and London: Harper & Row, 1965.

WALSH, MICHAEL. *The Triumph of the Meek: Why Early Christianity Succeeded*. San Francisco: Harper & Row Publishers, 1986.

5 | Medieval Christianity

INTRODUCTION

The conversion of Emperor Constantine to the cause of Christ marked a new era in Christian history. No longer an illegal religious sect on the margins of culture and society, Christianity found itself very much at the center of power. During the reign of Constantine and after, Christian worship was transferred from house churches and catacombs to grand basilicas. Christian bishops divided their time between the spiritual care of a Christian people and the temporal needs of a Christian society. And, together with temporal rulers, Christian bishops evolved new understandings of Christian authority.

Of course, not all Christians embraced this task of Christianizing the social order; not all welcomed the forces of church and society that would conform the church to "this world." And for individuals of this conviction monasticism held a strong appeal. Like early martyrdom, monasticism proved an important outlet for Christians with a vocation to bear witness to the New Testament's eschatological faith and to its hope for the new age, the age to come. Yet, even monasticism was enlisted in the service of the church's great work of translating the Christian faith into the unified and integrated Christian order known as Christendom. Just how this was achieved in the areas of church order and papal authority, worship and popular piety, and religious thought and theology during the centuries known as the Middle Ages is the subject of this chapter.

The Christian Middle Ages—Key Dates

Dates	Persons and Events
c. 251–356 C.E.	Anthony, father of Christian monasticism
c. 390–346 C.E.	Pachomius, founder of the first Christian monastery in Egypt
354–430 C.E.	Augustine of Hippo, one of the influential theologians of all time and author of the *City of God.*
c. 480–550 C.E.	Benedict of Nursia, founder of western monasticism and author of an influential monastic rule
c. 540–604 C.E.	Pope Gregory I, founder of the medieval papacy
680–754 C.E.	Boniface, missionary to the Germanic tribes
800 C.E.	Charlemagne, crowned first emperor of the Holy Roman Empire by Pope Leo III
910 C.E.	monastery founded at Cluny, beginning of a widely imitated reform movement
1054 C.E.	the division of Christendom between rival centers in Rome and Constantinople
1073–1085 C.E.	Pope Gregory VII, reforming pope who asserts the supremacy of the papacy over his rival, Emperor Henry IV
1095 C.E.	Pope Urban II, announces the First Crusade
c. 1182–1226 C.E.	Francis of Assisi, founder of Franciscan friars
1215 C.E.	Lateran IV, council that defined the West's Eucharistic doctrine
1225–1274 C.E.	Thomas Aquinas, theologian and author of *Summa Theologica*

MARTYRS AND MONKS

Christian Martyrs

Even before Constantine, Christianity was losing its character as an apocalyptic sect in the shadow of Christ's imminent return. Its social, political, and cultural environment were becoming more important. Yet, baptism in the first Christian centuries was still a politically suspect and often personally hazardous rite of initiation. It signified membership in an illegal and despised religious sect. For the Romans, usually tolerant in matters of religion, Christianity was a nuisance, an "accursed foreign superstition." The point at which the Christian community and the Roman state officially clashed, however, was over Rome's expectation that citizens pay homage to the gods and the emperor. Christians were willing to meet the state's expectations of good citizenship in certain matters. In morality and personal conduct, they tended to be model citizens. In their worship, they offered prayer for civil authorities. In their theology, they affirmed a sovereign, all-ruling God who establishes and by his providence preserves even the secular kingdoms of the present age. And Christians had the example of their savior who commanded his disciples to "render unto Caesar the things that are Caesar's" (Luke 20:25).

Yet, implicit in the Christian world view was a relativizing of imperial authority in the name of the transcendent authority of God. Here was the dilemma. What should the Christian response be when political loyalty, loyalty to Caesar, clashed with their ultimate loyalty to God, when their dual citizenship in an earthly and a heavenly kingdom pulled in different directions? We know from Roman writers of the time that, when tested, some Christians yielded under the pressure of public trial and the threat of torture and death. In the words of the Roman historian Pliny the Younger, these persons "did reverence, with incense and wine, to [the emperor's] image." Pliny writes that others obstinately refused to "curse Christ" and sacrifice to the emperor. Though troublemakers from the point of view of a regional governor like Pliny, Christians of this tougher mettle were looked upon as heroes and saints, and were honored by the title confessors. Those among them whose ordeal terminated in death were called *martyrs*.

Today the martyr is often thought of as gloomy, joyless, even pathological. Yet, this is not the image that emerges from the church's early literature of martyrdom. Christian apologists were first of all keenly aware of the political ramifications of the Christian's ultimate loyalty to Christ, a loyalty that conflicted with the temporal loyalties of Roman citizenship. In these circumstances every Christian was potentially a martyr. But of more importance was the religious significance the church attached to the deaths of the martyrs.

As the name indicates, martyrs were witnesses to Christ, their lives exemplary and imitable patterns of Christian discipleship. And to be a martyr was to be united to Christ in a special way—to be assimilated to the redemptive pattern of his sacrificial death and resurrection. To be a martyr was to be buried with Christ in a second baptism, a baptism of blood. Martyrdom was even given the properties that the church associated with its Eucharistic meal. As the church commemorated Christ's sacrifice in bread and wine, so the martyr presented anew in his or her action the church's thanksgiving offering in blood and broken bone. It was as a sacrificial lamb and burnt offering that the *Martyrdom of Polycarp* pictured the death of the famous second-century bishop of Smyrna. And it was as Eucharistic bread that Ignatius of Antioch wrote of his own impending death in the Roman circus to his fellow bishops. "Let me be fodder to wild beasts," he urged them,

> . . . that is how I can get to God. I am God's wheat and I am being ground by the teeth of wild beasts to make a pure loaf for Christ. . . . Then I shall be a real disciple of Jesus Christ when the world sees my body no more. Pray Christ for me that by these means I may become God's sacrifice.

Some did vigorously object to the state's policy of charging Christians like Ignatius with disloyalty and state treason. Christian theologian Tertullian protested that "Christians alone are not allowed to say anything to clear themselves, to defend truth, to save a judge from injustice." Yet, in spite of such protests, there can be no doubt that the church cherished its martyrs and found in their action a meaning that transcended politics and imperial policy. For earliest Christianity, martyrs were living exemplars of Christian meaning. In the words of Polycarp, they were true "disciples and imitators of the Lord." Like Jesus Christ, according to Ignatius "the true and faithful witness," their death was a perfect emblem of Christ's own death at the hand of the state. The church even came to regard the tombs of martyrs as sacred places of pilgrimage where intercessory prayer might be offered or the liturgy celebrated. And, having been thus assimilated to Christ, the source of sacred power, the remains of martyrs themselves were thought to be holy objects, channels of divine power and healing, holy *relics* with miraculous power. Even when the peace of Constantine brought an end to the age of martyrs, this form of exceptional discipleship survived in what has been called the white martyrdom of Christian monasticism, a martyrdom of conscience.

Monastic Beginnings

Christian *monks*, like the martyrs, took Christ's passion and sacrificial death as an exemplary pattern for their own living. Yet, for them the *via evangelica*—the way of the gospel—led not to the martyr's bloody witness. Though some monks desired martyrdom, theirs was to be a different kind of self-denial and sacrifice. In their personal struggle with sin and evil, they freely severed social and economic ties to society and to an increasingly worldly church and withdrew to do solitary battle with the flesh and the devil. These *anchorites* (originally meaning "withdrawn" or "fugitive"), as they came to be known, retired to deserted places. The Egyptian monk Anthony made an abandoned fortress on the shore of the Red Sea his home for twenty years. In such isolated retreats, monks spent their time in prayer, in the recitations of psalms, in the memorizing of Scripture, and in manual labor that would not interfere with their meditation. They also trained themselves as spiritual athletes or *ascetics* (Greek *askesis* meaning "exercise" or "training") in order that they might prevail against besetting temptations of all sorts.

Often the extremity of the ascetic practices took bizarre form. The Syrian, Simeon the Stylite (c. 390–459), for example, prayed and preached to pilgrims for thirty years atop a pillar. Nevertheless, even such eccentrics found admiring audiences, were esteemed for their holiness of life, marveled at for their extraordinary powers, sought out for their wisdom and counsel, and imitated by innumerable persons who wished to be like them. No early monk, however, was more esteemed in all these respects than the founder of Christian monasticism whom Athanasius memorialized in the *Life of St. Anthony*.

Born to relatively wealthy parents, Anthony inherited a comfortable income while still a young man and might have lived in ease but for an event that changed his life. Attending church services, he heard the story from the Gospel of Matthew of the rich young man. The circumstances of the man who questioned Jesus about eternal life must have struck Anthony as very much like his own. Certainly, Jesus' response spoke to Anthony's condition when he replied that to be perfect one must "go, sell what you possess and give to the poor, and you will have treasure in heaven" (19:21). In a sense these words can be taken as a summary of the monastic goal of perfection through renunciation. If one would be perfect in the solitary life (Greek *monachos* means "solitary"), monks have reasoned, the mind must be unencumbered of possessions that distract and trouble it with cares. Otherwise, the poor soul will be "well-nigh crushed and smothered under its load, creeping down the road of life."

The description is Henry David Thoreau's of a young New England farmer, but Thoreau's farmer, pushing before him barn, fields, pasture, and woodlot, might well be taken as a monastic analysis of the human condition. *Walden*, we may assume, was Thoreau's antidote for this condition and for all those "so occupied with the factitious cares and superfluous coarse labors of life that its finer fruits cannot be plucked by them." [1] Anthony's antidote, like that of countless others who followed him in the monastic life, was to dispose of his inheritance and, after arranging for the care of his sister, leave human society for the solitude of the desert.

Even the most dedicated anchorite, or solitary monk, however, requires spiritual direction, and so it was that Anthony's first years in the desert were under the tutelage of an old hermit. Later in Anthony's life he reluctantly allowed others similarly to live nearby and profit from his wisdom and experience. Still, too much company was never to his liking, and Anthony moved farther from human society to occupy a tomb in an abandoned cemetery. The final stage of his life was lived in an empty fort east of the Nile River. There he continued his defense against inward temptations and assaults from demons with night vigils, fasts, and prayers. But, as the history of monasticism shows, society follows monks and ascetics into the wilderness. Anthony was not only pursued by those who wished to imitate his life or who sought him out for his reputed powers of healing. He was twice called from the desert, once during the Diocletian persecution to court martyrdom and again during the Arian controversy to defend orthodoxy.

The image of the eccentric, solitary athlete of Christ doing battle against the world and the body captures only part of the truth about the monks of the Egyptian desert. A sampling of their sayings, collected and translated by Thomas Merton as *The Wisdom of the Desert,* [2] helps us appreciate another, more social side of monasticism. Let me quote just four sayings that speak for themselves:

> One of the brethren had sinned, and the priest told him to leave the community. So then Abbot Bessarion got up and walked out with him, saying, I too am a sinner. (*Verba* XL)

> If you see a young monk by his own will climbing up into heaven, take him by the foot and throw him to the ground, because what he is doing is not good for him. (*Verba* LXII)

> A monk ran into a party of handmaids of the Lord on a certain journey. Seeing them he left the road and gave them a wide berth. But the Abbess said to him: If you were a perfect monk, you would not even have looked close enough to see that we were women. (*Verba* XXI)

> One of the monks, called Serapion, sold his book of the Gospels and gave the money to those who were hungry, saying: I have sold the book which told me to sell all that I had and give to the poor. (*Verba* XXXIV)

Practical, common sense wisdom, mutual care, and wry humor—this side of the monastic life is best represented by the *cenobite* (meaning ''common life'') monasticism whose pioneer was an Egyptian named Pachomius (c. 299–346).

Converted to Christianity on leaving the Roman army, Pachomius found himself drawn to the desert. Like Anthony, he apprenticed himself to an old recluse and seemed destined to be an anchorite. He was even reluctant to abandon his plan in the face of a divine call to serve humankind, objecting that he had come to the desert to serve God. Perhaps remembering an earlier vow, Pachomius had a change of heart. He enlisted his brother to build with him a large enclosure at Tabennisi to house a community of monks. He hoped that this new community would be dedicated to prayer, meditation, and mutual assistance. After an abortive initial beginning, Pachomius's project eventually bore fruit, and by the end of his life a federation of several monasteries with as many as three thousand monks had been established. His sister Mary founded a community for women also to be incorporated into this first Christian monastic order. These several communities, each with its own cluster of enclosed buildings and self-sustaining economy, were organized in a hierarchy of obedience with final authority residing in the abbots.

Experience no doubt taught Pachomius that no human society flourishes without a constitution, and to this end he prepared a *Rule* to govern the new order. According to the Rule, the ideal of a common life was to be strictly enforced. All monks were to eat together, dress alike, hold property in common, work at manual labor, sleep in the same reclining position, fast at the same times, pray at regular hours twice daily, and twice a week attend Eucharist at a nearby church or within the monastery compound. Persons wishing admission to the community were subject to a long probationary period and before taking their place among the brothers were expected to demonstrate humility, a firmness of commitment, and a capacity for obedience. Those accepted as monks also embraced poverty and chastity and were not permitted to accept ecclesiastical appointments. It is interesting in this respect that the person who was most responsible for spreading the Pachomian form of monasticism in the East after Pachomius himself was Basil of Caesarea (c.330–379). Because Basil was drawn by theological controversy into the general life of the church and finally into administrative service as a bishop, he was not free to live as a monk himself. Yet, others asked him to provide directions for the ascetic life. As Basil's Rule, his instructions served the eastern church much as the Rule of Benedict of Nursia became the standard for cenobite monasticism in the West.

Benedict and Western Monasticism

The desert of Egypt has been described as the cradle of Christian monasticism, but monasticism arose spontaneously and flourished in other parts of the East. It was, however, through the influence and example of the East that monasticism was introduced to the West. Athanasius's *Life of Anthony*, for example, played an important part in promoting the ascetic ideal in the Latin church, influencing such prominent church leaders as Augustine of Hippo. But asceticism in the West was to be less extreme than that of Egypt, less fantastic than that of Syria. Its special gift was rather for shaping great institutions, and its greatest genius was Benedict of Nursia (c. 480–c. 550).

While still a young man, Benedict resolved to be a recluse, living a solitary life apart even from the company of other monks. Taking up residence for a time in a cave at Sabiaco east of Rome, he practiced an extreme asceticism akin to Anthony's, but his fame attracted others. Sometime around 525 he removed this community to Monte Cassino, a remote place where the inhabitants still observed ancient pagan religious customs. Felling the sacred grove there and destroying its altar, Benedict founded a self-contained monastic community dedicated to the principles of stability, obedience, communal prayer, the study of Scripture, and physical labor. His sister Scholastica established a similar community for women nearby. Benedict's Rule established the terms under which monks and nuns entered the monastic life and progressed in the spiritual life. Drawn from earlier models and the fund of his own experience, his Rule embodied an ideal of mutual support and corporate worship within the framework of an economically self-sufficient community.

Each monastery was to be equipped if possible with "water, a mill, a garden, a bakery" and served by different trades. This ensured that monks would not have to leave their community, but rather follow lives of permanence and stability, distinctive Benedictine features. Manual labor was prescribed as well for all monks, and the Rule set aside a fixed time each day for such activity. In addition, the monks were expected to pledge perfect obedience to the abbot. Benedictine monasteries, however, were not to be totally isolated from the world but were encouraged to receive visitors and for that reason became in time the hostels of Europe. Above all, Benedict gave instructions for corporate prayer, the monk's primary work, the *opus Dei* as this work of God was called. Citing the Psalmist's admonition to pray seven times daily, the Rule enjoined fixed hours for community prayer during the day—matins, lauds, prime, terce, sext, none, vespers, and compline—and prayer in the middle of the night. At these times, the community gathered in one place to recite the Psalms and other designated portions of Scripture in an act of celebration known as the *Divine Office*. Meals were also accompanied by the reading of Scripture and the Rule, a fact that together with the literary character of prayer made learning a prerequisite of Benedictine monasticism.

The monastery at Monte Cassino was destroyed in 589 by a Germanic tribe, the Lombards, but western monasticism seemed destined for success. It was carried north by monks like Augustine of Canterbury who at the behest of Pope Gregory the Great (590–604) traveled to England to convert the Anglo-Saxons. Among the Irish, whose legendary founder was Saint Patrick (c. 389–c. 461), monasticism flourished and its houses became centers of sacred and secular learning in the seventh and eighth centuries. It has been said that when the white-robed monks of Ireland, monks like Columba (c. 521–c. 597) and Columbanus (c. 543–615), set out to evangelize the pagan Anglo-Saxons of northeastern England or to establish religious foundations on the continent, they brought with them not only liturgical texts and the writings of the Christian fathers. They also carried the classics in their leather bags.

Monasticism spread in German territories with the encouragement of secular rulers. Charles Martel, the Frankish king famous for halting the advance of the armies of Islam at Tours in 732, extended his support to English missionaries, the most renowned of whom was Boniface. Known as the Apostle of Germany, Boniface (680–754) established bishoprics in Thuringia, Hesse, and Bavaria and generally sought to enhance episcopal authority. He himself was summoned to Rome where he pledged his loyalty to the pope who ordained him bishop. Boniface also founded the monastic center of Fulda, important for its use of the Benedictine Rule and as a center of learning and theological education. And, as a consequence of his efforts on behalf of the Frankish church, the way was prepared for an alliance between the papacy and the Frankish kings—an alliance sealed when Pope Leo III on Christmas day 800 crowned Charlemagne (Charles the Great) Holy Roman Emperor.

To share in his commission to the Germans, Boniface summoned Lioba of Wilborne, an Anglo-Saxon nun esteemed for her holiness and learning—qualities that help us understand the confidence she apparently inspired in Boniface. Lioba was learned in Scripture, the church fathers, and the teachings of the councils. She was also an accomplished classicist. And, as one commentator put it, "in the world of the eighth century, such erudition gave her an almost magical authority, and in addition afforded practical power in the vast administrative task of bringing order to the raw new church of Germany." [3]

The story of monasticism was, however, not just the history of holiness, missionary zeal, and the rolling back of Europe's geographical boundaries by heroic men and women of faith. It was also a story of decline followed by reform, renewal, and adaptation. Often through the intervention of secular or ecclesiastical rulers or during periods of social instability, monasticism suffered decline as it did during the seventh and eighth centuries in western Europe. At that time monastic communities became pawns of church and state policy, or they were dispersed through successive invasions of Vikings from the north and Moslems from the south, or they suffered simply from an internal relaxation of discipline. But then would follow monastic revival, usually through the efforts of exceptional individuals like Benedict of Aniane (751–821) who restored the strict observance of the Benedictine Rule to the monastic houses in the realm of King Loius the Pious.

A reform of far greater scope and influence came a century later when in 910 the duke of Aquitaine, having grown old and concerned about salvation, established a monastery at Cluny on the advice of Berno, abbot of Baume. According to the agreement, the land was bestowed upon the apostles Peter and Paul under the protection of the pope to be used for a monastery under the Benedictine Rule, with Berno as its first abbot. The deed further specified that the land belong to the monastery in perpetuity without interference from pope, bishop, or secular ruler. This—and the monks' right to elect their own abbot—removed one cause for monastic decline and a major obstacle to reform. Finally, the grant provided a peasant labor force to work the lands, thus freeing the monks from the need to perform manual labor. Though contrary to Benedict's original intention, the reform nevertheless allowed other occupations to substitute for physical labor, and in time Cluny and its associated communities came more and more to regard the celebration of the Divine Office as the exclusive occupation of monks. It became possible even to regard the choir of monks in unremitting prayer as a kind of *via angelica*, ''the way of angels.''

Cluny's constitution reasserted monasticism's separateness from the world, but certain features of the movement inevitably entangled it again in worldly affairs. Not only did the rule of hospitality encourage the development of large guest houses capable of supplying visitors with everything from stables for their horses to clean towels and silver spoons. The Clunaic reform was aggressive in its purpose of permeating church and society with the monastic ideal. It sought to restrict feudal warfare, encourage peace among the nobles, and promote the use of force only on behalf of the weak and in defense of the church. It endeavored to restore spiritual and moral authority to the church and its clergy. It worked to restore clerical celibacy and end the trading in church offices, measures with important implications for the separation of the church from the world. Most important, however, Cluny's program prompted the church to reaffirm its authority against secular rulers in the election of popes and the investment of bishops with ring and staff, the episcopal signs of office.

The remarkable achievement of this reform was attributable in part to the leadership of the early Cluny abbots, in part to the establishing of second Clunys, eventually some fifteen hundred, all of which were dependent on Cluny's abbot. The reform movement could thus enlarge its moral and spiritual authority from a strong center—as long as the monarchical abbots of Cluny were strong. But again prosperity proved Cluny's Achilles' heel and again a movement arose to restore monasticism to Benedict's ideal of a life separate from the world dedicated to poverty, simplicity, rigorous asceticism, and physical labor. Known as Cistercians after the place of their founding, the order's greatest luminary was Bernard of Clairvaux (1098–1153). A person of boundless energy, Bernard was a model of ascetic discipline and prayer and one of the Middle Ages' greatest mystics. Yet, summoned from his principal work, he served as adviser to popes and princes and counselor to the founders of religious orders. He mediated ecclesiastical and political disputes, organized a crusade, hounded heretics, and crossed intellectual swords with Abelard, the most brilliant theologian of the age. Yet few could balance the active and the contemplative callings as Bernard nor were the Cistercians wholly successful in their purpose to be separate from the world. This ideal, however, was not so central to the monastic revival of the thirteenth century.

Thirteenth Century Mendicant Orders

The thirteenth century saw expansion of trade, the development of a new monetary economy, and the growth of towns and cities. It also witnessed the emergence of a new kind of religious order. Better adapted to the spiritual needs of the urban masses than the rural cloistered monasticism of the Benedictines, the *mendicant* (or begging) *friars* (Latin *frares* meaning "brothers") ministered as preachers, teachers, and missionaries. But, as was so often true of monastic reform and innovation, the emergence of the friars began with the decision of an individual to live simply in the light of the Gospel. That individual was Giovanni Bernardone (1181/2–1226), popularly known as Francis of Assisi.

Francis was the son of a wealthy cloth merchant who, in spite of an early life of extravagance and youthful dreams of chivalry and military glory, committed himself rather to "Lady Poverty," as he called the life he embraced. In a characteristically dramatic gesture, Francis appeared with his father before the bishop of Assisi in 1206, removed his clothes, bundled and put them at his father's feet, and announced that his father was the Father in heaven. It was thus that he gestured his intention to abandon the world, and for the next two years he lived in the manner of a traditional hermit. Then, during Mass on February 24, 1208, he heard the reading of Matthew 10:7–14 where Christ charged his disciples to preach repentance and the Kingdom of God. Francis resolved to obey the gospel's command to preach, to manifest a Christlike love, especially for the sick, the leper, and the outcast, and to practice absolute poverty, a condition he believed necessary for true repentance and genuine peace.

Francis prepared a Rule, largely taken from quotations from the Gospels, to guide the union of those who, like himself, wished to imitate Christ in poverty, simplicity, and humility. And in 1210 he secured the verbal approval for his Order of Friars Minor, known popularly as Franciscans, from Pope Innocent III. The Poor Clares, a sister order for women

Prayer and devotional reading still guide Christian monks in their quest for holiness and service.

founded by Clare of Assisi (1194–1253), followed. Forbidden to pursue an itinerant ministry, the Poor Clares inverted Francis's summons to New Testament poverty and developed what proved to be a profound and influential piety of inward poverty. A third order, the Order of Penitents, spread the Franciscan ideal among *lay* Christians, Christians outside of holy orders. Francis, however, was not a gifted organizer and so turned over to others the running of the order. He himself retired to a hermitage on Mount Alverna where in 1224 he received the stigmata, thus bearing the wounds of Christ on his own body. During his last years, his early love of Provençal song bore fruit in his *Canticle of the Sun.* And, when two years later he died in a little hut near a stone chapel known as Portiuncula, his order was already becoming one of the most influential of the Middle Ages.

Contemporary with Francis and also founder of a mendicant order was Dominic de Guzman (1170–1221). Dominic's mendicants were officially the Order of Preachers but were popularly named Dominicans for their founder. Preachers, missionaries, and teachers, the Dominicans felt called, as had the Franciscans, to active service in the world. As a begging order, they adopted corporate poverty. Yet, for Dominic and his friars poverty had a more programmatic importance than it had had for the romantic Francis. Dominic had early learned the value of apostolic poverty while attempting to win back to the Catholic fold the heretical Waldensians and Albigensians of southern France. Poverty was found no less effective in connection with preaching among the growing population of new urban poor. Dominican poverty even gave rise to a flowering of mystical piety among Dominican nuns, who, denied the mendicants' service beyond the cloister, cultivated the virtue of interior poverty.

The Dominican cultivation of learning further distinguished the two great luminaries of thirteenth century mendicancy. While Francis is said to have chided that a friar who owns a Psalter will want a breviary (a liturgical book) and soon will be discovered mounting the pulpit as a bishop, one of Dominic's first acts was to send his friars to the university towns of Paris and Bologna where they distinguished themselves as teachers and where they were soon to claim as their own such theological luminaries as Albertus Magnus and Thomas Aquinas. It should be noted that the Franciscans too claim more than their share of distinguished scholars, among them Alexander of Hales, Roger Bacon, Bonaventure, John Duns Scotus, and William of Occam. Yet, as with poverty, Dominic early recognized the value of learning for preaching and missionary work, and from the beginning his order reflected their founder's emphasis on letters and learning.

THE CHRISTIAN STATE

A Sea Change

The coming of Constantine represented a major shift, a sea change in the social and political circumstances of the Christian church. Once a persecuted minority gathering for secret worship in catacombs and house churches like the one discovered at Dura-Europos, Christians emerged to enjoy not only religious liberty but a privileged social status as the Roman Empire reallocated and shifted its religious resources to the churches of the once illegal sect. Christian clergy were exempted from conscription into the army and other civil duties. The Christian day of worship, the first day of the week, was set aside as a holiday. Constantine even forbade crucifixion in honor of the crucified Christ. And of immense importance, Christian churches were granted the right to receive gifts and legacies and accumulate property. Thus, at the time when the ranks of Christian monks were swelling with those in flight from the world, the church was becoming more worldly. Even the basilica churches, Christianity's now public places of worship, announced the church's greatly improved social standing. In large rectangular buildings bearing striking resemblance to the audience halls of emperors, worshippers stood facing the altar, the clergy, and the bishop, symbol now of religious and social authority.

Constantine's vision of the Christian cross emblazoned across the sun at the Milvian Bridge (312) and his conversion to Christianity, however, marked much more than the prospering of the Christian cause. It signaled a momentous shift in Christian authority. Not only were Christian bishops to enjoy imperial privilege and power; Christian emperors aspired to sacral authority as God's anointed on earth, an authority Christian bishops viewed as their own prerogative. It was thus that Constantine interpreted his vision of the cross and the legend bearing the words, "In this sign conquer." The future emperor took this sign to be a divine call, a heavenly commissioning like the commissioning of the Twelve, to rule by divine right. And, having entered thus the company of the holy apostles, it no doubt seemed the correct thing to locate his own sarcophagus amidst monuments of the Twelve in a basilica bearing their name.

While neither Constantine nor subsequent eastern emperors sought to displace bishops in their sacramental function, the eastern churches held that sacred authority was the shared prerogative of the church's principal clergy, its patriarchs, and the emperor. Together patriarchs and emperors aspired to a unity of spirit, purpose, and will—a union that Orthodoxy spoke of as a *symphonia*. According to this cooperative system, the patriarchs of the church were charged with responsibility for the celebration of the sacraments, the enrichment of the liturgy, the presiding over synods, and the cultivation of the contemplative life of the monasteries. The emperors were in the words of Constantine "ordained of God to oversee whatever is external to the Church." They were, in other words, guardians of the Christian people, custodians of a Christian society, a conviction to which the mosaics of Ravenna's church of San Vitale are eloquent testimony. On the ceiling of that church, Christ, portrayed as a heavenly or cosmic king, an imperial Pantocrator, sits enthroned in glory surrounded by his heavenly court; below and to one side is Emperor Justinian, nimbus encircling his head and flanked by his bishop, priests, and soldiers. In this icon of sacral authority, the emperor is God's viceroy and visible image; the empire is a temporal, earthly reflection of Christ's heavenly Kingdom.

Church and State in the West

The situation of the Roman popes in the West differed from that of the patriarchs of Constantinople in the East and prepared the way for the separation of the two churches at the time of the Great Schism in 1054. The Roman church had from an early time enjoyed a privileged ecclesiastical standing among Christian churches by reason of its location in the ancient capitol of the Roman Empire. Its bishops claimed primacy too as successors of the apostle Peter, whom tradition regarded as the first bishop of the city. Political and social conditions were also important in defining the part popes were to play in western society. Heirs by default to the aura of emperors when Constantine removed his imperial government to Byzantium and established a new Rome named for himself, the popes were looked to as overseers and defenders of the city, and with good reason. It was Pope Leo I (440–461) who in the absence of imperial forces went out from Rome's gates to confront Attila and avert the siege of the city by the barbarian Huns. Other popes followed Leo's example. Yet, none of the early popes combined as well the office of civil administrator and pastor of the church as Gregory I (590–604). Amidst the social disarray and economic instability that accompanied the collapse of the Roman Empire, this pope negotiated with Christian and barbarian rulers, dispatched missionaries to England, fostered monasticism, reformed the clergy, instituted land reform of the church's properties, the "patrimony of Peter" as these lands were called, and with the revenue of church lands fed Rome's poor. This first of the medieval popes, who preferred the title "servant of the servants of God," believed the ideal Christian bishop to be above all a shepherd of souls.

Gregory's theological writings were immensely influential in giving direction to the medieval church as well. It was Gregory more than any other who mediated the thought of Augustine of Hippo to the Middle Ages. He is to be credited for the emphasis the western church placed on satisfaction as one of the essential elements of *penance*. He did not originate but elaborated the doctrine of purgatory. He stressed the sacrificial character of the Eucharist as Christ's self-offering, an offering that could be applied to the living and the dead. And important for the contours of Christian society in the West, Gregory's conception of the bishop was not—and in the West would not be—confined as it had been in the eastern church.

This is not to suggest that western rulers did not cherish the idea of the divinely anointed king into whose hand God had entrusted the care of Christian people. The western emperor Henry II referred to himself as "servant of the servants of Christ" and believed himself to rule by "the will of God and our savior and Liberator." In this role the western emperors took it upon themselves to reform the church and the monasteries, to appoint and remove bishops, even to discipline popes. Yet these quasi-priestly acts of emperors, accepted as the course of things in the East, were treated as presumption by the popes of the West. Sacred authority originating with Christ (see Matthew 28:18), the popes maintained, was conferred on the apostle Peter and through Peter's successors on emperors and kings. As the successors of Peter, the bishops of Rome exercised a divine authority and wielded the two swords of spiritual and temporal authority—the spiritual sword directly over the affairs of the church and the temporal sword indirectly through secular rulers over political government.

The Monarchical Papacy

The political vacuum in the West when Constantine shifted his capitol to the East, combined with able Roman bishops, gave substance to the theories of papal supremacy at the dawn of the Dark Ages. But energetic western emperors, Roman and Italian politics, and a succession of weak or corrupt popes checked papal powers until the beginning of the eleventh century. Then with Leo IX (1049–1054), a succession of gifted popes ascended to the throne of Peter. These reforming popes were committed to the related purposes of disciplining and purifying the church, strengthening their own position against temporal rulers, and pursuing the ideal of a unified Christian society. Instrumental in this program was a clergy separated from the world and pledged without reservation to the church. The reformers worked to accomplish this objective by enforcing the long established but frequently ignored church regulations governing clerical celibacy. Clergy were to be wed to the church alone. The loyalty of the higher clergy was similarly a matter of concern. At issue was the appointment of bishops and abbots—powerful political as well as ecclesiastical figures—by temporal rulers, often for financial or other consideration, a practice known as simony.

To accomplish this last goal, the reforming popes took the radical step of attacking the role temporal rulers played in the installation of bishops. The power to invest the bishop with the traditional signs of office, with the staff and ring, was viewed by these reformers as a priestly and especially a papal prerogative. Lay *investiture*, it was believed, usurped this priestly prerogative and violated the divine constitution of church order. This papal view that the Roman church was founded by God alone and the Roman pontiff alone can be called universal had been spelled out in earlier church documents, most notably in the *Donation of Constantine* and the *Pseudo-Isidorian Decretals*. So too had the claims that the pope alone may depose emperors and absolve subjects from fealty oaths to temporal rulers. What was new in these circumstances is that here were popes sufficiently independent and powerful to convert teaching into policy.

Nicholas II (1058–1061) took the monumental step of establishing a system of papal election intended to insure papal autonomy. In 1059 he saw to it that a Roman synod decreed that popes were to be elected by the *cardinal clergy* of Rome—a decree still largely observed today. But implementation of papal teaching on sacral authority fell to Gregory VII (1073–1083), a reforming firebrand who squared off with Emperor Henry IV in one of the most dramatic confrontations of the Middle Ages. Henry provoked the confrontation when he made an appointment to the politically significant archbishopric of Milan. The pope rebuked the emperor, who in turn summoned a council at Worms where Gregory was denounced and his authority summarily rejected.

Gregory's response was decisive and bold. He convened a Roman synod, excommunicated the emperor, forbade him to exercise his royal prerogatives in Germany and Italy, and released his subjects from oaths of allegiance. Opposition within imperial territories mounted, and the emperor marched south to confront the pope, not however as king but as suppliant. At Canossa, the castle of Matilda of Tuscany, Emperor Henry IV presented himself, a humble penitent, seeking the pope's forgiveness. Faced with Gregory's reluctance to give him an audience, the emperor stood before the castle gate, barefoot and in the snow, on three successive days before Gregory was persuaded to relent and lift the excommunication. Who won? The political victory went to Henry who, regaining power, marched south again, invaded Italy, and drove Gregory from Rome into exile where he died. On the other hand, the papal humiliation of the emperor at Canossa came to symbolize the triumph of the idea of a Christian society under the universal authority of the popes.

The Crusades

In the year 1095 at the Council of Clermont, Pope Urban II proclaimed the first of a series of military campaigns (from 1096–1300) known as the Crusades. The pope's announcement was met with cries of *Deus vult*—"God wills it." With that, Latin (or western) Christendom commenced its intermittent, pathetic, and often tragic military ventures against the forces of Islam that occupied Jerusalem and other historic sites of Christianity's birth and that threatened the great center of the Byzantine Empire at Constantinople. Other crusades were launched against groups considered by the popes either religiously or politically dangerous—the Moslems in Spain, heretical sects like the Albigensians, even the political opponents of the papacy. One of the most tragic episodes of the whole period occurred when the armies of the Fourth Crusade sacked Constantinople and in that center of Byzantine Christianity established a Latin patriarch. Seen by Pope Innocent III as God's will to reunite the church, the event only further divided the two great branches of historic Christianity.

For many Christian knights, however, the Crusades were a holy cause that at once advanced God's glory and secured personal salvation for the crusaders. It was believed that all who vowed to "take up the cross" pledged themselves to a solemn obligation for which, however, the faithful might expect great spiritual benefit. A full or plenary *indulgence* for the remission of the temporal penalty of sin was granted to all who took part in the crusades; for those who died on a crusade the forgiveness of sin was offered. "All who go thither and lose their lives," declared Urban II, "be it on the road or on the sea, or in the fight against the pagans, will be granted immediate forgiveness of sins."

For other crusading knights, the military campaign was approached as a holy journey. In many ways resembling a penitential pilgrimage, the Crusades afforded a unique opportunity to travel to holy sites in Jerusalem and along the way to see—perhaps to carry home—holy relics sanctified by Jesus himself. For still others who formed themselves into quasi-military religious orders, the defense of the Holy Land was itself a high and sacred calling. The first of these orders was the Knights Hospitallars (officially, "Knights of the Order of the Hospital of Saint John of Jerusalem"). The most famous of the new monastic orders spawned by and dedicated to the service of the Crusades was the Knights Templar. Like other monks, the military monks of these orders took monastic vows of poverty, obedience, and chastity. In addition to the usual vows, however, the monks of the crusades pledged themselves to defend the Holy Land, fight against the infidels, extend protection to Christian pilgrims, and offer charity to the needy and the sick.

WORSHIP, DEVOTION, MYSTICAL PRAYER

Public Worship

The celebration of a sacred meal was central to Christian worship from the earliest times. Called variously the Lord's Supper, Holy Communion, the Eucharist, the Mass, this ritual memorializes and reenacts Jesus' last fellowship meal and commemorates his sacrificial death and resurrection. Open only to those initiated through the rite of baptism, Christians in the first centuries gathered in private homes or at the tombs of martyrs to celebrate this communal feast of spiritual food and experience anew the redemption of Christ's sacrificial death. After the flood of converts filled the churches upon Constantine's conversion, and Christian worship was transferred from house churches to great basilicas, however, this ritual meal underwent important alterations.

We will discuss the themes and liturgical elaborations of this Christian rite as it took shape in the Orthodox churches of the East later in the book. As for its formation in the western church, its character as a communal meal was de-emphasized when great basilicas became the setting for Christian worship. Here Christians gathered not so much as a Christian family for "the breaking of bread." They assembled in cathedrals, like the one at Amiens that could accommodate ten thousand faithful at a time, as witnesses to a great mystery. Before them on the altar, it was held, Christ's propitiatory *sacrifice* was memorialized and enacted anew, and the spiritual benefits of this oblation were conferred on the faithful according to their devotion. Moreover, the ancient belief that the symbols of the rite—the bread and wine—were channels of sacred power was further magnified by

Gothic churches like the Lincoln Cathedral in England were imposing centers of medieval life.

the doctrine of *transubstantiation* developed in connection with medieval scholastic theology. Officially approved at the Fourth Lateran Council in 1215, the new teaching held that at the moment of consecration the bread and wine remained only in appearance; in substance and reality worshippers ate and drank of the body and blood of Christ.

Other related practices surrounding the Mass contributed as well to the mystery and miracle of the altar. It became customary to withhold the cup—perhaps for fear of spilling—from the laity at communion, to elevate the sacrificial offering or *host* (meaning ''victim'') at the time of consecration, and to reserve the consecrated Eucharistic bread in a vessel known as a monstrance for adoration in private devotion or public procession. By the thirteenth century, the Mass had become so much a part of popular piety that Innocent III designated a special feast commemorating its institution, the feast of Corpus Christi, and the great medieval theologian, Thomas Aquinas, was moved to prepare the office (the form or service of worship) for it.

The magnificent cathedral churches of Christendom not only provided space large enough often to include the whole Christian population of a town. They were architecturally and aesthetically designed to enhance Christian mystery and the drama of salvation. And their immense size must have accentuated the already mysterious character of the liturgy and magnified the hieratic, almost magical powers of the clergy who presided at the church's great miracle, the miracle of the Mass. All around too, worshippers would have been aware of the scenes from the Christian drama of salvation. It has been said that the cathedral itself functioned as a scripture in stone and glass for the great majority of Christians who could not read Scripture. The stations of the cross took the pious through the stages of Christ's passion and crucifixion. The windows unfolded the story of redemption from the Old and New Testaments. And stone gargoyles leered from the partial darkness as a reminder of sin and guilt and of the dark, satanic forces that fill this world and portend disaster and the soul's ultimate damnation. Yet, the first and dominant impression of the Gothic cathedral is one of height, of upward thrust, and of the almost mystical light flooding the whole space from above. An impression encouraged by elongated clusters of columns, pointed arches, and stained glass of radiant reds and blues, the very design of the cathedral gave form to the medieval aspiration to be free of earthly encumbrance in the heavenward ascent of the Christian pilgrim.

Pilgrimage

Like the Gothic cathedral, medieval life appears to have been one of arresting contrasts. It is impossible not to think of this period in the West's history without calling to mind its shining accomplishments in theology, philosophy, architecture, art, and literature. It was during this period too that some of Europe's greatest institutions came into being, among them the first universities. But what of the life of ordinary people? Here the darker side of the age is evident especially in the themes of popular piety where the reality of disease and death and the fear of judgment and damnation were ever present. Yet, even ordinary life for all its harshness was not unrelieved. There were the holy days and festivals which gave form and meaning to time in ways that the modern secular calendar does not.

There were in addition to the Eucharist other *sacraments* for spiritual assistance. Religious rites communicating sacred reality and divine blessing, the sacraments of baptism and Eucharist were always included, but the number of sacraments in fact was fluid during the medieval period. Peter Damian held that there were twelve, and Hugh of Saint Victor counted thirty. It was not until the fourteenth century that the traditional seven sacraments (i.e. baptism, Eucharist, confirmation, penance, marriage, ordination, extreme unction) were accepted by general agreement. Spiritual assistance came also through intercessory prayers to saints, and by the eleventh century the Virgin Mary became the object of popular piety. We hear for the first time, for example, of the *Ave Maria* or "Hail Mary," and Innocent III endorsed the popular feast celebrating the Immaculate Conception.

Of special interest among the features of medieval piety was the religious *pilgrimage*. Pilgrimage, of course, is not unique to Christianity. Religious believers in all cultures have felt drawn to distant holy places and by the hope of miracle or spiritual renewal. Hindus travel to Benares, Buddhists to Bodh Gaya, Moslems to Mecca, Japanese to the shrine at Ise, Jews to Jerusalem. Yet, no culture has been more enthusiastic about pilgrimage or used the metaphor of pilgrimage more extensively in its literature, art, and theology than medieval culture. And, if the spirit of pilgrimage is communicated faithfully by Geoffrey Chaucer (c. 1340–1400) in the *Canterbury Tales*, no society embraced pilgrimage with more gusto, more *joie de vive*. As Chaucer pictured pilgrimage, it was an occasion for an extended outing, for the experience of good fellowship and community, no doubt even for a temporary reprieve from the inhibitions of social and religious convention as the pilgrims assumed what anthropologist Victor Turner called a marginal or liminal status.

Visits to popular pilgrim sites, whether they were close to home as Canterbury for Chaucer's crew or to distant tombs of martyrs and saints or to the Holy Land itself, pilgrimage was also a pious act of religious devotion. For some it was undertaken in thanksgiving for a blessing received or in fulfillment of a vow made; for others it expressed a desire akin to the monastic impulse for purification and holiness through self-denial. In connection with the sacrament of penance (involving contrition, confession, and satisfaction), the pilgrimage became a penitential act begun with a formal blessing and a full confession of sins and embarked upon with a devotional seriousness that guided the pilgrim from shrine to shrine. At journey's end, the pilgrim could hope to be restored to spiritual health and wholeness, having successfully fulfilled the obligation of penance; or spiritual renewal, having made contact with holy relics; or a greater confidence in the power of their votive prayers to the patron saint, having visited places sacred to the saint. And, because the Christian life was itself viewed as a pilgrimage, perhaps, the holy journey gave weight to the pilgrim's hope that the spiritual journey toward the heavenly city had been well begun.

Mysticism

Mysticism was another feature of medieval Christianity, and yet, like pilgrimage, mysticism is not unique to Christianity. Evidence of the immediate knowledge of ultimate reality is found in all the world's religions. In the great religions of the East—Hinduism, for example, or Buddhism—such direct apprehension of the holy tends to be a more characteristic feature of religious experience and practice, more so certainly than it is of the prophetic traditions of Judaism, Christianity, and Islam. Nevertheless, Judaism can point to a vital mystical tradition known by the generic term Kabbalah; Sufism appeared as early as the eighth century in Islam; and traces of Christian mysticism are found already in the New Testament. Unlike much of the mysticism of India and China, however, western mysticism is theistic. It does not think of mystical aspiration as leading to a unity with an underlying, impersonal, ineffable source—the Brahman of Upanishadic Hinduism or the Tao of China's Taoism. Western religions envision the ultimate as a dynamic, transcendent, and personal reality knowable primarily as a consuming divine love.

For Christians wishing to walk in the way of the mystics, the approach to God is through Christ, the one believed to be both the teacher of the way and the way itself. We see this role assigned to Christ, for example, in passages like the one from John's Gospel where Jesus prays that "all may be one; even as thou, Father, art in me, and I in thee, that they also may be in us" (17:21). Paul too uses language that is decidedly mystical to describe his relationship with God through Christ, a relationship that begins with ecstatic vision. Of his conversion on the road to Damascus, he tells of being "caught up into Paradise—whether in the body or out of the body I do not know, God knows—and he [Paul's self reference] heard things that cannot be told, which man may not utter" (2 Corinthians 12:3). Here and in the Gospel of John the mystical knowledge of the divine Father is inseparable from a knowledge of Christ.

Mystical language and thought are employed to describe the experience of God in other early Christian writers as well. Augustine of Hippo, Pope Gregory I, and a fifth- or sixth-century author known as Dionysius the Areopagite all talk of a transforming inner light, akin to the divine light of Neoplatonism, to account for the interior experience of God. Light symbolism also played a major role in the mysticism among Orthodox churches of the East. According to this tradition, the sanctifying vision of the uncreated light of God that permeates the world and that shown from Christ at the time of his transfiguration on Mount Tabor is the aspiration of every Christian, contemplative and lay alike. Every Christian, according to Orthodoxy, hopes to be a partaker in the divine nature through the mystical burial of baptism and the sanctifying power of holy communion.

Yet, there were individuals for whom the cultivation of the mystical life meant discipline and method over and above—though never apart from—the sacramental life of the church. Building upon the thought of Simeon the New Theologian (949–1022) and others, there developed a distinctive Orthodox mysticism dedicated to the mastery of contemplation. This mystical tradition, known as *Hesychasm* (Greek meaning "stillness"), made use of rhythmic breathing and body posture reminiscent of Hindu yogic technique to quiet the body. Hesychasm also cultivated mystical experience by using the Jesus Prayer for deepening meditation much as Hindus focus consciousness through the repetition of the mantra. By the silent repeating of this simple contemplative prayer—"Lord Jesus Christ, Son of God, have mercy on me a sinner," the aspirant, it was held, penetrated that interior space where God is known most directly—a place that Orthodox speak of as the center of the heart. Here, at the place most open to the divine Presence, the mystic knows God as uncreated light.

Light symbolism also entered the West through the influence of Augustine and Dionysius the Areopagite. Yet western mysticism more characteristically joined God's eternal love with the experience of the divine light. The great epic poet and author of the *Divine Comedy*, Dante Alighieri (1265–1321), thus presents the consuming sight of God, the *visio Dei*, as the foundation of blessed communion. The path that winds through the lower regions of hell, then ascends the Mount of Purgatory, and finally rises through the spheres of heaven brings the pilgrim/poet of the *Comedy* to gaze on the Primal Love that informs and moves all things.

It is appropriate too that in this context Dante honors the great mystic, Bernard of Clairvaux, whom he pictures as "Rapt in love's bliss." Like Dante, Bernard used the popular motif of pilgrimage for the mystical path, a path that has been aptly called the pilgrimage inward. For Bernard the inward journey ascends by degrees to the love of God—from a carnal love of self to a mercenary love of God for the self's sake and then to a filial love of God for duty's sake. But only when the mystic reaches the last stage, Bernard believed, can it be said that the soul loves with the highest form of love, a wedded love that loves God for himself alone. In language that is often sensuous and even erotic, Bernard imagines the wedded love of God as a kiss passed between the soul and Christ, the bride and the Bridegroom. Though more cerebral and analytic, the Franciscan Bonaventure (c. 1217–1274) in *The Mind's Road to God* similarly conceives of the highest degree of illumination as one of "burning affection." Even the fourteenth-century Dominican mystic Meister Eckhart (c. 1260–1327), who stressed the otherness of God and spoke of the mystical way as a negative or *apophatic* path, nevertheless believed God to be as close as our own souls. And, though the Rhineland mystics like Eckhart think of God as enveloped in a "dark silence," it is a silence, as John Ruysbroeck (1293–1381) put it, where "all lovers lose themselves."

Perhaps because of this emphasis on love, the western church took Christ's passion and cross as important touchstones for mystical experience. And, whereas the great mystics and saints of the eastern church associated bodily radiance with holiness, the West found in the stigmata of Saint Francis a divine sign more expressive of its spirituality. The great Franciscan theologian Bonaventure was inspired, for example, to write one of the Middle Ages' great mystical works, *Mind's Road to God* (1259) while he meditated on top of Mount Alverna, the mountain where Francis received the stigmata. A vision of Christ crucified was given also to Catherine of Siena (c. 1347–1380) as a sign of divine love and as a seal of human salvation. The vision of a wounded, bleeding Christ, the cross mounted on his shoulders, was for Catherine of Genoa (1448–1510) the experience that aroused in her a desire for union with God in selfless love. But perhaps the most extraordinary of the late medieval mystics was the fourteenth-century English anchoress Julian of Norwich (c. 1342—after 1413).

In *The Revelations of Divine Love* (1393), Julian recorded her meditation on sixteen ecstatic visions given her on May 30, 1373. Julian saw in her visions the crucifixion; she had a spiritual vision of God's love; she beheld also the Virgin Mary. Other "shewings" or revelations brought her understanding of the Trinity and God's love. God's love in particular moved Julian, and she wrote of it using powerful feminine metaphors. She spoke of God's mothering action in bringing forth the world at creation; she wrote of the motherhood of God who nurtures, comforts, corrects, and instructs as a mother would her child. And of Christ Julian used one of her most arresting images, naming him "Mother Jesus."

> The human mother will suckle her child with her own milk, but our beloved Mother, Jesus, feeds us with himself, and with most tender courtesy, does it by means of the Blessed Sacrament, the precious food of all true life. . . . The human mother may put her child tenderly to her breast, but our tender Mother Jesus simply leads us into his blessed breast through his open side, and there gives us a glimpse of the Godhead and heavenly joy—the inner certainty of eternal bliss. [4]

Julian's choice of a maternal model for understanding God's action was not unprecedented, yet she went beyond all others in developing the model in her remarkable theological meditation on divine love. She also expressed as few others did how profound was "the sacramental, incarnational and even material character" [5] of western medieval spirituality.

MEDIEVAL THOUGHT

The disciplined reflection on faith and doctrine known as *theology* is more central to Christianity than to any of the other world religions. Not surprisingly, theologians have featured among the most prominent and influential figures in the Christian story. None, however, has more claim to preeminence than Augustine of Hippo (354–430). Living at a formative time for Christian thought and experience, Augustine exercised immense influence on theological reflection through the Middle Ages and beyond. But, as bishop during a volatile age, Augustine's thought was formed not in the study or the reading room of a library. It was shaped in the course of his duties as a churchperson and in response above all to heated controversies that embroiled him as representative of the Catholic faith in the North African city of Hippo where he served as bishop from 396 until his death. Against the Manicheans, he developed the view that evil was not a material reality but a turning away from God. Against the Donatists, he developed a theology of the church and sacraments. He distinguished between the visible and invisible church and defended the objective character of sacraments as gifts of Christ not dependent on the worth or character of the priest. Against the optimistic view of human nature set forth by the theologian Pelagius, he taught that humanity inherited Adam's sin and guilt and that, apart from the unmerited grace of God, there is no hope of escaping judgment and divine justice. And against those who held Christianity responsible for the fall of Rome in 410, he expounded a magisterial theology of history in the *The City of God* (413–427). Human history, he argued, is a drama of two cities, an earthly city whose motive is self-love and a heavenly one whose love is for God and divine things. Though the two coexist in time, those destined for heaven fix their love on things eternal. Above all, theologians ought to fix their devotion on things of heaven and strive for the wisdom that comes of personal faith and the contemplative experience of God.

Even so cerebral a thinker as Anselm of Canterbury (c. 1033–1109) shows Augustine's influence in joining contemplative prayer and theology. It was while at prayer during Mass that Anselm intuited the form of a logical proof for the existence of God. Set forth in the *Proslogion* ("A Discourse"), Anselm's famous ontological argument states that God is the greatest conceivable being. As the "highest thinkable," Anselm reasoned, God exists in understanding. But does he exist as well in truth? Since it is greater to exist in reality than in thought alone, Anselm concluded, God must by definition exist in truth. Here is confirmation of Augustine's conviction that reason is in the service of faith and that theology begins with faith and advances from faith to understanding (*credo ut intelligam*). And as confidence in the intellect gained momentum in the eleventh and twelfth centuries, theologians went even further. Faith seemed to invite a reason. Thus Anselm sought the logic of the Incarnation in the feudal notion of honor. Sin, he argued in *Cur Deus Homo* ("Why the God Man," 1090) is an infinite affront to God's majesty and demands proportionate satisfaction. Only a divine-human being, a being able as human to make amends and as divine to offer infinite satisfaction—only such a being as God incarnate can repair the injury to the divine dignity caused by sin.

Esteem for reason did not always mean a happy wedding of faith and thought, of knowledge and the church's orthodox belief. The twelfth-century's new breed of professional, peripatetic teacher often exhibited more passion for learning than prayer, more reverence for the intellect's authority than for church tradition. Attached to cathedral schools and later to the newly emerging universities, these scholars carried their work forward outside the context of monasteries where learning was supervised by abbots and spiritual directors to enhance worship and prayer. Skilled in the application of logic to philosophical and theological problems, this new breed of theologian took as its purpose rather the analysis and explanation of church teaching. It is perhaps not quite fair to say that they inverted Anselm's motto to read, "I understand in order that I may believe" (*intelligo ut credam*). Nevertheless, their spirit was basically critical and their method—a dialectical procedure of examining the pro and con of every question—submitted Christian doctrine to the arbitration of reason.

In *Sic et Non* ("Pro and Con," 1122), for example, Peter Abelard's (1079–1142) strategy was to assemble and place in opposition contradictory texts from Scripture and the writings of the early church fathers, confident that the sifting would reveal the truth. Church authorities, however, thought otherwise and at the Council of Soissons (1112) condemned his basic conclusions. What finally did win approval was his method for theological inquiry. Peter Lombard (c. 1100–1160), whose *Four Books of Sentences* (1155–1158) became the handbook for medieval theological study, demonstrated that dialectic need not foster doctrinal innovation. It could be used to establish the essential harmony beneath apparent contradictions in the church's teaching. And in this form, dialectic became one of the primary instruments of medieval thought in service of the church.

The theology associated with Anselm, Abelard, and Lombard attained its highest expression in the thirteenth century. The proponents of this scholastic theology, as it was called, took it upon themselves to prepare comprehensive summaries or *summae* of Christian doctrine. Encompassing the articles of faith from creation to the last things, these *summae* resemble in aspiration and achievement the age's other monumental achievement, the Gothic cathedral. And, reminiscent of the symmetry of the Gothic churches, accomplished through thrust and counterthrust of vault and buttress, the *summae* wrought theological unity from the diverse voices of apostolic tradition. Persuaded by the rediscovered philosophy of

Aristotle, however, Thomas Aquinas (1225–1274) believed it possible not only to harmonize doctrine; he was convinced that Christian doctrine could be reconciled with reason and philosophy.

In his *Summa contra Gentiles* ("Against the Heathens," 1259–1264) and in the *Summa Theologica* ("Sum of Theology," 1265–1273), Thomas held that natural reason without the assistance of grace is competent to discover basic truths about the world, humankind, and even God. In the cosmological argument, for example, he held that empirical knowledge of motion, cause, and contingency provides proof for the existence of God as prime mover, first cause, and necessary being. Yet, Thomas also held that beyond the natural order there are sacred truths—like the knowledge that God is a trinity—that cannot be established by reason. Touching the ultimate mysteries of faith, philosophy must be completed by divine revelation contained in Scripture and interpreted in the writings of the church fathers. An impressive synthesis that neither destroys reason's integrity nor separates it from the realm of faith, Thomas's accomplishment won him the title "Doctor of the Church" in 1567. His thought was officially declared the standard for all Catholic theological students by Leo XIII in 1879.

SUMMARY

Religious experience, if we accept the testimony of religious people, indicates an Other that transcends culture. Yet, religion is very much a part of human culture, at once shaped by and shaping the world around. Sometimes the mutual influence of religion and culture is subtle and indirect, sometimes deliberate and self-conscious. Without claiming too much for the formative figures of medieval Christianity, their synthesis of religion and culture is undoubtedly one of the great achievements of all time. Even monasticism, which aspired to a renunciation of the world, contributed positively to this medieval synthesis. Monks were enlisted as defenders of orthodoxy, as missionaries, as preachers and reformers, and as custodians of learning and teachers in Europe's first universities. We have seen too that monasticism itself changed its character to accommodate new social circumstances and spiritual needs.

Others, however, were responsible for defining the meaning and exercise of Christian authority in a Christian society, though with different results in the eastern and western churches. In the East, Christian emperors early established themselves as the focus of sacral authority; in the West, emperors and popes strove for supremacy with a qualified victory going to the Roman pontiff. The idea of a unified Christian society under pope or emperor, however, was not to last. The rise of the nation state and the sixteenth-century Protestant Reformation undermined the dream in the West; the inroads of Islam and the fall of Constantinople to the Ottoman Turks in 1453 ended Orthodoxy's cultural hegemony or at least shifted it north to Moscow. Yet, much of what we know today as Roman Catholic or Eastern Orthodox in theology, prayer, and worship derives from this remarkable age of monks and mystics, prelates and princes, theological *summae* and soaring Gothic cathedrals.

REVIEW AND REFLECTION

1. Who were the early Christian martyrs? What religious meaning did the early Christians assign to the act of martyrdom?
2. In what sense was monasticism considered a "white martyrdom"?
3. Who were the first monks? What religious truths did they seek to express in their way of life?
4. Western monasticism is also the story of institutional reform. Can you describe the major western reform movements of western monasticism?
5. How was western monasticism related to western culture?
6. Describe the different models for relating church and state. What accounts for the differences between the East and the West?
7. What steps did the Roman popes take to insure the independence of the church from secular interference?
8. What were the major features of worship in the western church of the Middle Ages?
9. What were some of the important features of popular religious life during the Middle Ages?
10. Characterize the mysticism that flourished in the eastern and the western churches of the Middle Ages. What is the aim of mysticism?
11. What is theology? What changes took place in theology during the Middle Ages? How do we explain those changes?

END NOTES

1. Henry David Thoreau, *Walden*, ed. J. Lyndon Shanley (Princeton, NJ: Princeton University Press, 1971), p. 5.

2. *The Wisdom of the Desert: Sayings of the Desert Fathers of the Fourth Century,* trans. Thomas Merton (New York: New Directions Publishing Corporation, 1970).

3. Eleanor McLaughlin, "Women, Power and the Pursuit of Holiness in Medieval Christianity" in Rosemary Ruether and Eleanor McLaughlin, eds., *Women of Spirit: Female Leadership in the Jewish and Christian Traditions* (New York: Simon and Schuster, 1979), p. 104.

4. Julian of Norwich, *Revelations of Divine Love,* trans. Clifton Wolters (New York: Viking Penguin Inc., 1986), p. 170.

5. Eleanor L. McLaughlin, "Women, Power and the Pursuit of Holiness" in Ruether and McLaughlin, eds., *Women of Spirit,* p. 126.

SUGGESTED FURTHER READING

BROWN, PETER. *Augustine of Hippo: A Biography.* Berkeley, CA: University of California Press, 1969.

BROWN, PETER. *The Cult of Saints: Its Rise and Function in Latin Christianity.* Chicago: The University of Chicago Press, 1981.

COCHRANE, CHARLES NORRIS. *Christianity and Classical Culture: A Study of Thought and Action from Augustus to Augustine.* New York: Oxford University Press, 1957.

CAMPENHAUSEN, HANS VON. *Ecclesiastical Authority and Spiritual Power in the Church of the First Three Centuries.* trans. A. J. Baker. Stanford, CA: Stanford University Press, 1969.

DAWSON, CHRISTOPHER. *Religion and the Rise of Western Culture.* Garden City, NY: Image Books, 1958.

FREND, W. H. C. *Martyrdom and Persecution in the Early Church: A Study of Conflict from the Maccabees to the Donatus.* Oxford: Basil Blackwell, 1965.

GEANAKOPLOS, DENO J. *Byzantine East and Latin West: Two Worlds in the Middle Ages and Renaissance: Studies in Ecclesiastical and Cultural History.* Oxford: Basil Blackwell, 1966.

HAPPOLD, F. C. *Mysticism: A Study and Anthology.* Baltimore: Penguin Books, Inc., 1970.

KNOWLES, DAVID. *The Evolution of Medieval Thought.* Baltimore: Helicon Press, 1962.

KNOWLES, DAVID. *Christian Monasticism.* New York: McGraw-Hill Book Company, 1969.

LECLERCQ, JEAN. *The Love of Learning and the Desire for God: A Study of Monastic Culture.* trans. Catherine Misrahi. New York: Fordham University Press, 1961.

LOSSKY, VLADIMIR. *The Mystical Theology of the Eastern Church.* Cambridge and London: James Clarke & Co., Ltd., 1968.

PELIKAN, JAROSLAV. *The Growth of Medieval Theology (600–1300).* Chicago: The University of Chicago Press, 1978.

SIMSON, OTTO VON. *The Gothic Cathedral.* New York: Harper & Row, Publishers, 1964.

SOUTHERN, R. W. *Western Society and the Church in the Middle Ages.* New York: Penguin Books, 1970.

SZARMACH, PAUL E. ed. *An Introduction to the Medieval Mystics of Europe: Fourteen Original Essays*. Albany, NY: State University of New York Press, 1989.

ULLMANN, WALTER. *A Short History of the Papacy in the Middle Ages*. New York: Methven, Inc., 1974.

WORKMAN, HERBERT B. *The Evolution of the Monastic Ideal*. London: Epworth Press, 1927.

6 | The Age of Reformation

INTRODUCTION

Historians have used the words *dissolution* and *waning* to describe the late medieval world. Yet, it is also accurate to speak of the late Middle Ages as a time of disequilibrium. Social, political, and intellectual developments were causing basic changes in European life that challenged the very idea of a unified Christian culture whose control extended to every aspect of life. There was in the first place the prominence of a new class of merchants and bankers whose interests and tastes were essentially secular and pragmatic. As patrons of artists and scholars, collectors of books, and builders of public monuments, this class rivaled the church's monopoly in education and culture so that it became possible for life and the arts to have a separate existence apart from the church.

As vigorous supporters of strong, stable, centralized governments, this middle class allied itself with a second important element of late medieval life, the "new" national monarchs. These national monarchs, anxious to consolidate power, frequently found themselves at odds with the popes who still aspired to that delicate balance of authority symbolized in the two keys of Peter. To the political pretensions of the papacy, fourteenth-century European monarchs devised policies to limit papal powers of ecclesiastical appointment and taxation and extended protection to radical programs for church reform within their territories. A third centrifugal element in late medieval life was the spirit of nationalism. Europeans came to think of

Christianity in the Age of Reformation—Key Dates

DATES	PERSONS AND EVENTS
1304–1377 C.E.	Avignon Papacy, called by Petrarch the papacy's Babylonian Captivity
1378 C.E.	Great Schism begins, one pope in Rome and one in Avignon
c. 1406–1457 C.E.	Lorenzo Valla, Italian humanist and reformer
1414–1417 C.E.	Council of Constance, ends the papacy's schism, establishes conciliarism, and condemns John Wycliffe (c. 1330–1384) and John Huss (1369–1415)
1453 C.E.	Constantinople falls to the Turks; Greek scholars flee to the West
1454 C.E.	Gutenburg's Bible printed
1516 C.E.	Erasmus's Greek edition of the New Testament
1517 C.E.	Luther (1483–1546) publishes the Ninety-five Theses in Wittenberg; Protestant Reformation begins
1484–1531 C.E.	Ulrich Zwingli, Protestant reformer of Zurich
1524–1526 C.E.	Peasant Revolt, application of reformation principles to a popular uprising
1527 C.E.	Schleitheim Confession, the Anabaptist consensus statement of belief
1534 C.E.	Act of Supremacy, the Church of England declares separation from Rome
1536 C.E.	John Calvin (1509–1564), publishes his *Institutes of the Christian Religion* and arrives in Geneva
1545–1563 C.E.	Council of Trent, Roman Catholicism affirms its traditional teaching against Protestantism

themselves as English or French or Spanish and to have these separate national identities confirmed in national literatures which rivaled the international Latin culture of the church.

These social and cultural conditions further intensified the contemporary alienation from a church whose spirituality had become arid and mechanical and whose leadership reacted with defensiveness or inflexibility. We begin this chapter, therefore, with a look at a major impetus for fourteenth- and fifteenth-century reform, namely, the failure of papal Christianity to renew itself. This failure led to calls for reform from extra-ecclesiastical movements concerned with the restoration of the church to its original apostolic condition, and from churchmen committed to reforming councils as instruments in church renewal. But the recovery of papal power in the middle of the fifteenth century dimmed the hope without satisfying the need for reform by a general church council for another century. In the late fifteenth and early sixteenth centuries, a group of Christian scholars known as *Renaissance humanists* were hopeful that the alliance of scholarship and piety would bring about a general renewal of Christendom. But their role in sixteenth-century reformation diminished as more strident voices called for a more radical reform. It is to these voices that we turn in the chapter's discussion of the sixteenth-century's major reformations, which resulted ultimately in the division of the western church into Protestant and Roman Catholic camps.

FOURTEENTH CENTURY REFORM

Papal Christianity

On September 3, 1303, with three hundred horsemen and a thousand foot soldiers, a henchman of France's Philip the Fair entered the Italian town of Anagni and kidnapped Pope Boniface VIII. This same Boniface had only a year earlier published the bull *Unam Sanctam*, in which he boldly reasserted the temporal power of the papacy over the whole of the Christian social order. Not two years after the incident at Anagni, the papacy under Clement V was removed to Avignon just across the Rhone from France, beginning a seventy-year period described by the great Italian poet Francesco Petrarch as the papacy's "Babylonian Captivity." This period of the papacy seriously compromised the popes' claim to be international arbiters in Europe's spiritual and temporal affairs. At the same time, the popes found it necessary to increase their revenues to meet the cost of maintaining a court in exile and so added to the alienation of Europe's monarchs who resented the drain of moneys from their own national coffers. Certainly, some prelates must have objected to the fiscal machinery, judging from the papal record. In a single audience in July 1328, no fewer than one patriarch, five archbishops, thirty bishops, and forty-six abbots were excommunicated for default on their taxes. The prestige of the popes further declined in the period known as the Great Schism (1378–1417), when Europe's allegiance was divided between the papacy's "two heads," the popes in Rome and those in Avignon. The spectacle of Christendom with three popes followed the Council of Pisa (1409–1410). Little wonder that Dante consigned several Roman pontiffs to the eighth circle of hell.

It is important to keep in mind that even at this period the papacy was not without loyal defenders. There were saintly figures like Catherine of Siena (1347–1380) who energetically worked for justice and Christian unity under the church. It was at least in part through the efforts of Catherine, for example, that Gregory XI returned from exile in Avignon to Rome. Yet, the papacy seemed incapable of disentangling itself from events destined to make it more worldly and less a symbol of unity. In spite of the best efforts of popular, charismatic figures like Catherine, disaffection with the papal church mounted. Others like the Waldensians sounded a more schismatic note of protest.

The Waldensians believed that the church had long ceased to represent the simple religion of the Gospels. Tracing the fall of the medieval church to the Donation of Constantine (a document in which Emperor Constantine allegedly transferred vast land holdings in the West to the popes, making them temporal lords), the Waldensians rejected all postapostolic practices and beliefs without Scriptural justification. John Wycliffe's followers in England, the Lollards, held similar views of what they called the "Caesarian" clergy and the importance of a spiritual church in imitation of Christlike poverty.

The popes responded by condemnation. Already by the fourteenth century, repressive measures had been taken against the Albigensians, the Beguines and the Beghards, and the Waldensians. These sectarian movements emphasized the laity's role in the church, the ideal of apostolic poverty, and the importance of Christ and the apostles as exemplars of the Christian life. Among late medieval sectarian Christian movements, we find too that women emerge in the roles of prophets, founders, and exemplars of what Joachim of Fiore spoke of as the Age of the Spirit—an age he believed that would supersede the Age of the Son and the clerical church. Prous Boneta, founder of a Provençal Beguin sect, was regarded by her followers as "the incarnation of the Holy Spirit, the new Eve who would bring final salvation to all humanity." [1] And the Guglielmites of Milan believed that "in the new church, built on the foundations of the Spirit . . . women will be spiritual leaders." [2] The official church also took steps to suppress these groups and their teachings.

The fourteenth-century church was especially anxious to suppress the ideal of poverty which it took to be a threat to its authority. And a prime target of such repressive measures was the Spiritual Franciscans.

With the coming to the papal throne of John XXII in 1316, steps were taken against the Spiritual Franciscans, that branch of the Franciscan Order which clung to the order's primitive ideal of poverty. Against this potentially subversive doctrine, this pope stated the church's official position in no uncertain terms. To hold, as the radical Franciscans did, that absolute poverty was a necessary condition of perfection or that those who embraced such poverty were more perfectly reproducing the example of Christ and the apostles was heresy.

The ideal of the church in Dante's words as "no other than the life of Christ" was not limited to popular piety, nor was opposition to the secular pretensions of the popes limited to heterodox religious communities. Opposition to John XXII also centered in the imperial court, where Louis IV assembled around himself such eminent figures as Michael of Cesena, General of the Franciscan Order, and William of Occam, the century's pre-eminent theologian. The Emperor's political theorist in his quarrel with the pope was Marsilius of Padua. In his *Defender of the Peace* (1324), Marsilius challenged the medieval view of the church as a divinely sanctioned hierarchical reality in whose head, the pope, is entrusted both spiritual and temporal authority. He argued that the popes falsely aspired to temporal jurisdiction, an aspiration destructive of the church's peace and unity, and that the church is a human, not a divine, institution. On the question of ecclesiastical authority, Marsilius advocated the transfer of power from the papacy to general church councils of laity and priests.

The emerging nationalism of the European states meant that antipapal criticism of this sort would not be silenced. The English theologian and reformer John Wycliffe (c. 1329–1384) supported the government's policies to restrict papal powers of ecclesiastical appointment and taxation in England. His heterodox teachings also raised searching questions about the nature of the church and religious authority. He held, for example, that the sole criterion for the church's action was the gospel, that the true church imitated Christ's humility and poverty, and that the king ought to disendow the church and divest it of its property. A century and a half later, King HenryVIII took this advice to heart when he dissolved the English monasteries.

Wycliffe's controversial teaching spread to Bohemia through the influence of a popular preacher and theologian, John Huss (c. 1372–1415). Like Wycliffe, Huss was a popular preacher, closely associated with the national spirit of his own people and his king's international policies. He too appealed from papal to biblical authority in the church and from the Roman church to the church of the apostles. The papal office, as the apostolic one, he wrote, "consists in preaching the Word of God, in administering the sacraments, and praying diligently to God on behalf of the people." The administration of "temporal possessions," on the other hand, is a secular responsibility, in which popes and prelates ought not to meddle. That Huss should be condemned to the stake not by a pope but by the delegates to a general church council convened to reform the papacy shows how sadly reform itself was divided in this age.

FIFTEENTH-CENTURY DEVELOPMENTS

Conciliarist Reform

We have been looking at reform from outside official ecclesiastical channels. *Conciliarism* was an attempt from within to restructure church authority. This fifteenth-century movement had as its purpose to heal the schism of the papacy, institute church reforms, and through general church councils provide for greater representation in church government. Gaining strength during the Great Schism, the conciliarists criticized the popes' identification of the church's interests with their own. As elected heads of the church, the conciliarists held, the popes have a special responsibility for church unity and peace. Yet, the full power of the church resides not in the popes who are but a part of the church. The power of the church resides rather in the whole body of the faithful whose common will is best expressed through the church's general councils. Thus the conciliarists sought to reverse the trend begun in the eleventh century by Gregory VII who set the tone of the medieval papacy by arguing for the supremacy of popes within the church.

Conciliarists opposed this position and saw their views triumph at the most effective of the reforming councils, the Council of Constance that met at the Swiss city of that name in the years 1414–1417. In a return to ancient custom, the call for the council was initiated by the Emperor Sigismund, but it was dominated by the French party of reformers, among whom were Jean Gerson and Peter d'Ailly. In a first order of business the council fathers in a declaration entitled *Sacrosancto* (1415) asserted their authority as deriving directly from Christ and as binding even on popes. On this basis they claimed the right to pronounce on matters of faith, to end the papal schism, and to reform the church "in its head and members."

To make good on these claims, the council delegates deposed the three papal claimants and elected a new pope, Martin V. Anxious to remove any taint of heresy, they scrutinized and criticized the works of John Wycliffe and John Huss, and condemned Huss to be burned at the stake. In the document *Frequens* (1417) the delegates provided for the frequent and regular assembly of councils and so ensured the implementation of conciliar reform in the future. Thus, at the council's close, conciliar principles had been asserted and a means for their implementation had been settled upon; heresy had been dealt with and the Great Schism ended. But this apparent victory was short-lived for by mid-century a unified papacy once more reasserted its authority, disclaiming, in the words of Pope Pius II, conciliar principles as "erroneous and abominable" and "completely null and void."

Renaissance Humanism

The *Renaissance* was a cultural movement of immense importance for European art, architecture, and literature. It began in the fourteenth century but flourished in the great fifteenth-century Italian city states, most notably in Florence, and at the ducal courts of Ferrara, Mantua, and Urbino and the papal court in Rome. It enjoyed the patronage of bankers, politicians, generals, and popes, men in many respects as remarkable as the artists and scholars they sponsored. Cosimo de Medici, member of a powerful Florentine banking family, built the library of San Marco within whose vaulted rooms ancient manuscripts were preserved, catalogued, and studied. Federigo Montefeltro, first duke of Urbino, combined martial prowess with cultivation and a love of books. The portrait of him by Justus of Ghent, in full military dress, helmet at his feet, reading in his library, summarizes perfectly the Renaissance ideal of the man of action and culture.

But not to be surpassed as partisans or patrons of the Renaissance were the popes of this age of art and culture. Though unsurpassed in their worldliness, we nevertheless owe to them the Vatican Library, the Sistine Chapel, and the beginning of the Basilica of Saint Peter's. Yet, the true greatness of the Italian Renaissance was its artists and scholars, among whom are numbered Petrarch and Boccaccio in poetry and literature; Giotto, Raphael, and Titian in painting; Leonardo da Vinci and Michelangelo in art and sculpture; Filippo Brunelleschi in architecture; and Marsilio Ficino and Pico della Mirandola in philosophy. Diverse though these figures were, they shared an enthusiasm for classical culture, a fascination with the natural world, and a confidence in the dignity, intellectual capabilities, and creativity of the human being.

Especially important for religious reform was the literary movement of the Renaissance. Known as *Renaissance humanism*, this movement included poets, chancellors of cities, and scholars, all of whom were united in the commitment to a program of education from which they derived their name, the *studia humanitatis*. Essentially a liberal arts program, the *studia humanitatis* concentrated on literary and historical subjects, the Greek and Latin classics, and the ancient church fathers. The first impetus for humanistic studies came before the middle of the fifteenth century with the arrival of Greek scholars and manuscripts from Constantinople. The earliest humanists were poets and orators, men who provided cultural and civic leadership and who looked to the ancients for their political and cultural ideals.

For the most part the humanists did not challenge the church. But their refinement of historical and textual criticism opened official papal documents to a fresh and more critical scrutiny. And in this new critical task no fifteenth-century humanist proved more adept than Lorenzo Valla (1407–1457). Typical of the humanists, Valla was a dedicated classicist and wrote a widely read text in Latin philology, *Elegancies of the Latin Language* (1444). Yet it was in his study of ancient religious texts—to which he brought the humanist passion for objectivity and historical truthfulness—that we see the relevance of literary studies for reform. He established, for example, that a letter from king Abgar of Edessa to Jesus was apocryphal, that the writings of Dionysius the Areopagite were not composed, as believed, by a contemporary of Saint Paul, that the Apostles' Creed was not the work of the apostles, and that the Latin Vulgate (the official Bible of the Roman Catholic Church) contained grammatical errors. But Valla's most famous discovery was that the Donation of Constantine, a document on which papal claims to temporal dominion were based, was an eighth-century forgery. On the basis of its Latin style and its historical references, Valla offered conclusive proof that the document could not have been contemporary with the Emperor Constantine. These findings would later be used in the Protestant arsenal against the Roman church.

In the North, humanism was more sober. By contrast to the Italians, humanists like Lefevre d'Etaple in France, John Colet in England, and Johann Reuchlin in Germany were less exuberant about pagan values, more serious about religion and ethics, and more concerned with using humanistic learning in the service of the Christian tradition. The greatest of these Northern humanists was Desiderius Erasmus (probably 1469–1536). Known as the "Prince of Christian Humanists," Erasmus was wary of the revival of paganism. The study of the classical authors, he was careful to observe, ought not to be an "end in itself"—as it tended to be in the south—but a means to a worthier goal, namely, the study of sacred Scripture and the writings of the ancient church fathers. "It was not for empty fame or childish pleasure," he wrote in the *Handbook for the Christian Soldier* (1504), "that in my youth I grasped at the polite literature of the ancients, but by late hours gained some slight mastery of Greek and Latin. It has long been my cherished wish to cleanse the Lord's temple of barbarous ignorance, and to adorn it with treasures brought from afar, such as may kindle in generous hearts a warm love for the Scriptures." Erasmus dreamed that scholarship would be instrumental in reform and that the use of the new learning in biblical studies would effect a Christian spiritual renewal.

Erasmus looked forward to the day when Scripture above all else would be the touchstone for Christian living, [3] and in *Paraclesis* he expressed a dream that the Protestants would come more nearly to realizing. "I would to God," he wrote, "that the plowman would sing a text of the Scripture at his plow and that the weaver would hum them to the tune of his shuttle. . . . I wish that the traveler would expel the weariness of his journey with this pastime. And, to be brief, I wish that all communication of the Christian world be of the Scriptures." To the end of restoring to Christendom its ancient literary heritage, he published before his death thirty critically edited folio volumes of patristic texts and a monumental critical edition of the Greek New Testament (1516), used by Luther in making his own German translation of the text. In preparing these scholarly editions, Erasmus hoped that he would thereby hasten Christianity's return to the simple, undogmatic religion of the gospel, in whose light the theological vagaries and the accumulated religious observances and superstitions of the medieval church would be burned away as morning mist by the sun. Yet by the 1520s it was clear that reform was to follow another course than the one Erasmus envisioned; it would be accomplished through decision, action, and faith rather than enlightenment and toleration.

LUTHER'S PROTEST

Martin Luther

Born of a successful Thuringian miner, Luther (1483–1546) went to school at Madgeburg and Eisenach, and earned the bachelor's and master's degrees from the university of Erfurt. He entered the Augustinian monastery at Erfurt in the summer of 1505 and was ordained a priest in 1507. About his years as a monk, Luther wrote that "if ever a monk could have gained heaven through monasticism, I should have done so." Yet, the prospect of addressing God in his first Mass filled the new priest with religious dread, so great was his awe of divine majesty. A sense of God's righteousness and the magnitude of sinful unworthiness proved paralyzing and relief would not come to Luther until he had cast off the medieval notion of salvation as at once God's grace and human effort.

Release from what can be described as a form of spiritual paralysis came from Luther's so-called "Tower Experience." Luther saw for the first time that sinners do not achieve righteousness through their own efforts. The righteousness that Paul spoke of in Romans 1:17 is rather a "passive righteousness, by which a merciful God justifies us through *faith*." We cannot be certain when Luther had this experience. But it may have occurred while he was lecturing on the Psalms (1513–1515) at the new university at Wittenberg, where he had become a doctor in theology (1512). Had it not been for Luther's pastoral duties, however, he may not have been thrust so prominently into the international spotlight when in 1517 he published the famous theses protesting the sale of *indulgences* in the neighboring territory of the archbishop of Mainz.

Attack on Indulgences

Reading for the first time of the events leading to the Protestant Reformation, we might think it strange that a proposal for an academic disputation on a minor point in Catholic theology should provoke a controversy that would embroil Europe and result in the second great schism of the Christian church. But that is what happened when, on the eve of the Feast of All Saints, October 31, 1517, an obscure Bible professor nailed to the chapel door of the Wittenberg Castle Ninety-five Latin Theses on indulgences. It should be stressed that Luther in principle was not at the outset opposed to indulgences. We might note too that the idea of some sort of ritual exchange involving the accumulation of spiritual merit is a feature common to many religious traditions. In Hinduism's *Agni Purana*, to cite only one example, a financial commitment to the building or the restoration of a temple is a pious act with the incentive of release from "the sins of a thousand births"—an attractive incentive indeed if one desires to be free of the karmic cycle of rebirth.

A ritual exchange akin to that recommended in the Hindu scripture cited above became a part of the church's practice as early as the eleventh century. At first the exchange was in consideration for an especially meritorious deed. Pope Urban II (1088–1099) extended the practice by declaring a complete indulgence for all who enlisted in the First Crusade. Medieval theologians paved the way for a still more elaborate understanding of the indulgence by joining the practice to the idea of a spiritual treasury of merit at the disposal of the church. According to the theologians, there exists a heavenly treasury consisting of the superabundant merit of Christ and the saints that is available to all members of that invisible fellowship of the church known as Christ's mystical body. This merit, it should be stressed, is not the same thing as the grace of God's forgiveness communicated to sinners in the sacrament of penance. The ritual exchange made possible by the indulgence is rather the remission or cancellation of a temporal penalty extracted as punishment for sins committed—a punishment to be satisfied in this life through meritorious works or after this life in purgatory.

Though the indulgence reflected a general religious wisdom and was based on sound Catholic theology, the danger inherent in ritual exchange was that it became an economic exchange. And that is what had occurred in the territory adjacent to Luther's Wittenberg. The twenty-three-year-old archbishop of Mainz, Albert of Brandenburg, had arranged to pay the

Medici pope, Leo X, ten thousand ducats for a dispensation to hold simultaneously the diocese of Mainz, Madgeburg, and Halberstadt. To assist in raising this sum, the pope permitted the sale of indulgences in the archbishop's territories for eight years, half of the proceeds returning to Rome for the building of Saint Peter's and half to be divided between Albert and the Fuggers, the German bankers who financed Albert's ambition.

Of course, had Luther known of this deal he would have been incensed, but then what he did know of the indulgence affair in Albert's Mainz was enough to ignite a powder keg. Johann Tetzel, the Dominican preacher secured to promote the indulgence sale, was without shame. He called upon his audiences to hear the souls from purgatory—"Don't you hear the voices of your dead parents and other relatives crying out?" And he encouraged a popular belief that the release from purgatory was the automatic effect of the indulgence for the dead. Erasmus voiced the liberal Catholic objection to this abusive practice. Writing to the archbishop of Mainz, he expressed his fear that indulgence preaching was undermining "the vigor of the Gospel teaching." But the Ninety-five Theses raised doubt about the practice itself. In them, Luther not only condemned the false security that indulgence preaching encouraged—he questioned the pope's power over purgatory. If there existed such power, he wrote in thesis eighty-two, "why does not the pope empty purgatory on account of most holy charity?" He doubted also the existence of a treasury of merit, pointing to the gospel as the real treasury of the church.

Luther sent a copy of the theses to the archbishop of Mainz who forwarded the theses to Rome. The ecclesiastical machinery was now in place, but not until the following summer were proceedings against Luther begun. When it became evident that Luther was expected to answer charges of heresy in Rome, Luther's prince, the Elector of Saxony, intervened to ensure that his Bible professor would receive a hearing on German soil. Appearing in October 1518 before Cardinal Cajetan, Luther presented the papal legate a written statement in which he held that the pope could and did err and that general councils of the church were superior to the popes. A year later at Leipzig, Luther went still further in debate with Johann Eck. He not only denied divine authority to the popes but impugned the authority of church councils as well. The chief function of the church is to teach the Word of God; the sole authority in matters of faith is Scripture.

When Luther was summoned before Emperor Charles V to defend his writings at the imperial Diet meeting in Worms (1521), he again made it clear where he would stand. "Unless I am convinced by the Scriptures and plain reason—I do not accept the authority of popes and councils, for they have contradicted each other—my conscience is captive to the Word of God. I cannot and I will not recant anything, for to go against conscience is neither right nor safe. God help me. Amen." Over the authority of the Bible, the line was drawn between Luther and Rome and for the future between Protestantism and Catholicism. A month later Luther was placed under the ban of the empire and for protection he went into hiding at the Wartburg Castle, where he translated the New Testament into German.

Luther's Reformation Treatises

When Luther was called before the Diet of Worms, he had already outlined his biblical faith in three pamphlets of 1520, the reformation treatises. The first, *The Address to the German Nobility*, swept aside the medieval distinction between the clergy and the laity. "It is pure invention," he wrote, "that pope, bishop, priest, and monks are called the spiritual estate while princes, lords, artisans, and farmers are called the temporal estate." Expressing a doctrine that would become basic to Protestantism, Luther announced a *priesthood of all believers*. Christians are all of one status and within the church differ only in respect to office. The supremacy of the spiritual over the temporal was thus avowed a false distinction. The exclusive authority of the pope to interpret Scripture or to call church councils was rejected as having no biblical justification. The secular princes, Luther concluded, had the right and the responsibility to intervene in church reform.

The second treatise appeared in October. Titled the *Babylonian Captivity of the Church*, this work dealt with the sacraments and above all the Mass. Echoing Huss and Wycliffe, Luther rejected the practice of withholding the communion cup from laity, and the doctrine of transubstantiation. The practice of reserving the cup for the priest magnified the false distinction between laity and clergy; the doctrine of transubstantiation made the rite seem magic. Luther's theology of the Eucharist treated the body and blood of Christ as a consubstantial reality, present with the bread and wine. But most important in his attack on Catholic sacramental teaching, Luther disavowed the view that the Mass is a sacrifice. The idea that humans can offer sacrifice to God or perform any meritorious act was antipathetic to Luther's doctrine of salvation by faith. The Lord's Supper is not a sacrifice, an offering made to God, but rather a testament of God's love and mercy in offering his Son for sinful humanity. Of the other Catholic sacraments, only baptism retained sacramental status as an efficacious sign of God's promise instituted by Christ.

The first two treatises announced Luther's views on the priesthood of all believers, the superiority of Scripture to tradition, and the spiritual character of the sacraments as a rite instituted to "nourish faith." *The Freedom of the Christian*, the last and the most enduring of the 1520 reformation treatises, expressed what Luther believed essential to Christianity or, as he put it in his open letter to Pope LeoX, "the whole of the Christian life in a brief form." He began with the New Testament paradox on the freedom of the spirit: "A Christian is a perfectly free lord of all, subject to none. A Christian is a perfectly dutiful servant of all, subject to all." By this he meant that, since justification is by faith alone and cannot be earned by good works, the Christian is free from the compulsion to merit God's approval through ceremonial, legal, or moral works. All that is required for God's approval is faith. By faith's power God's word and the gospel of Christ are imparted to the soul, as "the heated iron glows like fire because of the union of fire with it." Or, to shift to Luther's other metaphor, all that is needed is Christ's "grace, life, and salvation," the soul's property by virtue of a royal marriage that weds the soul to Christ.

The metaphors describing this central Christian experience indicate the immediacy, intimacy, and profoundly personal character of faith, but Luther's faith was neither pietistic nor antinomian. Certainly, he was unrelenting in his refusal to assign ceremonial or moral work a role in salvation. Against Erasmus's defense of human freedom in *The Liberty of the Will* (1524), for example, Luther upheld God's majesty and inscrutable justice. In *The Bondage of the Will* (1525), he compared the human will to a beast of burden, ridden either by God or the Devil. Intemperate though it seems, this response serves to underscore his opposition to good works in salvation. Nevertheless, Luther disclaimed any charge that "we will take our ease and do no works, and be content with faith." Though works contribute nothing to justification, they are, if faith be present, done for the glory of God. Similarly, his evangelical ethic of service balanced the requirements of faith and love in the religious life. "Although the Christian is thus free from all works, he ought in this liberty to empty himself, take upon himself the form of a servant. . . . and to serve, help, and in every way deal with his neighbor as he sees that God through Christ has dealt with him." With respect to God, the Christian responds with faith, trust, and gratitude; yet, toward the world, faith is expressed as spontaneous love and willing service in imitation of Christ, who himself assumed the form of a servant.

DIVERSE PATTERNS OF PROTESTANT REFORMATION

Reformation Beyond Luther

Once the break with Rome had been initiated, the reforming spirit was given diverse expressions. Even at home, Andreas Carlstadt, Luther's old colleague on the faculty at Wittenberg, took advantage of Luther's absence at the Wartburg Castle to introduce his own radical reforms and innovations. In an egalitarian application of the priesthood of all believers, Carlstadt dressed as a peasant, renounced the use of his title, preferring the address Brother Andreas to Doctor Carlstadt, rejected church music and religious images, and interpreted the Lord's Supper as a spiritual meal. The situation worsened with the arrival of a group of radical preachers from Zwickau who claimed direct divine inspiration and prophesied the end of the world. Luther returned from hiding to curb the excesses and to restore Lutheranism to a middle course between Rome and the radicals. Following the principle that "what is not contrary to Scripture is for Scripture and Scripture for it," he preserved much of postapostolic tradition. He regarded, for example, confession as desirable preparation for communion and approved the use of candles, the crucifix, and religious images as aids for worship and instruction. By contrast, the reformation in Switzerland followed another, independent course. The Swiss Reformed churches, in a different application of the biblical principle, rejected all traditional ceremonies, practices, and teachings lacking a solid scriptural basis.

Ulrich Zwingli

The theologian Ulrich Zwingli (1484–1531), a leading figure in the Swiss reform movement, approached the Protestant Reformation by a different path than Luther. Educated at Bern, Vienna, and Basel, Zwingli came into active contact with Christian humanists. At Basel, he met Erasmus, who persuaded him to put aside medieval theology for the classics, the church fathers, and the New Testament. It was thus as a humanist that Zwingli commenced biblical preaching at Einsiedeln, where he became a priest in 1516. He also undertook there the serious study of Greek and Hebrew. In 1519 he was asked to serve as a stipendiary priest of the Great Minster church in Zurich. The move marked the beginning of his evangelical activity, to which he would devote himself until his death in 1531, as a patriot and a Protestant, defending Zurich against the Catholic cantons (states) at the second battle of Kappel.

Reform in Zurich

The Swiss reform party initially welcomed Luther's ideas. Nevertheless, the events in Zurich, and the theology guiding them, pointed to Switzerland's independent reformation. A first step in this reformation came in 1519 when Zwingli abandoned the *lectionary*, the traditional cycle of readings from Scripture. He expressed his intention rather to preach in continuous exposition from the New Testament starting with Matthew.

"The Word of God," he wrote, "will take its course as surely as does the Rhine." And so it did. Moved by Zwingli's preaching, the printer Christopher Froschauer and several associates decided to break the Lenten fast by dining on "two dried sausages." The breaking of the fast was a serious matter, but Zwingli defended Froschauer on biblical grounds. Doctrine and practice, he held, must have scriptural warrant. "If I saw that a teaching could bear the test [of Scripture]," he wrote, "I accepted it; if not I rejected it." The veneration of saints, belief in purgatory, the priest's wearing of vestments, and the use of images and music in worship were also submitted to this test, and in 1524 "cleansing" of the churches commenced. Images were smashed, relics were disposed of, statues and ornaments were carted away, priestly vestments were discarded along with other ornaments of the Mass, the organs were boarded up, and the paintings on the walls of churches were whitewashed.

While Luther refused to separate spirit and flesh, Zwingli insisted on a literal application of the saying from John's Gospel—"the flesh is of no avail." The opposition between flesh and spirit was basic for his program of reform. Denying that things accessible to the senses can be the object of faith, Zwingli repudiated the doctrine of Christ's real presence in the consecrated communion bread and wine, a position that ended in a stormy confrontation with Luther at the Marburg Colloquy of 1529. At that conference, Luther declared that the words, "This is my body," should be accepted at face value. Zwingli countered that the command, "Do this in memory of me," was decisive for interpreting the communion meal. The meal, he believed, was a commemorative act, joining believers in fellowship and in loyalty to Christ. Instructions for the Zwinglian rite, therefore, featured table fellowship, a remembering of Christ's redeeming act, and thanksgiving and praise for God's grace. The congregation was to assemble around a simple table. The minister presided not as a priest before an altar but as a servant of his fellow believers. Reading from the Bible accompanied the distribution of the bread and wine in plain wooden utensils. Though austere in outward form, the Zwinglian rite spoke eloquently of the meditative (as distinct from the sacramental) in religious experience. Its purpose was to focus the mind by a contemplative act whereby the great mystery of faith, the mystery of Calvary, became for the worshippers a reality contemporary with their experience.

Anabaptists

Anabaptism was a radical reformation that developed in Zwingli's circle. Called Anabaptists because they practiced rebaptism, these reformers under the leadership of Conrad Grebel grew impatient with the slow pace of reform in Zurich and disillusioned with Zwingli's refusal to act without permission of the city council. They believed that there should be no delay and no compromise in putting Christian practices to an exacting biblical test. Finding no biblical warrant for infant baptism, they rebaptized one another. Grebel began by first baptizing George Blaurock, and Blaurock proceeded to baptize the others present. In less than a week, thirty-five persons had received the rite, laying the foundation for the first Anabaptist congregation. Adult baptism thus became associated with the Anabaptists who interpreted the rite as a condition for admission to the church and a sign of repentance and the amendment of life. By advocating a believer's baptism, however, the Anabaptists called into question a deeply held sixteenth-century belief that together the church and the state form one Christian society.

Government repression followed, and in June of 1527 the Zurich authorities made Felix Mantz the first Anabaptist martyr. Other Anabaptists were to follow Mantz's example in witnessing to their New Testament faith with their lives. Yet the Anabaptists took comfort in the example of the earliest heroes of faith whose courage they imitated. In the words of Elizabeth, a Dutch Anabaptist, "it is the way which the prophets and the apostles went, and the narrow way which leads into eternal life, for there shall no other way be found by which to be saved." [4] It is interesting too that the political circumstances of these irenic people of faith should resemble so nearly the condition of the first Christians. Catholic Emperor Charles V made rebaptism a capital offense throughout the empire, and Protestant princes concurred with the imperial decree at the Diet of Speyer in 1529. In the course of events, Anabaptists suffered persecution and banishment and many became martyrs through burning or drowning.

From the outset, Anabaptism was a heterogeneous movement dispersed over Switzerland, northern Germany, the Netherlands, and Spain. Yet, the Schleitheim Confession (1527) represented a consensus statement of their belief. In that confessional statement, the Anabaptists distinguished between the world and "those who have come out of the world." Christian citizenship, they held, is heavenly, and those who are Christians should have no dealings with the world or fellowship with the churches that have not separated from the world. That is why, in part, Grebel rejected Zwinglian reform. Like Luther, Zwingli allowed the state a role in the church's reformation. But the Anabaptists went further still by rejecting all customary contact with ordered society. They agreed to hold no public office, make no appeal to the magistracy for the settling of disputes, swear no oaths, and bear no arms in their own or others' defense.

There were notable exceptions to this standard among some who were identified with this branch of the reformation. Thomas Munster (1489–1525), an *apocalyptic* prophet, led the unsuccessful Peasant Rebellion of 1524–1525. And a band of apocalyptic visionaries took control of the city of Munster in 1534, called it the "New Jerusalem," and sought to establish a utopian Christian community along New Testament communitarian lines. Yet, the rule for Anabaptists was and continues today to be a Christian pacifism, a renunciation of physical force in matters of faith. Anabaptists did retain *excommunication* to discipline recalcitrant members and preserve the integrity and holiness of their separate communities.

In many respects, the Anabaptists bore greater resemblance to the quasi-monastic communities of the Middles Ages or to the Waldensians than to other churches of the Protestant Reformation. Like the Waldensians, many Anabaptists believed that the adoption of Christianity by the Roman Empire marked the fall of the church. The church, elevated to official status within the state, thereby ceased to be a community of decision and obedience and became instead a birthright symbolized by infant baptism. Renouncing both infant baptism and the church's alliance with the state, Anabaptists turned to the New Testament as a pattern for the church, a guide for Christian practice, and a code for Christian living. Interested far more in life than in theology, they took the ethics of the Sermon on the Mount as their standard of perfection—a perfection required of all who experienced new life in Christ and anticipated his imminent return in the Second Coming. In innocence of life, Erasmus wrote of the Anabaptists, they excelled all others. They refrained from profanity, lying, strife, intemperate eating and drinking, and practiced humility, patience, uprightness, meekness, honesty, temperance, and straightforwardness. They observed simplicity in diet, speech, dress, and the furnishings of their homes and communal buildings. Concerned that covetousness inhibits Christian charity, some held property in common. Affirming an equality of function as well as status, Anabaptists interpreted the priesthood of all believers to mean the dropping of all distinctions between clergy and laity. These same values continue to be held by the Amish, the Hutterites, and the Mennonites, contemporary descendants of sixteenth-century Anabaptism.

John Calvin

Calvin (1509–1564) was a French theologian, reformer, and father of Calvinism. Born in the cathedral city of Noyon in Picardy, he seemed destined for the ministry. His father, an advisor to the bishop, secured for him a church income when he was twelve and from this fund his education at Paris and law studies later at Orleans were financed. During this formative period, he became aware of the French humanist reform movement and, as a humanist, wrote a commentary on Seneca's *Treatise on Clemency* (1532). But he despaired of humanism as an effectual means of reform. In the year 1534 Calvin experienced "a sudden conversion," resigned his church income, and prepared his first statement of Protestant belief. Yet, it was not until 1536 that he was actively enlisted in the Protestant cause. On his way to Strasbourg, where he planned to pursue his literary studies, he stopped overnight in Geneva. The city was newly won to the Protestant cause, and its people had pledged "to live according to the Law of the Gospel and the Word of God and to abolish all Papal abuses." William Farel was the preacher charged with implementing this pledge. Learning that Calvin lodged in the city, Farel went to his hotel and prevailed on the young scholar to join the city's ministry. Reluctantly, Calvin agreed and in his own words found himself thus "thrust into the game."

Calvin's Religious Thought

Calvin may have been a reluctant player. Yet, he was the most influential figure in shaping the character of the Reformed tradition in Switzerland, France, Holland, Scotland, England, America, and elsewhere. No small part of that influence is attributable to his *Institutes of the Christian Religion*—described by one historian as the single most influential book of the Protestant Reformation. Calvin finished the first edition (1536) when he was twenty-six and expanded it over four revisions, the last one being published only a few years before the author's death. Organized in four sections, the *Institutes* presents a clear, systematic statement of Calvin's beliefs about God, Christ, creation, sin, redemption, the Christian life, sacraments, and church order.

The *Institutes* was thus a comprehensive statement of Protestant belief and owes its influence to its clarity and organization. Yet, Calvin's religious thought had its own character, in part attributable to the importance of creation and providence in his theology. Acutely aware of the dependency of all things on the Creator, Calvin stressed gratitude and praise as basic religious attitudes. Conscious too that nothing in creation is left to chance, he held that what happens in the world happens according to the will and providence of God. In consequence, faith for Calvin was the knowledge of God's will, revealed in Scripture as law and expressed toward the elect (saved). The idea of law in particular distinguished Calvin's theology from the theologies of other reformers. In particular, Calvin thought of law as a necessary and inherent condition of creation and a positive good in the ordering of society.

The Bible was also related to God's will as its unique revelation, apart from which nothing can be known of God's otherwise inscrutable purposes. Repentance was joined with faith in Calvin's thought as the expression of faith's obedient submission to the divine will and manifest in a sanctity and purity of the whole life. Christian vocation consisted in divinely appointed duties and tasks to be performed in the diverse spheres of life. Salvation—a matter about which individuals should not be too anxious—was subject to God's "secret counsel," according to which one is either predestined to eternal life or damnation. In sum, the object of the religious life for Calvin was knowledge of God's will and obedient submission to it in the fulfillment of the divine commandments.

Calvin's view of the church and its worship also reflected his own distinct emphases. Concerning the church, Calvin was more optimistic than Luther about the possibility of identifying the elect by positive signs and more confident about the sanctity of the visible church. Calvin felt as strongly about the independence of the church from state supervision and was embroiled with the Genevan civic authorities over this point for the better part of his ministry there. Indeed, not until 1555 was he able to secure victory for the principle that the church alone has the power to discipline and in extreme cases to excommunicate unworthy members. Yet, Calvin did not envision, as the Anabaptists did, the church's separation from society. He regarded civil government, along with the church and the sacraments, as a divine institution. It is the purpose of the state, he believed, to protect the church and uphold religious orthodoxy. He further believed it was possible for the church, state, and citizenry to cooperate in the creation of a holy commonwealth, ruled by the saints and dedicated to God's work and glory in the world. Calvin's Geneva was the exemplar for Calvinists of what such a society might look like.

Concerning the church's worship, Calvin adopted a position somewhere between Luther and Zwingli. He was less puritanical than Zwingli in his willingness to allow "some external exercise of piety" because of human weakness. He approved, for example, the congregational singing of Psalms as an enhancement of religious devotion. Nor did he follow Zwingli in understanding the Lord's Supper merely as the symbolic focus of a devotional act. Without denying its spiritual character, Calvin affirmed Christ's real presence in communion. In other respects, however, Calvin gave little scope to the externals of religion. True worship, he believed, has nothing to do with ceremonies. What God requires is obedience to his word expressed in gratitude, praise, faith, prayer, purity of heart, and innocence of life.

Reformation in England

The way for reformation in England had been prepared as early as the fourteenth century. English monarchs asserted their authority against popes by curtailing papal taxation and judicial appeals to Rome. The English theologians William Occam and John Wycliffe upheld royal against papal prerogatives in church affairs. During the reign of HenryVII (1485–1509), the arrival of Christian humanism sparked a cultural renewal and the advocacy of liberal Catholic reform. Erasmus himself found England a congenial intellectual climate and at Cambridge prepared the Greek New

Testament (1511–1513). The 1520s saw also the arrival of Lutheran ideas circulated among the Cambridge scholars who met at the White Horse Inn.

Yet, the introduction of reformation to England had its immediate cause in the politics of Henry VIII's marriage to Catherine, the daughter of the Spanish king and queen, Ferdinand and Isabella, and the aunt of Emperor CharlesV. At issue was dynastic succession, for the queen had failed to produce a male heir. The obstacle was Pope Clement VII who refused Henry's request for an annulment for fear of the emperor's reprisal. The solution to the affair—at least from Henry's perspective—was suggested by a young Cambridge scholar, Thomas Cranmer (1489–1556). Cranmer urged the king to submit his case for annulment to the university canons, from whom Henry could expect a favorable answer. In 1533 when the king married Anne Boleyn, he made inevitable a break with Rome. The next year Parliament issued the Act of Supremacy, declaring the king to be "the supreme head in earth of the Church of England called *Anglicana Ecclesia.*" A national English church was born.

Reform made unsteady progress during Henry's religiously conservative reign. The monasteries were dissolved. Some doctrinal concessions were forwarded for the sake of a hoped-for defensive alliance with the German Protestants. The king drafted the Ten Articles (1536), a doctrinal statement that affirmed among other things the sole authority of the Bible and the church's ancient creeds. But the most important advance came at the instigation of Cranmer, archbishop of Canterbury since 1533. Cranmer's first concern was for an English Bible and at his urging the "Matthew" Bible (1537) appeared with the king's authorization. Two years later, the Great Bible was issued and placed in every parish church. Cranmer's desire that the English church have a suitable instrument for instruction, private edification, and public worship had been realized. Its successors were the Bishop's Bible, the Geneva Bible (used by Shakespeare), and the King James Bible (1611).

With the English Bible, the English Prayer Book was the second major contribution that Cranmer made to the English reformation and the formation of the Anglican church. Prepared largely by Cranmer, the Book of Common Prayer appeared in two editions (1549, 1552) during the reign of Edward VI. By act of Parliament, it was made the official service book of the English church; it contained daily offices of morning and evening prayer, the forms for the administration of the sacraments and other rites, and the Psalter and Lessons based on the Great Bible. As an instrument of worship, the Prayer Book has been favorably compared in power, beauty, and dignity of expression to the best medieval liturgies, and its religious prose was described by C. S. Lewis as burning with "a white light" rarely surpassed outside of the New Testament. One of its distinguishing marks was its skillful joining of ancient and medieval traditions with reformation elements. The two Prayer Books of Edward's reign also reflected change in English theological opinion as loyalty shifted from Lutheran to Zwinglian views of worship. This change can be seen, for example, in the words used to administer the bread at communion, in the use of *table* instead of *altar*, and in the designation *minister* instead of *priest*.

But the doctrinal consistency of the 1552 edition was muted when Elizabeth I gave the Prayer Book its decisive form in 1559. Elizabeth's religious policy aimed at an inclusiveness that comprehended all but Roman Catholics and the most extreme Protestants. When the queen reissued the 1552 Prayer Book, she had it amended to retain much of the church's medieval appearance. She also combined the Lutheran/Catholic and the Zwinglian formulas used to distribute the communion bread. The Prayer Book now read: "The body of our Lord Jesus Christ which was given for thee preserve thy body and soul unto everlasting life. [from 1549] Take and eat this in remembrance that Christ died for thee and feed on Him in thy heart by faith with thanksgiving. [from 1552]" The same policy can be seen in the Thirty-nine Articles (1562), which became the Anglican doctrinal statement. The great apologist of England's *via media* was Richard Hooker who wrote the *Laws of Ecclesiastical Polity* to defend England's episcopal form of government and its middle course between Rome and the extreme English Protestant party, the Puritans, to be discussed in the next chapter.

ROMAN CATHOLIC REFORM IN THE SIXTEENTH CENTURY

Catholic Reformation

At the time of Luther's Ninety-five Theses, a fellowship, dedicated to spiritual renewal through regular devotions and the cultivation of ethical piety through acts of charity, was established in Rome. Known as the Oratory of Divine Love, this confraternity of clergy and laity included among its members future leaders of the Catholic Reformation—the Venetian Gaspar Contarini, described as "the heart and soul" of reform, Gian Caraffa, the future Pope Paul IV, and Gaetano da Thiene, later canonized Saint Cajetan. It was to this group that Pope Paul III turned to establish a nine-member commission (1537) of progressive cardinals to study the question of church reform. But the commission's blunt criticism of the management and fiscal policies of the papacy was not well received by the papal court.

Spiritual revival, moral reform, and organizational renewal, however, found other avenues of expression. Gian Caraffa and Gaetano da Thiene established the Theatines, a new religious order whose purpose was to reform the parish clergy and raise the level of their spirituality. The Barnabites were also to revive spirituality among the clergy. The Capuchins were

The sixteenth-century vision of women religious still has
examplars in figures like Mother Teresa of Calcutta.

organized to restore Saint Francis's primitive ideal of apostolic poverty. Of
importance for the women of the Catholic Reformation, Angelica de Mer-
ici, Mary Ward, and Louise de Marillac founded respectively the Ursulines,
the Institute of the Blessed Virgin Mary, and the Daughters of Charity.
These communities, called congregations or societies, were instruments of
a new vision of Christian vocation for women outside the inherited framework of conventual life. They allowed for an apostolate in the world where
their members were at liberty to function as teachers, ministers to the sick,
and agents of charitable work. The great Spanish mystics, Teresa of Avila
and her friend and disciple, John of the Cross, initiated a more traditional
reform of the Carmelites aimed at the revival of contemplative spirituality.

At the diocesan level, Gian Giberti, another member of the Roman
Oratory, restructured his Veronese diocese, raised the educational standard for its clergy and the standard for preaching, pastoral care, and the

performance of the liturgy. Many of Giberti's decrees for Verona were later incorporated as part of the general legislation of the Council of Trent (1545–1563), reforming council of the Catholic Reformation. An effort, supported by Charles V, was also made to resolve the doctrinal differences with the Protestants, and in the late 1530s a series of conferences was initiated for discussion between conciliatory Catholic and Protestant theologians.

But the conciliarists' hope of a possible reunion was not shared by the delegates of Trent whose first concern was the organizational disarray of the church. Among the most important reforms was the requirement that bishops reside within their own diocese, preach regularly, conduct annual visitations of parish churches, hold regular provincial councils, provide for the education of their priests, and oversee hospitals and charitable organizations. With the strengthening of episcopal control over the diocese, these measures enabled the bishops to provide for needed spiritual and moral discipline within their diocese. Steps were taken also to reaffirm and preserve papal supremacy. The pope was declared Christ's vicar upon earth and all patriarchs, archbishops, and bishops were to promise him their obedience. And, in Pius IV's bull *Injunctum nobis* (1564), all bishops and clergy were required publicly to affirm this authority, pledging to recognize "the Holy Catholic and Apostolic Roman Church as the mother and mistress of all churches" and swearing "true obedience to the Roman Pontiff, the successor of blessed Peter, the chief of the Apostles and the representative of Jesus Christ." Perhaps the most striking symbol of obedience, however, was the religious order founded by Ignatius Loyola (1491–1556). The Society of Jesus, or simply the Jesuits, took obedience as its central tenet, requiring its members to subject personal will to the will of the pope. Finally, Trent put to rest the conciliar principle of church government by acknowledging the subordination of the council to the pope. The post-Tridentine church, as the church after Trent has been called, thus effectively countered Luther's rebellion with absolute obedience to the pope and the hierarchy.

Correcting the church's organizational breakdown and restoring internal discipline were two of the council's concerns. Another objective was the dispelling of the doctrinal confusion threatening the church in the wake of the Protestant Reformation. To that end, the council uncompromisingly rejected Protestant doctrine and reaffirmed traditional Catholic teachings. By contrast to the Protestant insistence on the sole authority of Scripture and salvation by justification alone, Trent reverted to the historical Catholic balances. Both Scripture and tradition (that is, the rulings of popes and councils) were held to be authoritative for faith and teaching; both faith and good works were required for salvation. The Tridentine faith also preserved the traditional number of sacraments, the form of penance, the sacrificial nature of the Mass, the doctrine of transubstantiation, the withholding of the communion cup from the laity, and the celibacy of the clergy. It endorsed purgatory, indulgences, the worship of saints, and the veneration of relics and sacred images. In 1564 the decrees of the council were confirmed by Pius IV.

Though the legacy of Trent was conservative and reactive, its great achievement was, in the words of one historian, to get the church in "fighting trim," ready for a counteroffensive to recover ground lost to the Protestants. In the front ranks of this offensive were the Jesuits who worked to win Protestants back to Catholicism and new converts in the mission fields of Asia, Africa, and the Americas. The Jesuits also contributed to the revival of Catholic spirituality. That spirituality had four prominent features. It was first and foremost a sacramental, in particular, a Eucharistic piety. Not only were the sacraments the principal channels of grace for the members of the church; the council had taught that the sacrament of the altar was to be accorded the adoration due God. Frequent communion—a practice not common during the Middle Ages—and confession were encouraged. A second feature of Catholic spirituality was its encouragement of a special meditative form of mental prayer. Ignatius Loyola's *Spiritual Exercises* popularized the systematic meditation on sin, its consequences, Christ's passion and his resurrection, and the use of physical sense impressions to bring these meditations vividly to mind. Third, Tridentine spirituality demanded of its practitioner self-discipline, self-control, and regularity in prayer. Here too one sees the influence of Trent and the disciplined spirituality of Loyola. The council decreed that faith is made perfect by charity; *The Spiritual Exercises* taught meditation as a technique for activating the pursuit of spiritual perfection. Finally, this spirituality involved a prayerful act of submission before the mystery of the church. Catholic Christianity had always believed the church to be both the context and a content of faith, and Trent crystallized this belief. For the Calvinist, God's predestination was the ground of faith in the world; for the Catholic, ultimate mystery was manifest no less surely in the visible, triumphant church, a fact still evident today in Catholic devotion to the pope.

SUMMARY

Erasmus was one of the greatest scholars of his age and about his age he was moved to write that "Wherever I turn my eyes I see things changed, I stand before another stage, and I behold a different play, nay, even a different world." Already in the fourteenth century major shifts were underway that would eventually alter the face of the Christian world. Political realities foreclosed a return to the religious and social order envisioned by Boniface VIII; a growing awareness of the historical difference between the contemporary church and the church of the apostles intensified the disillusionment with the church as a hierarchical, sacramental reality beyond time. During the period leading to the Council of Constance, the conciliarists expressed the desirability of constitutional changes to make the church more representative and reformable. But the Christian ideal of apostolic poverty, represented by the church of the New Testament and deemed recoverable by imitation or state policy, proved to be a common theme of the century's reformers.

The appeal to an age discontinuous with the present one also shaped the religious ideal of the humanists. The humanists, however, developed indispensable scholarly tools for the next phase of reformation. Applying what had been learned from textual and historical study of Latin and Greek classics to church documents and sacred Scripture, humanists like Valla, Colet, and Erasmus further undermined the religious authority of the contemporary church and more importantly threw open the windows on the world of the New Testament. The Christian humanists contemplated the world mirrored in the New Testament; the Protestant reformers used it for laying a new foundation for the Christian tradition. Soon after Luther burst upon the world with his Ninety-five Theses, Protestantism itself splintered into separate church traditions.

Protestants did, however, agree on fundamentals: the authority of Scripture, the importance of evangelical preaching, a believers' priesthood, and the sanctity of common life. Still, Lutherans, Reformed, and Anabaptists evolved unique expressions that underscored Protestant theological, religious, and cultural diversity. Anglicanism also separated from the Roman church and established an independent national church committed to a comprehensive or middle way, a *via media*, between Roman Catholicism and continental Protestantism. The medieval synthesis of Christianity and culture, in spite of an attempted revival of this ideal by fifteenth-century Renaissance popes, had lost historical viability. The Roman church at Trent did, of course, reaffirm traditional beliefs and practice and its continuity with the medieval church. Yet, in this it only postponed its own constructive encounter with cultural and religious diversity of the emerging modern world.

REVIEW AND REFLECTION

1. Identify the conditions that brought about the weakening of papal Christianity.
2. Discuss the negative reactions to the official fourteenth-century church. What reforming steps were taken by the church's critics? What steps were taken by the church's friends?

3. What were the goals and accomplishments of conciliarism and then of Renaissance humanism?

4. What did the sale of indulgences have to do with the beginning of Protestantism? What other factors in Luther's career as a reformer led to Luther's break with Rome?

5. Describe the beginnings and the subsequent differences of the other churches that broke with the Roman church. Who were the major actors in this Protestant Reformation?

6. How did Roman Catholicism seek to renew and reform itself in the sixteenth century? What in particular was the role of the Council of Trent in this process?

END NOTES

1. Rosemary Radford Ruether, *To Change the World: Christology and Cultural Criticism* (New York: The Crossroad Publishing Company, 1981), p. 50.

2. Ibid., p. 51.

3. Hans J. Hillerbrand, ed. *The Protestant Reformation* (New York: Harper & Row, Publishers, 1968), p. 148.

4. For a discussion of Erasmus's religious program and the general spirit of his work, see my essay "Enchiridion Militis Christiani" in Frank N. Magill and Ian P. McGreal, eds., *Christian Spirituality: The Essential Guide to the Most Influential Spiritual Writings of the Christian Tradition* (San Francisco: Harper & Row, Publishers, 1988).

SUGGESTED FURTHER READING

ASTON, MARGARET. "Popular Religious Movements in the Middle Ages." in *The Christian World*. ed. Geoffrey Barraclough. New York: Harry N. Abrams, Inc. Publishers, 1981.

BAINTON, ROLAND H. *Erasmus of Rotterdam.* New York: Charles Scribner's Sons, 1969.

BAINTON, ROLAND H. *The Reformation in the Sixteenth Century.* Boston: Beacon Press, 1956.

BREEN, QUIRINUS. *Christianity and Humanism.* Grand Rapids, MI: William B. Eerdmanns Publishing Co., 1968.

CHADWICK, OWEN. *The Reformation.* New York: Viking Penguin, Inc., 1964.

CLEBSCH, WILLIAM A. *England's Earliest Protestants, 1520–1535.* New Haven: Yale University Press, 1964.

DICKENS, A. G. *The English Reformation.* New York: Schocken Books, 1964.

GERRISH, BRIAN A., ed. *Reformers in Profile*. Philadelphia: Fortress Press, 1967.

HARBISON, E. HARRIS. *The Age of Reformation*. Ithaca, NY: Cornell University Press, 1955.

HARBISON, E. HARRIS. *The Christian Scholar in the Age of Reformation*. New York: Charles Scribner's Sons, 1956.

HILLERBRAND, HANS J. ed. *The Protestant Reformation*. New York: Harper & Row, Publishers, 1968.

KRISTELLER, PAUL OSKAR. *Renaissance Thought*. New York: Harper & Row, Publishers, 1961.

KUNG, HANS. "The Permanent Necessity of Renewal in the Church," in *The Council, Reform and Reunion*. Garden City, NY: Image Books, 1965.

LEFF, GORDON. *The Dissolution of the Medieval Outlook: An Essay on the Intellectual and Spiritual Change in the Fourteenth Century*. New York: Harper & Row, Publishers, 1976.

McNEILL, JOHN T. *The History and Character of Calvinism*. New York: Oxford University Press, 1967.

OLIN, JOHN C. ed. *The Catholic Reformation: Savonarola to Ignatius Loyola*. New York: Harper & Row, Publishers, 1969.

OZMENT, STEVEN. *The Age of Reform, 1250–1550: An Intellectual and Religious History of Late Medieval and Reformation Europe*. New Haven: Yale University Press, 1980.

7 | The American Experience

FIRST IMPRESSIONS

From the beginning America was an idea as much as a place on the map; America's discovery and settlement would give shape and content to the idea. When Columbus sailed west from Palos on August 3, 1492, the cultural renewal known as the Renaissance had already instilled in cultivated Europeans the dream of a purer, simpler age than the one inherited from the Middle Ages. In less than thirty years after Columbus's first voyage, another great movement swept Europe, the Protestant Reformation. The Reformation intensified the desire to restore and purify the church, and it looked to the New Testament and the apostolic church for its guiding principles. Those early explorers and settlers who sailed toward the setting sun could not, or at least did not, fail to see in the new continent the cherished promise of hopes kindled by the Renaissance and Reformation.

Though European rivalries, prospect of economic gain, and refuge from repressive religious policy were all factors in exploration and colonization, those first "horizon crossers" [1] came to America with a heightened sense of purpose. Among them, one senses that a golden age or a new religious order had become an imminent possibility. So it was that Columbus saw in the New World evidence of lost innocence, signs of the

The American Experience—Key Dates

Dates	Persons and Events
1492 C.E.	Columbus sails from Palos, discovers the New World
1607 C.E.	the first Anglican church established at Jamestown, Virginia
1620 C.E.	the Pilgrims land at Plymouth, Massachusetts
1630 C.E.	the Great Puritan immigration begins
1636 C.E.	Roger Williams (1604–1772) founds Providence as a haven of religious conscience
1734–1735 C.E.	Jonathan Edwards (1703–1758) stimulates religious revival in New England
1739 C.E.	George Whitefield (1714–1770) arrives in Virginia and the Great Awakening becomes a colony-wide revival
1774 C.E.	Mother Ann Lee (1736–1784) leads a group of Shakers to America
1787 C.E.	Constitution drafted in Philadelphia, establishes the principle of separation of church and state
1790s C.E.	the first stirrings of the Second Great Awakening
1794–1796 C.E.	Thomas Paine's *Age of Reason*, advocates Deism in its most anti-Christian form
1801 C.E.	Cane Ridge, famous camp meeting
1830 C.E.	Joseph Smith (1805–1844) founds the Mormons
1843 C.E.	William Miller (1782–1849) announces date for the end of the world
1848 C.E.	John Humphrey Noyes (1782–1849) leads a group of followers to Oneida, New York

primitive state from which the human race had fallen. Recording his impressions of the new peoples he encountered, he observed that "all go naked, men and women, as their mothers bore them." Unlike Europeans, the natives seemed to him to live in harmony with one another, free of the force of law or the coercion of government, and without the instruction of creeds they exhibited a natural reverence, believing that "power and good are in the heavens." One Protestant, George Alsop, even read in the geography of the New World "Hieroglyphics of our Adamitical or Primitive State."

While some saw in the New World a pristine condition analogous to the Garden of Eden, others interpreted the discovery and settling of America as a sign of a great work yet to be accomplished. For these mostly Protestant Christians America was the next, perhaps even the last chapter in God's universal plan of salvation envisioned by Luther less than a century earlier. Those who crossed the vast expanse of ocean believed themselves a destined people with a special, providential mission. Their gaze was not directed back to an age that was, but forward to an age that was yet to be. Identifying with the Israelites who passed through the Red Sea, they too passed over a wide sea and were delivered into a wilderness. In the words of John Rolfe, famous otherwise for marrying the Indian princess Pocahantas, they believed themselves to be "A peculiar [chosen] people marked and chosen by the finger of God, to possess it, for undoubtedly He is with us." Or, as the Puritans of New England conceived the mission, theirs was a holy experiment, nothing less than the purification of the church and the state and the dedication of both to the will of God.

The images to which those first horizon crossers appealed in their attempt to understand the meaning of America did not always correspond to the realities of the world they had entered. They were convinced nevertheless that the discovery of America would be a new chapter in the story of Christianity and that it was their sacred duty to write the script for that chapter. Important features of that story are the subject of this chapter. We will look at the new order of church and state that emerged during the colonial period, the Great Awakening, and the American Revolution. This social order in which church and state were officially separated was significant as the first time since Constantine that the church was to be separate from the state with a plurality of religious expressions allowed to flourish. Once that separation of church and state was officially accomplished with the adoption of the Constitution (1789), Christian churches redirected their energies from politics to society. Revivalism, reform, and *millenarianism* became basic elements in the American experience after the Revolution. These movements help us understand what is distinctive about Christianity as it developed in the context of America to the mid-nineteenth century.

THE BEGINNINGS
OF THE AMERICAN EXPERIENCE

The Church of England in Virginia

On April 10, 1606 James I of England chartered two companies to support settlements in the New World. On April 26, 1607 the members of the expedition sent out by the London Company first sighted the Virginia coast. Soon after landing, Robert Hunt, minister to the group, celebrated the colony's first Holy Communion. The Church of England had arrived in the New World, and the charter issued by the king made explicit the terms of its settlement. The religious life within the territory, in short, was to conform to the worship, doctrine, and discipline of the Book of Common Prayer and the Church of England.

While there were dissenters from state-enforced uniformity in religion, the idea was in no sense novel. *Establishment* in religion—whereby the state authorized and enforced uniformity in worship and discipline, and financially supported the church and its ministry—was a widely accepted practice among both Protestants and Catholics at this time. Indeed, since the days of Constantine, the unity of church and state was recognized as the rightful, even the divine order of things. Speaking of this arrangement in the Church of England, Richard Hooker articulated the common rather than the exceptional view when he wrote that "there is not any member of the Church of England but the same man is also a member of the commonwealth; nor any member of the commonwealth which is not also [a member] of the Church of England." The king's explicit instructions concerning religion, then, would not have struck his contemporaries as anything unusual. Religion was to be "preached, planted, and used" in the new colony "according to the doctrines, rights [rites?] and religion now professed and established within our realm of England." In theory, then, there would be no diversity in religious profession or practice for state policy would tolerate no religious dissent.

In practice, however, the transplanting of the Church of England to the New World, as the Virginia experience proved, was frustrated for two major reasons. First, there was the incorrigible fact of geography. The population of Virginia scattered over a vast territory that reached inland along miles of rivers and tributaries. A parish might measure from 30 to 100 miles in length and require a minister weeks to complete the visitation of a flock scattered in small settlements over the whole width and breadth of the parish. The centuries-old view of the parish as the basic unit of church life, the geographical focus of its worship, instruction, and discipline, proved under the circumstances impracticable. Of necessity funerals, religious instruction, even baptism took place in the family home, not in the parish church. The home became the stage where the great human drama of life and death was enacted. The parish church, the traditional center of religious life, was nudged to the edge of social existence.

A second factor making Establishment impracticable in Virginia was the absence of bishops. In the Church of England, bishops played a vital role. It was the bishop who ensured orthodoxy in belief, enforced ecclesiastical discipline, oversaw theological training, and provided for ordination to the ministry. With the Bishop of London three thousand miles across Atlantic waters, episcopal oversight of the church and its clergy was all but impossible. Much of the bishops's supervisory and disciplinary authority transferred to the colony's governors. Much of the direct responsibility for the affairs of individual congregations was assumed by an elected lay committee known as the vestry. It was, for example, at the discretion of the vestry that a newly ordained minister sent over by the bishop was presented to the governor for official installation as parish minister. But vestries preferred more often than not to defer the presentation indefinitely and so keep the minister in perpetual dependence. Thereby they reserved power over church affairs in themselves. This practice once prompted the Archbishop of Canterbury to complain that clergy in Virginia were treated by vestries like "domestic servants." The custom of lay governance in church affairs nevertheless had established itself in the episcopal churches in the colonies, and there even the Church of England took on a congregational coloring. But to understand the development of the *congregational principle* we have to turn to the Puritans.

The Puritans

Puritanism arose in the sixteenth century within the Church of England as a reaction against the Catholic elements that persisted in Anglicanism after England's official break with Rome. As their name implies, the Puritans wished to purify the church of its Catholic "corruptions," and in this spirit they gave English expression to the Calvinist spirit of reform. Like the Swiss reformer, John Calvin, the Puritans believed that Scripture was a sufficient guide for both Christian worship and church order, and their program entailed among other things the restoration of the church to its New Testament perfection. Indeed, the Puritans are an important part of our narrative of Christianity primarily because their practical application of church reform involved a radical departure from the old style state-church pattern. In New England this new church order was known as Congregationalism, and in giving institutional reality to what seems a simple idea—namely, that church membership is voluntary and that ecclesiastical authority rests with local congregations—the Puritans exhibited penetrating insight and considerable organizational skill.

We miss something of the essence of Puritanism if we do not also see that its drive to reconstitute the church was organically related to an intensely personal Puritan faith. As instrumental in their reform program as the New Testament was their experience and understanding of faith and conversion. Of course, Puritans referred their experience of God's saving grace to Scripture which provided them the theological frame for understanding the experience. Finding that the Bible, and in particular the Old Testament, conceived of faith as a compact or *covenant* relation between God and God's chosen, they took the idea of covenant as their preferred way of speaking not only about faith but also about the church and even the state. Like the covenant faith of Old Testament patriarch Abraham, Christian faith was both grace and summons, gift and call to an obedient willingness to act one's part in the larger historical drama of salvation.

Significantly, while faith for the Puritans was deeply personal, it was never private. The Bay Colony Puritans, for example, believed themselves summoned to make manifest Christ's reign in both church and commonwealth. And it is precisely in the Puritan sense of being called to a special work, to restore holiness to the church and righteousness to society that we see most clearly the connection between Puritan faith and Puritan institutional reform. The holiness of the church—we will discuss the Puritan social experiment later—was to be achieved not in addition to but because of personal, experiential faith.

Assurance of the church's sanctity, and hence of the success of the experiment, hinged on the sanctity of its members. Restriction of church membership to committed or experiential ("saved") Christians was their means to that assurance. Thus, individuals who sought admission to the church had to demonstrate a sincerity of faith and to give public evidence of "their knowledge in the principles of religion, and of their experience in the ways of grace, and of their conversation among men." Beginning, therefore, with a covenant theology of faith, Puritans came to view the church as a special community not coextensive with the general population, but based and built on personal decision or an inward covenant of grace, a congregational church of covenanted members in whom full ecclesiastical authority was vested.

This view that the church is a congregation or "gathered" community of committed believers had radical political as well as ecclesiastical consequences, and clashes with the English establishment were inevitable. For a brief time they hoped that King James I would favor their reform programs, but their hopes were short-lived. Only a year after ascending the English throne (1603), the king at Hampton Court declared that he would "make [Puritans and other dissenters] conform themselves [to the state church] or I will harry them out of the land." Under these circumstances, some Puritans withdrew from the Church of England altogether to form separate or independent congregations.

John Robinson's Scrooby congregation—later the Pilgrims of Plymouth Colony—were Puritans of this type. These *Separatists,* as they were called, despaired of reform from within, and yet not all Puritans wished to leave the Church of England. However corrupt their native church, they felt strongly that the English church in the words of Francis Higginson was "the Church of God in England." Political conditions in England, however, worsened when James's son Charles I became king. Many nonseparating Puritans, though still regarding themselves as loyal sons and daughters of England, saw immigration to England's American colonies as their best option. In New England they would do what they were blocked from doing at home. They would carry forward their program for the purification of church and state and, as a kind of saving remnant in the New World, they would be a model for fellow Christians left behind, "a city on a hill," to use the image of Governor John Winthrop, for all the world to see.

On June 12, 1630 Winthrop with other members of the Bay Colony stepped ashore at Salem. They brought with them all the stockholders of the trading company and also the king's charter for the colony. This was a bold stroke, for in removing the whole company of stockholders and the royal charter to New England they also transferred authority and the legal warrant to govern themselves as well. Their first act in the New World was even bolder. On October 29 they held an open meeting to elect by "general vote of the people" certain individuals who from among themselves were to select a governor and deputy governor. The trading company had been transformed in effect into a commonwealth, and one of the conditions of the Puritan experiment in the New World was satisfied.

The other condition—namely, a free church organized according to congregational principles—was prepared for a full year before the Winthrop group arrived. The settlers at Salem resolved that a properly constituted church should be formed and for that purpose chose thirty persons to draft a church covenant. The result was an exemplary application of the congregational principle:

> We Covenant with the Lord and one with an other; and doe bynd our selves in the presence of God, to walke together in all his waies, according as he is pleased to reveale himself unto us in his blessed word of truth.

On this basis the Salem settlers entered into a voluntary association of committed believers with authority to rule on admission to church membership and to impose discipline. Shortly after the covenant was signed, the church also "ordained to their several offices" two ministers who had recently come over from England, thus confirming the congregation's power to call their ministry as well.

From the beginning, the church in Puritan New England asserted its autonomy as a community of committed believers, constituted according to biblical principles and, by reason of the inward covenant of grace, conformed to the sovereign will and purpose of God. But what of the state? How did these Puritans manage to fashion a holy commonwealth? The Massachusetts Puritans sought to create a biblical commonwealth, driven by the same religious motive as the church, yet independent of the church in organization and purpose. The commonwealth's way of achieving that goal was to prescribe carefully the electoral process. Only full church members were eligible to vote or to hold public office. Those Christians who experienced an inward covenant of grace directed the affairs of the church; those same Christians also governed the state.

This arrangement was only in a very loose sense a theocracy. However influential the church and the clergy, the church did not elect officers of the state nor did it govern, and the clergy did not make laws. The civil and ecclesiastical governments were distinctly separate, as they were not, for example, in England. Still, the Bay Colony was conceived as a religious state, a biblical commonwealth. Even though the churches were not directly involved in governing, their role was instrumental to the electoral and the governing process for they supplied the state "fit instruments both to rule and choose rulers." Likewise, the magistrates were dedicated to carrying out biblical principles in framing laws and implementing justice. As "nursing fathers" of the church, civil magistrates were committed to upholding church order. They examined ministers for their fitness, served as mediators when disputes arose between churches, and generally assured a Puritan monopoly by enforcing orthodoxy in belief and uniformity in religious practice.

But the Puritan monopoly in Massachusetts was not to go unchallenged. Almost from the outset dissent sprang up, questioning the legitimacy of the "New England Way" as the Puritan church/state system has been called. Puritans like Roger Williams and Anne Hutchinson, the Presbyterian Robert Childs, the Quakers Mary Fisher and Ann Austin, and the respected president of Harvard College, Henry Dunster who adopted Baptists' views, all clashed with the Bay Colony's policy of restricting worship and religious conscience. Quaker Mary Dyer and her fellow martyrs, William Robinson and Marmaduke Stevenson, paid with their lives for protesting the persecution of their coreligionists. Yet, like the sixteenth-century Anabaptists, these New World martyrs were persons of singular conviction, courage, and resolution—a fact evident in Mary Dyer's reply on hearing her death sentence pronounced by John Endicot.

I came in Obedience to the Will of God to the last General-Court, desiring you to repeal your unrighteous Laws for Banishment on pain of Death; and that same is my Work now, and earnest Request; although I told you, that if you refused to repeal them, the Lord would send others of his Servants to witness against them. [2]

However we judge the Puritans of the Bay Colony, we should not think that they came to the New World to establish the principle of religious liberty. That work fell to dissenters like Mary Dyer, Anne Hutchison, and Roger Williams. The Massachusetts Puritans dreamed rather of a holy church, a righteous society, and the liberty to bring them into being. Their dream to create an exemplary society on the shoulders of the saints was one of the first in a long series of religious or utopian experiments to appear in America. Nevertheless, theirs was a failed experiment. In trying to impose a doctrinal orthodoxy and a religious uniformity, the Puritans had pitted themselves against the more powerful centrifugal force of religious diversity in America. It was primarily for others to learn how to live with some measure of toleration in the midst of that diversity, and to those experiments we need to turn now.

First Experiments
in Religious Liberty

One of the most famous advocates of religious liberty during the colonial period arrived at Boston in February of 1631. Roger Williams (c. 1604–1683), dubbed by an opponent the "New England Firebrand," was a Puritan minister who was at first warmly received in the Bay Colony and invited to join the Boston ministry. His refusal of the position on the ground that the church in Boston was unwilling to break away from the state church of England foreshadowed things to come. Williams adhered to the radical Puritan position that the visible saints ought to be separate as "holy from unholy, penitent from impenitent, godly from ungodly." This would be the religious principle on which he would later advocate religious liberty in Rhode Island. But Boston's middle way of walking—neither fully within nor completely outside of the national church—compromised (in Williams's opinion) the integrity and the holiness of the church.

Nor did Williams stop with questioning the holiness of the Bay Colony churches. He rejected as well the second important element in their program to create a biblical commonwealth. The magistrates, he maintained, did not have authority to enforce uniformity in worship or orthodoxy in belief. As a good Puritan, Williams was willing to allow that all aspects of human life are under God, but he drew a sharp line between the spiritual and the secular areas of life so far as humans were concerned.

While the truth of the gospel could be applied directly in the spiritual sphere, its application to social and political life could only be indirect and voluntary, and then only imperfect and subject to the judgment of God. In his mind, the church and the state stand apart as two distinct areas of life, the one ruling according to human law and custom and the other according to the operation of grace. But the separation Williams proposed found little support among most New England Puritans, and to the Puritans of Boston it meant the failure of their experiment, an experiment they hoped would profit the church not just in Massachusetts but throughout the world.

After a brief stay in Boston, Williams retired to the Plymouth colony just south of Boston, but even among fellow Separatists his welcome wore thin. Once more he found himself back in the Bay Colony, this time at the invitation of the more sympathetic Salem congregation. Using his unofficial capacity there to promulgate his religious and social views, he further kindled the wrath of the colony's leadership who had him brought before the General Court, the colony's highest tribunal. The court's ruling that he be banished from the colony could have surprised no one. In January 1636 Williams set out from Salem, exposed to "winter miseries in a howling wilderness," to the headwaters of the Narragansett Bay where he founded Providence Plantation. Other dissenters from Massachusetts were to follow him, including Anne Hutchinson and John Clarke who settled on the island portion of what is today Rhode Island. Roger Williams's "lively experiment" in religious liberty had begun.

Rhode Island became a haven for religious dissent and for those fleeing persecution for conscience's sake, and in what is a classic in American religious literature, *The Bloody Tenent of Persecution* (1644), Williams argued that persecution for reason of religion was not only unjust but contrary to the welfare of the state. In this teaching he anticipated the future—but the time was not quite right to receive or act upon this perspective. Nevertheless, Williams thought of the spiritual as a separate sphere of life, related only indirectly to human social existence. In *Bloody Tenent* he took a further step, emphasizing the voluntary character of the church, calling it a "company of worshippers," and comparing it to a college of physicians or a corporation of merchants. With respect to the civil government, the church, he maintained, is like these several societies or associations. Like them it enjoys relative autonomy in overseeing its own affairs, and like them it is free to "dissent, divide, break into Schisms or Factions" without any necessary harm to the common weal or good because the "well-being and peace [of the state] is essentially distinct from those particular societies."

The test of Williams's envisioned state was Rhode Island itself. Working together with the Baptist John Clarke, Williams eventually secured from the English crown a Royal Charter (1663) that promised a "flourishing civil state" maintained "with full liberty in religious concernments." Baptists were already represented there. Williams himself for a brief time had been a convert to the Baptist persuasion and helped found the first Baptist church in America. Others were soon to come; none were to be turned away. French Protestants or Huguenots, Anglicans, Jews, even Congregationalists secured a place among the multiplying religious groups.

Rhode Island's commitment, however, was tested by the Society of Friends, known also as Quakers. The Quakers' pacifism has always put them at odds with civil authorities and that remains as true today as at the time of their founding in the seventeenth century. In addition, that century had serious difficulty with the Quakers' belief about revelation and their attitude toward clerical authority. Whereas it was a fundamental tenet of the Puritans that the Bible was decisive revelation and the definitive source for Christian doctrine, the Quakers emphasized rather a direct revelation of Christ, an "inward light." In the words of Robert Barclay, perhaps their greatest theologian, "true revelation [is] an experienced reality." For them, worship was simple, involving a quiet waiting for the inward witness of the Spirit, and to this end sacraments and other external or objective means of salvation were set aside, as was the expounding on biblical texts so central to the teaching and preaching offices of the Puritan clergy. The Quakers intrepid enough to bring these views to Boston received harsh treatment and by law were subject to imprisonment, whippings, banishment, and even martyrdom.

Thus, when Quakers landed in Newport (1657), the other New England colonies petitioned the governor to prevent their settlement. The reply was unequivocal; Rhode Island would not meddle in matters of conscience, since a meddling policy was more dangerous than the ones the Puritan colonies pursued. As a consequence, Quakers enjoyed their first opportunity for expansion in America. But this "liberal" policy was not the consequence of a reasoning similar to that which in the next century would give birth to "the rights of man." Roger Williams's restraint from wielding the sword in matters of religious conscience was deeply rooted in an essentially Puritan understanding of the inviolability of religious experience. He also had the Puritan confidence in biblical revelation as the source of religious truth. Quakers might prosper economically and flourish politically in Rhode Island, but the "New England Firebrand" would not permit religious error to go unchallenged. When the Quaker founder George Fox (1642–1691) visited the colony, Williams was already seventy years old. Yet he rowed a small boat thirty miles to Newport, hoping to debate Fox and refute the Quaker "heresy."

Other colonial extensions of religious toleration, if not religious liberty, met with mixed success. In Maryland, for example, the Toleration Act (1649) insured religious freedom for Christians, but conservative forces managed to secure the modification of the colony's religious policy so that Roman Catholics—even though Maryland was founded as a refuge for Catholics—were not at liberty to freely practice their religion. And by the last decade of the century, Maryland legislated the establishment of the Protestant religion and made provision for the division of the counties into parishes to be governed by vestries and supported by public taxes.

To the north, Pennsylvania, founded by Quaker William Penn, fostered a religious diversity rivaled only by Rhode Island. The Anglican missionary Thomas Barton, though not at all sympathetic to what he discovered in Pennsylvania, fairly summarized the religious circumstances there when he reported finding only five hundred Anglicans; "the rest are [he wrote] German Lutherans, Calvinists, Mennonites, New Born, Dunkers, Presbyterians, Seceders, New Light, Covenanters, Mountain Men, Brownists, Independents, Papists, Quakers, Jews, etc."

Penn's "holy experiment" was guided by the Quaker conviction that where the Spirit is concerned external force has no place. Wealthy Quakers from southern England were among the first to purchase tracts of land in the new colony. Philadelphia, whose name means city of brotherly love, was laid out by Penn himself only a year after the colony's charter (1681). In 1683, Germantown near Philadelphia was settled by German Mennonites and Dutch Quakers. Baptists arrived in sufficient numbers from Great Britain as well as from other colonies to establish an interchurch alliance, the Philadelphia Association (1707). Scotch-Irish Presbyterians moved to Pennsylvania's western frontier. The Amish farmed in Berk County. German Baptist Brethren known as Dunkers migrated to Penn's colony and upon arrival splintered, forming another sect, the German Seventh-Day Baptists. German Calvinists and Lutherans made the colony home. By 1750 Roman Catholics would number fourteen churches, second only to Maryland. And to the surprise of many like Thomas Barton the "swarm of sectaries" did not subvert the colony's peace or prosperity.

THE EIGHTEENTH CENTURY

The Great Awakening

The eighteenth century witnessed a general spiritual "quickening," with religious revivals in continental Europe and in England, Scotland, and Wales. In America, religious revival was manifest in the *Great Awakening* of the 1730s and 1740s. When it began to spread, first in New England and then throughout the colonies, religious life was at a low point; it was a time—in the words of one of the Awakening's leading figures—

"of extraordinary dullness in religion." That was also how Theodore Frel-inghuysen (1691-c. 1748) found conditions among the Dutch Reformed churches when he arrived in America in 1719. A perfunctory orthodoxy prevailed in the churches Frelinghuysen came to serve, when he and a young pastor to the Presbyterians in New Brunswick, a Gilbert Tennent, undertook a program of reform and evangelical preaching with striking results. By the end of the 1720s the local revivals they initiated had kindled and spread among the Dutch Reformed and the Presbyterian churches of the Middle Colonies.

The figure in New England to spark a regional revival was Jonathan Edwards (1703-1758). As pastor in Northampton, Massachusetts, Edwards had grown concerned about a drift towards moral and spiritual laxity among the young. He was also troubled by the spread among the New England clergy of "Arminianism," a doctrine that allowed for some human effort in the process of salvation. This theological tendency, Edwards believed, undermined the very foundations of the Christian faith. In response, he preached a series of five sermons in 1734 on the central Reformation tenet, justification by faith alone.

In a sense the remarkable success of these sermons and Edwards's fame as a revivalist was surprising, for neither in manner nor in disposition did he resemble what is popularly thought characteristic of a revivalist. His demeanor was scholarly; his interests were theological and philosophical; much of his time was spent sequestered in the study; his sermons were careful doctrinal expositions read from the pulpit. Yet, as anyone knows who has read his famous Enfield sermon, "Sinners in the Hands of an Angry God," Edwards's words, even at this distance in time, have evocative power, as when he asked his audience to imagine a guilty soul suspended, like a spider by a thread, over hell's pit. Edwards was a convinced Calvinist committed to orthodox Christian doctrine, but his Enfield sermon demonstrated a style of preaching that "convicted" his hearers of the consequence of sin and made them tremble at the thought of divine wrath. He was also of the conviction that lively, personal experience was required if Christian truths were to become an inward possession of faith.

Edwards's writing provided the revival its theological justification, but the English Methodist evangelist George Whitefield (1714-1770), whom Increase Mather of Harvard disparagingly called "a wandering Levite," joined the several threads of revival, making the Awakening a common heritage of the colonies. He made seven tours of the colonies, traveling from Georgia to Maine, preached before audiences of thousands, and by his own account delivered over fifteen thousand sermons during the thirty years of his ministry. By Benjamin Franklin's report, "his eloquence had a wonderful power over the hearts and [what impressed Franklin even more] purses of his hearers." Whitefield preached wherever he was invited or whenever he could. Clergy sympathetic to revival, pastors like Edwards and Tennent, welcomed him to their pulpits, but White-field broke convention by also availing himself of an open field where, according to newspaper accounts, he would address as many as twenty-five thousand persons.

Nor was Whitefield's ministry or preaching limited to any particular religious group. According to his belief, "true and undefiled religion, doth not consist in being this or that particular sect or communion." He promoted "heart religion." Yet in theology he was Calvinist like Edwards. The salvation he preached was no easy grace; the words he spoke were no comforting message. In his sermons he portrayed human unworthiness and dependency on divine election, putting his audience in mind of judgment and damnation. When Nathan Cole, a Connecticut farmer, attended one of Whitefield's preaching meetings, he reported that the revivalist's very appearance on the platform "put me in a trembling" and "my hearing him preach gave me a heart wound." Whitefield's theology was no new thing; the manner, the place, and the freshness of the preaching were.

The religious excitement stirred by Whitefield and others was enthusiastically welcomed by many but viewed with hostility by others. Open-air preaching, the elevation of experience over theological expertise, and the disregard of denominational distinctions provoked some established clergy, like antirevivalist Charles Chauncy of the old First Church of Boston, to accuse the revivalists of undermining both religious and social order. Very much like Roger Williams a century earlier, the revivalists found themselves pitted against the representatives of the established churches. But, as Williams's lively experiment in Rhode Island provided an early blueprint for the separation of church and state, so the Great Awakening fostered a pattern of religious thought and association that would supersede the established state churches. Formal church differences based on creed and worship would not be discarded in the process, but the revivalist spirit minimized their importance as it also relativized the exclusive claims of churches to religious truth. "Dost thou fear God," John Wesley, founder of Methodism, asked, "It is enough! I give thee the hand of fellowship." What was of transcending significance was Christian fellowship based on broad Christian principles.

Denominationalism

Although the Great Awakening divided some colonial churches into pro- and anti-revivalist camps, its spirit was "catholic" in the sense that Christian unity was elevated above institutional affiliation. While creed and external forms of worship were not set aside, revivalists minimized their importance. John Wesley, for example, took only "common Christian principles" to be the distinguishing marks of a Christian. George Whitefield told a crowd in Philadelphia that Abraham would greet them in heaven not as Episcopalians, Presbyterians, Independents, or Methodists—but as Christians. Being a Christian, in short, carried more weight with the revivalists than the names or "denominations" attached to any particular institutional expression of Christianity.

Yet, the view that the church is a denominational reality—a view with antecedents in seventeenth-century Puritanism—helped accommodate the antinomian spirit of the Awakening to the institutional and historical character of the Christian churches. The result was a peculiarly American pattern of church order which well suited America's prevailing religious diversity and its separation of church and state. Its ability to make these accommodations can be attributed to two factors in particular. Unlike the state church model, *denominationalism* repudiated the idea that the church should include all members of society; different from the sectarian view, denominationalism refused to equate the true church with its own institutional structure. This church order did allow for diversity in external forms of worship and belief, and churches were free to compete among themselves for members or cooperate in achieving common goals. But, as revivalist Gilbert Tennent put it, "all societies who profess Christianity and retain the foundational principles thereof, notwithstanding their different denominations and diversity of sentiment in smaller things, are in reality but one Church of Christ." Here we have the outline of a pattern of religious thought expressing the revivalist ideal of Christian fellowship. We also have a pattern of church order that would facilitate the adjustment of American religious life to the separation of church and state.

Religion in the New Nation

In a letter to the Baptists of Virginia, Thomas Jefferson wrote that by "fair experiment" the American people had dispelled the general uncertainty of the times that "freedom of religion is compatible with order in government, and obedience to the laws." In "Notes on the State of Virginia" he pointed to the example of Pennsylvania and New York where religion thrived without any state establishment of religion at all. The "experiment was new" but it was an assured success. In particular, Jefferson observed, churches managed to secure material and financial support without dependency on the state. Nor did the arrangement threaten social or civil peace as some had feared. Indeed, as Washington affirmed in a 1797 letter to the Philadelphia clergy, the contrary was true of religion and order. The "harmony and brotherly love which characterizes the clergy of different denominations," he wrote, presents "to the world a new and interesting spectacle, at once the pride of our country and the surest basis of universal harmony." The free or voluntary churches had been tested, in Jefferson's phrase, by "fair experiment" and had given the lie to two basic assumptions underlying religious establishment. First, the coercive power of the state was not required for the flourishing of religion, and second, a plurality of religious groups was not subversive of social order.

A wall or at least a "meandering line" was placed between the state and the churches. On the one hand, the natural rights of citizenship were guaranteed by Article IV of the Constitution: no religious test was required for any office or public trust. On the other hand, the voluntary practice of religion was ensured by the Constitution's First Amendment: "Congress shall make no law respecting an establishment of religion, or prohibiting the free exercise thereof." Even though establishment persisted in some states and was not abolished in Massachusetts until 1833, state neutrality in ecclesiastical affairs was assured and the voluntary principle in religion triumphed. James Madison even saw in the separation of church and state a revival of the "primitive" condition of Christianity wherein religious teachers leaned solely on the voluntary support of their people.

The separating of ecclesiastical and civil governments, however, did not bring an end to religion's role in American life. To be sure, the Great Awakening had encouraged the privatization of religious experience, fixing in the minds of Americans the image of religion as an intensely personal and inward transaction culminating in a saving experience. At the same time, the eighteenth-century expression of rational religion known as *Deism*—influential among such leading colonial figures as George Washington, Thomas Jefferson, Benjamin Franklin, and Thomas Paine—advocated the social importance of religion. The Deists held that religion was reducible to the following essential beliefs: That there is a deity who created the world and governs it by divine providence, who requires acceptable service and the practice of virtue, and who punishes crime and rewards virtue in this or the next life.

This list of Deist beliefs, taken from Franklin's *Autobiography*, at once shows the moral bias of the Deists' definition of religion and indicates how well the definition was tailored to their conviction that religion contributes to the peace, harmony, and moral integrity of civil society. With characteristic drollery Franklin remarked that for him religion got his approval, not for making good "Presbyterians," but for making "good citizens." Washington also expressed the Deist perspective when he wrote that "religion and morality" are the essential pillars of civil society. So too did James Madison, who held that religion and morality "alone can establish the principles upon which freedom can securely stand." The churches, in short, were charged with the moral integrity of the nation beyond what the nation's laws could ensure. This was the work of reform. Reform, along with the legacy of revivalism from the Awakening, gave the special mission to the American churches in the next century.

REVIVALISM AND MILLENNIALISM

Revivalism

When the eighteenth century became the nineteenth, the *Second Great Awakening* broke upon the new nation. In the East one of its first manifestations occurred at Yale College. Timothy Dwight (1752–1817), Yale's president and Jonathan Edwards's grandson, preached a series of chapel sermons with surprising results: one-third of the student body was converted! Revival enthusiasm soon spread to other colleges—Amherst, Dartmouth, and Williams—and from the colleges the Awakening spread to towns and villages.

Fear of Deist views and the spread of French "infidelity" in particular provided the revival with its themes. Men like Lyman Beecher (1775–1863), converted to revival faith at Yale, believed that the French infidelity imported by Thomas Paine had to be opposed. Views calling into question the sovereignty of God and casting doubt on scriptural revelation were felt to threaten both the Christian religion and the moral well-being of the nation. By contrast, Beecher believed that *revivalism* propagated a correct understanding of Christianity, instilled good morals, and provided government a solid foundation upon which to build. Later, Beecher led the attack on the Unitarians who, in the midst of New England Congregationalism, rejected the metaphysics of the Christian creeds and in particular the teachings that Jesus was a divine being. Yet, in spite of this hard line against Deists, infidels, and Unitarians, Beecher was typical of the Second Awakening's softening of the strict Calvinism that we encountered in Jonathan Edwards. The American people, having recently won liberty from the British, preferred a theology allowing a far more active involvement in the process of redemption.

The religious fervor of the Second Great Awakening spread beyond the Appalachians where revivalism adapted itself to the circumstances of the frontier by means of the camp meeting. The first such revival took place on July of 1800 at Gasper River, Kentucky, but the most famous camp meeting assembled a year later in August of 1801 in the same state at Cane Ridge. Sponsored jointly by the Presbyterians and the Methodists, Cane Ridge attracted families from all over Kentucky and from Tennessee and Ohio. They came great distances, brought provisions, set up camp, and settled in for nearly a week of preaching, prayer, and hymn singing. Services began on Friday and continued until Wednesday. Platforms were erected, a meetinghouse was built, felled logs served as convenient pulpits for lay exhorters. Twenty-five ministers from the Methodist, Presbyterian, and Baptist denominations preached in a marathon session. Estimates of the attendance ranged between 12,000 and 20,000 and the conversions numbered in the thousands.

Ministers at such revivals, concerned more about conversion than theology, were not orthodox in style nor were they always orthodox in the articles of faith they professed. Neither formally educated nor theologically sophisticated, many revival ministers qualified for preaching, in the words of Illinois Methodist circuit rider Peter Cartwright, more by "a Divine unction" in their words than by the ability to "conjugate a verb or parse a sentence." These revival preachers sermonized largely from their own conversion experiences and from the Bible with its store of "proof texts." Success was measured on such occasions by the power of the sermon to make sinners "fall like dead men" or as "men slain in battle." When sinners lay motionless on the ground for hours or when they were seized by what was called the "jerks" or convulsive shaking of the body, when they danced, ran, jumped, or "barked," the ability to "parse a sentence" seemed hardly necessary.

For traditional Protestant denominations emphasizing orthodox creeds and a formally educated ministry, revivalism was a mixed blessing. It swelled membership in the frontier churches, but it neglected or discarded basic articles of faith and altered the character of the ministry. Dissension was inevitable. Presbyterian minister Barton Stone, for example, withdrew in 1804 from the Synod of Kentucky to form the "Christian Church," which later merged with a group led by Alexander Campbell to become the Disciples of Christ—and a new denomination was born. Though not all churches thrived under revivalism as much as the Disciples, Baptists, and Methodists, the success of revivalism in enlarging church membership solely by persuasion assured it a permanent place in American Protestant Christianity. And in time it became—and continues today—an integral feature of a church system in which revivals provide an instrument for winning souls to Christ and local churches supply the setting where the converted display the effects of their religious experience.

But not until the 1820s did the individual who deserved the title, father of modern revivalism, appear. Charles Grandison Finney (1792–1875) began his professional life in law practice, until a dramatic conversion experience turned him toward the ministry. He wrote in his *Memoirs* that one evening in the fall of 1821 he was alone in his office with only a fire in the open fireplace when he "received a mighty baptism of the Holy Ghost." From that evening, he was resolved to preach. "I have enlisted in the cause of the Lord Jesus Christ," he announced to a deacon of the church, "I have a retainer from him to plead his case." The legal metaphor used here to describe his "call" to the ministry shows how Finney could draw on his legal training to make vivid his religious convictions. He studied theology privately, refusing to consider formal training at Princeton, and was ordained to the Presbyterian ministry in 1824.

Called first to the part of New York State known as the "burnt-over district," so designated because of the frequent revivals that swept through it, Finney introduced "new measures" for revival, measures that proved well adapted to urban revivals, much as the camp meeting was to frontier needs. His manner of addressing an audience in the second person "you" and his custom of calling individuals by name enhanced the psychological immediacy of his services. He encouraged women to pray in public meetings. Above all, Finney instituted the "protracted meeting," the "anxious bench," and the "inquiry room." At the preaching services held every day or evening several weeks running, Christians wishing to struggle with the spiritual life were invited to come down front to a pew— the anxious bench—reserved for that purpose. The service being over, those desiring private spiritual counseling were invited to join ministers or trained spiritual advisors in an inquiry room. Anyone who has seen a Billy Graham crusade will recognize these techniques in modern dress and adapted to the requirements of the electronic media.

Revivalism after Finney, and to some degree due to his packaging it, evolved a more restrained character, lacking not only the emotional and physical abandon of the frontier experience but also the psychological intensity associated with the anxious bench. As one historian observed, by mid-century "Calvinism disappeared, so did hell." The frontier revivalist's sermon brought down a hundred sinners; Finney's new measures heightened the psychological conviction of sin and the need for repentance; and, at the hand of a Theodore Weld, Finney's revival techniques were marshalled against the evil of slavery and in the cause of abolition. But the mood of revivalism changed. The preaching of Dwight Moody (1837–1899) and the hymns of Ira Sankey reflected a mid-century sentimental turn in religion. A new note was sounded, registering a wistful longing for a haven secure above a troubled world.

Millennialism

The American Revolution and the Second Great Awakening created a climate of expectancy. Americans foresaw the dawn of a new age; many even believed that the millennium prophesied in Revelation was imminent. Some, like Charles Finney, were optimistic about revivalism's role in preparing for the millennial day. Spiritual awakenings and reform, piety and moral regeneration, Finney thought, would hasten that thousand years of peace and prosperity associated with Christ's Second Coming. Others like Thomas and Alexander Campbell were convinced that the millennial age would commence with the restoration of the church's "primitive" or apostolic condition. The Campbells predicted that, if the church were restored to its primitive integrity, it would be "as perfect as Christ intended" it to be. Yet there were prophets and visionaries with a more radical interpretation of the meaning of the new age.

Joseph Smith (1805–1844), the founder of Mormonism, was one such individual. When he was a boy, Smith moved with his family to the "burnt-over district" of New York State where he received two visions of particular importance for Mormonism's future. In the first, two divine personages, the Father and the Son, instructed Smith not to give his allegiance to any of the competing religious groups of his day, for all were in error. In the second vision the angel Moroni revealed the existence of golden tablets, inscribed with an extrabiblical history of an ancient Israelite tribe and a pre-Columbian Christian church in America. The tribe in that history left Jerusalem shortly before its fall to the Babylonians, migrated to North America, was witness to a postresurrection appearance of Jesus, and vanished from the earth, leaving only Mormon and his son Moroni, who buried the golden tablets from which Joseph Smith later translated the Book of Mormon.

In the same year the Book of Mormon was published (1830), Smith joined with five others in Fayette, New York to restore "the Church of Christ in these days" (later renamed the Church of Jesus Christ of the Latter-day Saints). With the revelation of this sacred history to Joseph Smith, the true church was revived and America was assimilated to the history of salvation as the place where Zion would be built. Starting in New York, Smith's followers were pressed ever farther West, migrating to Ohio, to Missouri, and to Nauvoo, Illinois where a temple was built and a Mormon community of twenty thousand sprang up on the banks of the Mississippi. After the 1844 murder of Joseph Smith in the nearby Carthage jail, the majority of the Mormons regrouped around the patriarchal figure, Brigham Young. From Nauvoo, Brigham Young led the saints on a heroic trek that brought them finally to the Great Salt Lake basin, where they raised another temple and so planted a new Zion in the wilderness.

The return to ancient traditions was one theme in nineteenth-century millenarianism. For the Shakers and the Oneida Perfectionists, the new age had arrived in Christ's Second Coming on earth. Organized as the United Society of Believers in Christ's Second Appearing, the Shakers looked to their founder, "Mother Ann" Lee (1736–1784), as the female Messiah—Christ's "second appearing" on earth. In Jesus of Nazareth the Godhead was incarnate in its masculine aspect; in Mother Ann, Godhead now appeared in its feminine manifestation, thus completing the process of human redemption and establishing "a parity of male and female in redeemed humanity." [3] Related too, to this Shaker doctrine of a male and female Messiah was the Shaker doctrine of God as mother and father. In the words of a popular hymn from the Shaker hymnal, *Millennial Praises*:

The Father's high eternal throne
Was never fill'd by one alone:

There Wisdom holds the Mother's seat
And is the Father's helper-meet. [4]

This androgynous conception of God as both male and female received other concrete expression among the Shakers as well. Theologian
Rosemary Ruether sees a connection between Shaker theology and "a parity of male and female leaders in the messianic community." [5] The spiritual drawings that later developed among the Shakers—drawings regarded
as inspired by the Holy Mother Wisdom—were rich symbols of the mother-
father God. Perhaps, however, the feature of Shaker worship that best
illustrates the way theological conception and language shape worship and
the life of a religious community was their ritual dance. Women and men
joined in ecstatic dancing, fanning the air with upturned hands and whirl-
ing in opposite concentric circles, until the dance and the dancers were
one—experiencing "in a mystical union with one another in God and
Mother Ann a foretaste of the bliss of paradise." [6] Formed into one body,
female and male, the community thus became a living, moving image of
the millennial kingdom already in process of dawning with the coming of
Mother Ann.

John Humphrey Noyes's Oneida community was another nineteenth-
century millennialist group committed to living a communal life anticipatory of the new age. In his communities at Putney, Vermont and then at
Oneida, New York, he provided for a millennial freedom, equality, and
mutuality. In particular Noyes advocated a system of "complex marriage,"
as much a key to perfection in Noyes's view as celibacy was for the Shakers. Noyes held that ordinary marriage, like private property, was a part
of the "sin system." It caused jealousy and suspicion among men and
women; it disrupted social harmony. Noyes pointed to Jesus's admonition
that there will be no marriage in heaven. So on earth among the saints of
Oneida there were to be no permanent relations, no restrictive laws regulating the conduct of men and women toward one another. Each woman
was accorded the respect due a wife, each man that due a husband, and
all were married in Christ. No doubt, we can translate Noyes's meaning
into modern terms as "free love," but, as he conceived it, the freedom of
Oneida was a millennial freedom. Oneida no less than the Shaker settlements was an expression of the Perfectionist impulse universal in religion,
evident also as a prominent feature of American culture in the decades
immediately following the American Revolution.

For the Shakers and the Oneida Perfectionists, Christ's Second Advent had occurred; the new age was already a present reality, if only for
the saints in holy community. There were others, however, known as *pre-
millennialists*. They did not expect a gradual or progressive dawning of the
millennium, nor did they believe with the Perfectionists that the millen-

nium was already somehow present. The Second Advent, they believed, was a future event which would precede (not follow, as the *postmillennialists* believed) the millennium. For these Adventists the present time was one of anxious or hopeful suspense, a waiting for God's miraculous intervention, which no human effort could hasten or delay.

Yet, the popularity of the millenarian movement in the 1830s and early 1840s reflected a very human work. On the basis of biblical prophecy, William Miller (1782–1849), a devout Baptist, calculated that Christ's return to earth would occur during the year between March 21, 1843 and March 21, 1844. Persuaded also that he was called to tell the world of his findings, he published *Evidence from Scripture and History of the Second Coming of Christ, About the Year 1843* (1836). That book, along with the promotional campaign of Joshua Himes and a changed mood in the country due to the economic depression of 1837, did much to advance Miller's cause. Other evangelists were enlisted to assist in the work; camp meetings were held; tracts and pamphlets were distributed; even a hymnbook, *The Millennial Harp*, was issued. March 21, 1844 came and went; an error in calculation was discovered and a new date—October 22, 1844—was set. When the Second Coming did not materialize, the Adventist movement collapsed; many returned to their own churches while the remaining Adventists splintered into parties. One of these parties has been especially influential in keeping millennial hope alive. Stressing the observance of Sabbath (Saturday) worship as prescribed by the Decalogue, the imminent return of Christ, and the prophecy of Ellen G. White (1827–1915), the Seventh-day Adventists (1860) with a membership today of over half a million in the United States alone continue to be a major denominational expression of American millennialism.

SUMMARY

In his *Thoughts on the Revival*, Jonathan Edwards observed of America that it was "discovered about the time of the reformation, or but a little before: which reformation was the first thing that God did towards the glorious renovation of the world." As we have seen, Edwards's Puritan ancestors shared that same sense of America's importance for the continuing of the Reformation. They believed that in New England it would be possible to build a holy commonwealth where God's sovereign rule would be exercised directly in the affairs of the church and the state through Puritan "saints" and that ecclesiastical and civil governments, though distinct in administration, would stand and flourish together. But others, like Roger

Williams, objected to this "middle way" of walking and proposed another, more radical application of Puritan principles. They held that the spiritual and the civil realms are fundamentally different, and that the state, being essentially different from the church, ought not interfere with religious conscience. And so in Rhode Island, Roger Williams and his Baptist associate, John Clarke, drafted a colonial charter which extended civil and religious liberty to all citizens. William Penn applied Quaker principles to the same end in Pennsylvania. With Rhode Island and Pennsylvania in the lead, the American colonies were edging their way toward the view that diversity of religious expression was consistent with the interest of both the churches and the state.

The eighteenth century brought further changes in the traditional understanding of the church, its relation to the state, and its role in society. Two factors in particular were important for those changes. The first was the colony-wide spiritual "quickening," the Great Awakening. The Awakening contributed to the weakening of traditional ecclesiastical authority and to the decline of New England's Congregational establishment. It enhanced the status of the religious affections at the expense of theological precision. And it contributed to the development of the denominational concept of the church. Deism, fashionable in the upper class circles in the decades before the American Revolution, was a second significant element in the century's changing religious climate. Deism held that natural reason is a sufficient source for knowledge about the essentials of religious truth, that reason reveals a Creator whose world is ruled by law, and that this God holds rational creatures morally accountable in the next world for what they do in this one. Religion's social purpose, in the Deist scheme, followed from the essential truths of natural revelation: God had created a world governed by moral law; religion fulfilled its central mission when it promoted civic virtue or, in the words of John Adams, when it makes of us "good men, good magistrates and good subjects, good husbands and good wives, good parents and good children, good masters and good servants."

The social function of religion had thus become more restricted than, for example, it had been for the Puritans. Deists and revivalists both tended to agree that religion is a private affair, a matter of personal religious affections or of obedience to the moral laws of the Creator, that the church is a voluntary society, independent of the state for its financial support, and that the state is religiously neutral, acting to protect the natural rights and the religious consciences of all its citizens. Still, the state looked to the churches as a moral leaven for the nation. And in this at least the Puritan vision of church and state standing and flourishing together persisted as a feature of American culture. But, as the nineteenth century was to demonstrate, this cooperation was to take shape largely outside the political establishment through instruments such as revival and reform.

REVIEW AND REFLECTION

1. What is the principle of establishment? What difficulties faced those who wished to implement the principle in America?
2. Who were the Puritans? What was their religious objective? What was their political objective? How did they relate the two objectives?
3. How did Roger Williams apply Puritan religious principles in Rhode Island? What importance did his ideas have for the separation of church and state?
4. The Great Awakening was a religious revival. What did it contribute to the cause of disestablishment?
5. What is denominationalism? What made this form of church polity such a good one for the religious and political aims of the new American nation?
6. The American nation was pledged to the separation of church and state. Did that mean that the churches were no longer to have an active public role in American life?
7. Describe the purposes of revivalism and the phases it went through in the nineteenth century.
8. What forms did utopianism and millennialism take in nineteenth-century America?

END NOTES

1. The image of these explorers as horizon crossers was suggested by Edwin Scott Gaustad in his *A Religious History of America* (New York: Harper & Row, Publishers, 1974), p. 2.

2. Rosemary Radford Ruether and Rosemary Skinner Keller, eds., *Women and Religion in America, Volume 2: The Colonial and Revolutionary Periods* (San Francisco: Harper & Row, Publishers, 1983), p. 281.

3. Rosemary Radford Ruether, *To Change the World: Christology and Cultural Criticism* (New York: The Crossroad Publishing Company, 1981), p. 51.

4. Quoted in Barbara Brown Zikmund, "The Feminist Thrust of Sectarian Christianity," in Rosemary Ruether and Eleanor McLaughlin, eds., *Women of Spirit: Female Leadership in the Jewish and Christian Traditions* (New York: Simon and Schuster, 1979), p. 210.

5. Ruether, *To Change the World*, p. 51.

6. Catherine L. Albanese, *America: Religions and Religion*, The Wadsworth Series in Religious Studies (Belmont, CA: Wadsworth Publishing Company, A Division of Wadsworth, Inc., 1981), p. 156.

SUGGESTED FURTHER READING

AHLSTROM, SYDNEY E. *A Religious History of the American People.* New Haven: Yale University Press, 1972.

ALBANESE, CATHERINE L. *America: Religions and Religion.* Belmont, CA: Wadsworth Publishing Company, 1981.

BRAUER, JERALD C. *Protestantism in America: A Narrative History.* Philadelphia: The Westminster Press, 1953.

CLEBSCH, WILLIAM. *American Religious Thought: A History.* Chicago: The University of Chicago Press, 1973.

GAUSTAD, EDWIN SCOTT. ed. *A Documentary History of Religion in America Since 1865.* Grand Rapids, MI: William B. Eerdmanns Publishing Company, 1983.

GAUSTAD, EDWIN SCOTT, ed. *A Documentary History of Religion in America to the Civil War.* Grand Rapids, MI: William B. Eerdmanns Publishing Company, 1982.

GAUSTAD, EDWIN SCOTT. *Historical Atlas of Religion in America.* Rev. ed. New York: Harper & Row, Publishers, 1976.

GAUSTAD, EDWIN SCOTT. *A Religious History of America.* New York: Harper & Row, Publishers, 1974.

HUDSON, WINTHROP. *Religion in America.* (4th ed.) New York: Charles Scribner's Sons, 1987.

MARTY, MARTIN E. *Modern American Religion: The Irony of It All 1893–1919.* Chicago: The University of Chicago Press, 1986.

MEAD, SIDNEY E. *The Lively Experiment.* New York: Harper & Row, Publishers, 1963.

MEAD, SIDNEY E. *The Nation with the Soul of a Church.* New York: Harper & Row, Publishers, 1975.

MULDER, JOHN M. and JOHN F. WILSON. eds. *Religion in American History: Interpretative Essays.* Englewood Cliffs, NJ: Prentice-Hall, Inc., 1978.

RUETHER, ROSEMARY RADFORD and ROSEMARY SKINNER KELLER. eds. *Women and Religion in America.* 3 Vols. New York: San Francisco: Harper & Row, Publishers, 1983.

WILLIAMS, PETER W. *Popular Religion in America.* Englewood Cliffs, NJ: Prentice-Hall, Inc., 1980.

8 | The Early Modern World: Quest for Authority

INTRODUCTION

Mark's Gospel presents Jesus as a commanding figure, as one whose words and actions elicited the response, "With authority he commands even the unclean spirits, and they obey him." But, as in most religions, the question for the early Christians was not whether their founder possessed sacred authority. The question that vexed the church was on whom would the mantle of authority fall with the disappearance of the apostles, those on whom authority had originally been conferred by the founder. It was this difficulty that the church of the first centuries sought to resolve as it wrestled with the nature of Christian ministry. The eastern and western churches of the Middle Ages gave further refinement to Christianity's definition of authority in the context of a Christian society. The question of authority erupted with explosive force during the sixteenth century as Protestants and Catholics reevaluated Christian foundations and asked anew about the respective authority of Scripture and tradition for Christian faith and practice. Still, in spite of all the diversity and all the controversy, Christians through the centuries were at no time in doubt of God's sovereign authority; the God of Christian *revelation*, it was held, was the universal lord of human life and history. And the notion of a world without reference to Christian revelation or Christian tradition would have been simply inconceivable—at least for Christians up to the dawn of the modern era.

Yet, the modern world made the unthinkable thinkable. Where theology was once thought to be queen of human learning, in this new world

Christianity During the Age of Reason—Key Dates

Dates	Persons and Events
1610 C.E.	Galileo Galilei (1564–1642) discovers the four satellites of Jupiter with the newly invented telescope
1630 C.E.	Deist views of Matthew Tindal (1655–1733) published in *Christianity as Old as Creation*
1637 C.E.	philosopher Rene Descartes (1596–1650) publishes *Discourse on Method*, expressing the age's growing confidence in reason
1623–1662 C.E.	Blaise Pascal, religious thinker important for his emphasis on revelation and religion of the heart
1675 C.E.	Philipp Jacob Spener (1635–1705) publishes *Dia Desideria*, considered the charter of Pietism
1687 C.E.	*Principia* in which Isaac Newton (1642–1727) explains the heavens using mathematical demonstration
1694 C.E.	William Paley (1743–1805) publishes *View of the Evidences of Christianity*
1695 C.E.	*The Reasonableness of Christianity* sets forth John Locke's (1632–1704) thesis that Christianity is the most reasonable of religions
1722 C.E.	beginnings of Herrnhut, a Pietist community on the estate of Count Zinzendorf (1700–1760)
1738 C.E.	the Aldersgate conversion experience of John Wesley (1703–1791)
1774–1778 C.E.	Gotthold Ephraim Lessing publishes Hermann Samuel Reimarus's *Wolfenbuttel Fragments*, a work of biblical scholarship critical of miracles and revelation

of modernity philosophy and science vied for superiority by promoting the sufficiency of human reason in solving the world's mysteries. At first, agitation for autonomous reason was cautious. Seventeenth-century English philosopher Francis Bacon advocated a doctrine of "double truth." Reason and revelation were to have equal, but distinct and separate, standing. But others urged greater scope for reason in a spirit akin to Rene Descartes's claim that "there is nothing so removed from us as to be beyond our reach, or so hidden that we cannot discover it." The tutelage of reason to religion, many believed, had come to an end as the idea of mystery was shut out of first one, then another area of modern thought. Yet, Christianity found new ways to affirm the authority of its traditional witness to Jesus Christ in the face of the scientific, social, and cultural forces that shaped the modern secular world. In this chapter, we examine the form those affirmations took. We look at the efforts of Christian thinkers of the early modern era to reconcile reason and revelation and at the accomplishments of mystics and Pietists who sought religion and the truth of revelation beyond reason altogether. The second act in the drama of modernity and the quest of religious authority is set in the nineteenth century with a new set of challenges and supplied with new resources. This is the subject of Chapter 9.

THE AGE OF REASON

The New Philosophy

In *The Divine Comedy*, Dante's hero, having traveled upward through the planets to the ninth celestial sphere, beholds the whole of the revolving heavens. His companion and guide, the heavenly Beatrice, explains the meaning of the pilgrim's mystic vision in canto xxvii of the *Paradiso*.

> The nature of the world which, motionless
>   At core, the wheeling of the rest maintains,
>   Starteth from here the running of the race;
> Else this heaven no locality contains
>   Save the divine mind, whence enkindled glows
>   The love that turns it and the power it rains.
> Light and love always it in one circle close,
>   As it the other spheres; and this circuit
>   He only who guides it understands and knows. [1]

In this Dantean cosmology the earth is positioned motionless at the center, and, surrounding it, concentric crystalline spheres mount to the *Primum Mobile*, whose force moves the whole through the influence of divine love.

This was in sum the cosmology that still enjoyed favor when in the year of his death Nicolaus Copernicus (1473–1543) published *On the Revolutions of the Heavenly Spheres* and inaugurated the modern era in astronomy.

Copernicus is, of course, famous for dislodging the earth from its privileged position at the center of our planetary system. Yet Copernicus's importance was due as much to the method by which he came to his heliocentric theory of the universe. Using mathematics, he sought to construct a more rational, and from his point of view aesthetically pleasing, system of planetary motion. But not until the Italian astronomer Galileo Galilei (1564-1642) was the Copernican revolution given solid empirical confirmation. When in 1609 Galileo turned the recently invented telescope for the first time toward the sky, stars previously unseen came into view, mountains appeared on the moon and spots on the sun, and Jupiter was observed to have satellites. The heavens, it was discovered, were not as Dante had imagined. But of more importance for religion was Galileo's advocacy of scientific study without reference to theology. Galileo drew a sharp distinction between revelation and nature, God's two books, and argued that the book of nature is "written in the mathematical language, and the symbols are triangles, circles, and other geometrical figures, without whose help it is impossible to comprehend a single word of it, without which one wanders through a dark labyrinth." French philosopher Rene Descartes (1596–1650) came to a similar conclusion about the nature of the material universe. For Descartes the world is an autonomous, material reality, distinct from mind or spirit; its parts are related mathematically; and its properties—extension and space—are the properties of matter.

Traditional beliefs about the relation of revelation and the world or of nature and grace could not be assumed in the face of the new cosmology. Some, like the Anglican divine and poet John Donne, viewed Galileo's accomplishments with suspicion. Aware that old meanings and old authorities were weakened, Donne lamented that "the new philosophy," as he named Galileo's science, "calls all in doubt." Yet, the new science received warm welcome as well. Puritan poet John Milton declared on leaving Florence after visiting Galileo, "Now clear I understand what often my steadiest thoughts have searched in vain." Donne's doubt was well founded. Certainties arising from confidence in the authority of the Bible or the church were questioned in the age of the Enlightenment that followed. But Milton correctly sensed new certainties as old ones faded.

Natural Religion

Francis Bacon disparagingly compared the scientific speculations of theologians to the spinning of spiders. By contrast, the new philosophy had a remarkable track record. Reason had penetrated secrets of the natural world once believed to be the exclusive domain of revelation. Copernicus displaced the earth from the center of the solar system. Galileo turned his telescope skyward to discover that the imperfections of the earth were mirrored in the heavens. And Sir Isaac Newton (1642–1727) supplied mathematical demonstration for his theory that planets move, as do objects near the earth, through mutual attraction of what he called gravitation. Science was coming to view the universe as a great integrated, uniform machine, governed throughout by the same mechanics, and subject to scientific analysis. But the task fell to the *Enlightenment* to extend science's standard for truth and reason's authority to social, political, and religious spheres of life.

The Enlightenment was a cultural and intellectual movement of the seventeenth and eighteenth centuries known for its elevation of reason above all other authorities. By reason, the Enlightenment understood a "common sense" innate in all persons, mirrored in the regular, orderly, and harmonious laws of nature, and embodied in the method of science. To follow reason or imitate nature's law seemed to the Enlightenment the highest wisdom. Poets in this Age of Reason took nature, reason, and society as their themes and copied nature in the regularity of meter and rhyme. Social philosophers found society's ideal state mirrored in the state of nature. Metaphysicians discerned divine purpose in nature's design. Even Newton concluded that a system of such mathematical perfection and beauty "could proceed only from the counsel and dominion of an intelligent Being." Was it not reasonable to postulate an intelligence behind the design?

The idea of a higher purpose seemed built into the logic of the universe and just waiting for a William Paley (1743–1805) to give it form in the *Argument from Design*. Paley reasoned that, just as we infer the existence of a watchmaker from a watch, so from the design everywhere evident in nature we infer an almighty Designer. To be sure, Paley lacks the intellectual rigor of a Thomas Aquinas and is devoid of Dante's sense of mystery. Yet, Paley was of his age in his fascination with mathematics and mechanics and in his assurance in the divine architecture of a world that is orderly and purposeful. With the coming of the nineteenth century, confidence in intelligibility and meaning again would become problematic. But for a time the world of Paley and Newton, having displaced Calvin's inscrutable, arbitrary, willful deity, would trust that the world was purposeful, benign, and reasonable, because its Creator was these things.

The logical step was for the eighteenth century to grow more certain of reason's importance not only for scientific and social truth but for religious truth as well. And in this age of Newton this meant above all that religion would have to be more like science. It would have to be reasonable like science, and like scientific truths the truths of religion would have to be useful and universally applicable. The obverse of this was also held by the age. Whatever in religion was not apparent to plain reason and whatever was not useful or generally true, whatever tended to obscure, mystify, or localize—that religious belief or practice or ritual ought to be disdained. Memory of the senseless brutality of the Thirty Years War (1618–1648), fought ostensibly for religious reasons, of the schism and the splintering of Christendom following the Protestant Reformation, and of the doctrinal controversy of seventeenth-century Protestant orthodoxy further reinforced the age's suspicion of religion. It seemed that traditional religious doctrine and ritual practice in particular were the cause of much human misery. Religious truth, the Enlightenment thinkers held, ought not to be disruptive, divisive, and destructive. Rightly understood and practiced, religion ought to promote personal happiness and social concord.

The first earl of Cherbury, Edward Herbert, brother of metaphysical poet George Herbert and father of Deism, deserves credit for first formulating a justification for just such a religion, called by the age *natural religion*. In a work titled *De Veritate* (1624), Herbert expressed the view that we find an essential core of belief in all the great world religions. These beliefs, or "common notions," are self-evident, instinctive to all persons, are found even among the ancient pagans, and are independent of ecclesiastical authority or special revelation. According to Herbert's calculations, there are five such universal religious truths. Human beings everywhere have an innate knowledge of the existence of a supreme, providential God. They know too that this God ought to be worshipped, that virtue and piety are indispensable to proper worship, that all persons ought to abhor crime and repent of sin, and that reward or punishment are dispensed in a future life. These articles of natural religion, which we encountered in our discussion of Deism in Chapter 7, met the age's requirement for religious truth. They stood solidly on the testimony of reason and nature and the universal opinion of the human race. And they allowed religion a clear ethical utility by aligning religious sanction with social stability, order, and harmony in this life and with reward in the next one. But Christianity was a revealed religion, and Herbert's articles did not clarify revelation's role in authorizing the religious life.

Revealed Religion

Reason exercised such influence that even orthodox Christian thinkers took it as an article of belief that revelation should meet the test of reasonableness. John Tillotson (1609–1694), archbishop of Canterbury and the most popular preacher of his day, was representative in his view that "nothing ought to be received as a revelation from God which plainly contradicts the principles of natural religion." Implied in the archbishop's statement is a syllogism that might be phrased this way: Nothing comes from God that is not reasonable; revelation comes from God; therefore, Scripture is reasonable.

Apologist William Chillingworth (1604–1644) appealed to Scripture's reasonableness in the continuing Protestant controversy with Roman Catholicism. Chillingworth's defense turned on a logic very similar to Tillotson's. Since revelation publishes God's eternal wisdom and conforms to reason, the Bible's superiority to tradition as the source of belief is self-evident. Since revelation conforms to reason's standard of truth, the Bible provides a solid basis for consensus and Christian unity. Yet, whatever force this logic had, something of the unique character of Christian revelation was lost in the process. It remained for the proponents of rational theology, or what is also known as supernatural rationalism, to develop a defense of revelation's distinctive Christian character. The foremost seventeenth-century architect of this defense was English philosopher John Locke (1632–1704).

Locke's religious views were developed in his popular treatise, *The Reasonableness of Christianity* (published in 1695). Christianity was superior to natural religion, Locke argued, because it had been more successful in fostering both religious piety and moral duty among people of all stations in life. In basic agreement with theologians like Tillotson, Locke assumed that fundamental Christian truths were in harmony with reason. In this, Christianity was at one with all the major historic world religions as well as the natural religion of the ancient pagan. But Christian truths, Locke observed, were expressed in "plain and intelligible propositions" well within the grasp of the poor of the world. This could also be said of Christianity's ethical precepts. Pagan philosophy, he reasoned, failed where the gospel of Jesus succeeded because the gospel set forth "a full and sufficient rule for our moral direction" in the persuasive form of an exemplary holy life.

Locke's comparison in favor of Christianity would have stopped short had it concluded with this pragmatic test. A person of his age, he assumed a sufficiency of reason for the justification of natural religion's truths, but historic revelation went beyond "the clear and self-evident dictates of reason." The Enlightenment thought a universal consensus based on reason sufficient evidence for the existence of God or of ethical precepts. The common sense of the human race attested to these truths. But what status should be assigned the knowledge of religious truths originating with a historical person, albeit a divinely inspired one? What was required for historical testimony to be received with confidence as reasonable? According to Locke, knowledge based on historical evidence did not have the same degree of certainty as truth apprehended directly by reason.

Yet, knowledge of historic revelation under certain conditions could be said to have a high degree of probability. In one of the eighteenth century's most popular defenses of Christian Scripture, Locke maintained that, if the "proposers" of revelation are credible and their testimony is consistent with reason and experience, belief based on the testimony of, let's say, the original evangelists was worthy of assent by reasonable persons. Examining the New Testament, Locke found that Christianity proclaimed Jesus as the Messiah and called for a repentance of sin and a conversion to a life of moral earnestness. These articles of belief contradicted nothing in reason. He found too that prophecy and miracles attested to the divine authorship of Scripture. The credibility of the evangelists was thus established. Here then was a religion with the advantages of natural religion. Yet, here too was a religion whose teachings had a democratic appeal, whose moral precepts were augmented by the force of lively example, and whose proposers, the New Testament evangelists, were credible witnesses by reason of prophecy and divine signs.

Christianity not Mysterious

The Enlightenment saw the steady erosion of Locke's defense of Christian revelation. Attack was to come first from the Deists, then both Deists and supernatural rationalists were subjected to the philosophical skepticism of David Hume. Typical of the Deists was John Toland. In *Christianity Not Mysterious* (1696) Toland opposed the idea that special revelation adds anything to the truths reason makes known. "There is nothing in the Gospel," he maintained, "contrary to Reason, nor above it; and that no Christian Doctrine can be properly call'd a Mystery." Not surprisingly, his views were frequently answered from the pulpit, and, according to report, one Irish peer refused even to attend Sunday services because, he said, Toland was more frequently discussed than Jesus Christ.

Orthodox critics gave William Tindal's *Christianity as Old as Creation* (1730) similar reception. Tindal wrote that Christian revelation is but a "republication," and Christ merely a notable example, of truths known from the beginning of time. How could it be otherwise with reason? Since reason teaches that God is eternally the same, it follows that perfect religion can be neither increased nor decreased. Since human nature is the same and unalterable, a perfect God must dispense truth equally to all at all times. So Toland reasoned, and, though stopping short of dispensing with biblical revelation altogether, he thought special revelation superfluous, or at best derivative and supplemental.

From England, Deism spread to the Continent where attacks on revealed religion grew more virulent. Francois Marie Arouet (1694–1778), more generally known by his pen name Voltaire, was typical of such attacks. Like his fellow *philosophes*, Voltaire made use of his ample literary talent and a gift for biting satire to ridicule conventional religion. In a commentary characteristic of his genius for mockery, Voltaire called to mind the biblical story of Noah and the ark with its seven pair of clean and two pair of unclean animals. Then, appealing to his readers' common sense, he asked with feigned astonishment: "You can imagine what would be needed to feed fourteen elephants, fourteen camels, fourteen buffaloes, and as many horses, asses, deer, serpents, ostriches . . . !"

The Bible received no better treatment at the hand of the German Deist, Samuel Hermann Reimarus (1694–1768). In a work published posthumously as the *Wolffenbuttel Fragments*, Reimarus submitted Scripture to critical historical analysis. He argued that the biblical narrative was full of contradictions and impossibilities, that the conflicting resurrection accounts of the synoptic Gospels indicate a fraud perpetrated by the apostles, and that the New Testament pictured Jesus as a Jewish apocalyptic fanatic. The created world, he averred, was the only miracle, nature God's only revelation.

Gotthold Ephraim Lessing (1729–1781), editor of the *Fragments*, tried to soften Reimarus. He too doubted the supposition that prophecy and miracles are reliable as historical proofs. But he was less certain than either the Deists or the supernatural rationalists that reason was the final arbiter in religious truth. Anticipating nineteenth-century liberal theology, he believed that personal experience was a valid confirmation of biblical truth. Yet, Lessing was very much a man of the Enlightenment. For him as for the Deists, Christian revelation lacked finality. However authentic Hebrew prophecy or the apostolic witness, they were merely stages—albeit positive stages—in a progressive education of the human race, leading ultimately to a "new eternal gospel" and a universal religion of reason.

Skepticism and Doubt

The most serious challenge to eighteenth-century proofs for revelation and its arguments for the existence of God was posed by the English philosopher David Hume (1711–1776). Hume was, like Locke, an empiricist, believing that experience is our only guide in reasoning about the world around us. But Hume's radical empiricism did not allow for innate ideas or for universally knowable, self-evident religious truth. According to Hume, our simple ideas "derive from simple impressions, which are correspondent to them, and which they exactly represent." Complex ideas, such as the idea we have of the *world* or the *self*, are merely composites of our simple impressions. The notion that we have of a real, existing, substantial self is similar to the idea that we form of unperceived substances like the horse Pegasus of Greek myth. However remote we find perceived things—whether a flying horse or *me*—the ideas we have of unperceived substances are nothing more than bundles of simple impressions. Hume also reasoned that causation is without any rational justification. The impression that we form of causal relations among objects is nothing more than habit arising from a frequent conjunction of two objects. When one object appears, we infer the operation of the other, yet in reality the conjunction is only custom operating on our imagination.

This Humean epistemology, though it may seem confusing and abstract, had serious consequences for eighteenth-century religion. Hume's thoroughgoing empiricism called into doubt rational religion's fundamental belief that all people have "common notions" or innate ideas about God, worship, virtue, and a future life. It also seriously damaged rational religion's confidence in metaphysics. If there is no way of reasoning from an effect to its cause, how is it possible to construct, as Paley attempted, any cogent argument for the existence of God from design? Hume's *skepticism* was not any more comfort to those who followed Locke in pointing to miracles as authenticating signs of the authorship of Scripture. Hume argued that the law of nature has been established by firm and unalterable experience. By definition "a uniform experience [of humankind is] against every miraculous event." For miracles to stand as a proof, the miraculous must be very strong to contravene the certainty with which natural law is held. But, since evidence for miracles is based principally on the credibility of the witnesses' testimony, and witnesses to miracles are often ignorant, primitive people with a natural tendency to credulity about extraordinary events, it is more reasonable to believe that the witnesses were in error than to renounce the uniform experience of humankind.

RELIGION OF THE HEART

Pascal's Existential Doubt

There is a wonderful story of the famous biographer James Boswell's interview with David Hume shortly before the philosopher's death. Of interest to Boswell was Hume's skepticism. Would Hume relent in the face of his own imminent death? Boswell put the question to the great man. Was immortality a possibility? "It is possible," was Hume's response, "that a piece of coal put upon the fire would not burn" but it was an unreasonable idea that we should live forever. The doubt that the late eighteenth century harbored, I think, is nicely illustrated by Boswell's journal entry following the interview. Boswell wrote: "I was like a man in sudden danger eagerly seeking his defensive arms by momentary doubt while I had actually before me a man of such strong abilities and extensive inquiry dying in persuasion of being annihilated. But I maintained my faith." Hume's unsettling effect on Boswell is very much the effect philosophical skepticism had on Enlightenment confidence in the later eighteenth century. But skepticism had more than one meaning in the seventeenth and eighteenth centuries. In France, for example, skepticism was skillfully employed in the service of religious experience and revealed religion.

Blaise Pascal (1623–1662) was one of those remarkable geniuses who comes along only rarely. He was an innovative mathematician and scientist, a gifted writer, and a profound religious thinker. He did pioneering work in the field of calculus. He anticipated the digital computer with his mechanical calculator. He performed original experiments on the vacuum and on hydraulics. He even devised the first public transportation system for the city of Paris. And his *Provincial Letters,* a work attacking the ethical code of the Jesuits, has been said to mark the beginning of modern French prose. Yet, for all his successes in mathematics, science, and literature, Pascal was also a religious thinker of the first order whose *Pensees* ("Thoughts") published after his death seem even today surprisingly modern.

Yet, Pascal was also very much a person of his own day and concerned himself with the religious and theological issues of his time. Drawn to the theology and devotional thought of Jansenism, a movement named for Cornelius Jansen and associated with the convent at Port-Royal, he had a view of God and human nature that was more like Calvin's than Locke's. His was a tragic sense of the mystery of Adam's fall. Human nature was corrupt and human knowledge was hopelessly flawed, allowing genuine knowledge of neither God nor the self. In important respects Pascal anticipated Hume in his suspicion of reason's competency and Christian rationalism. The causes of his suspicion, however, were not philosophical or epistemological but theological and experiential. Especially in *Pensees,* Pascal was critical of the tradition of natural or philosophical theology which had been enshrined at the Council of Trent as Thomism. The problem with metaphysics was its remoteness from ordinary human experience or thought. While some souls whom God chooses may be enlightened by proofs based on nature, as a rule metaphysical reasoning is so complicated that it makes little, or at least no lasting, impression. What's more, Pascal believed rational theology of no relevance to religious experience.

Pascal's skepticism about reason's competency to produce certainty may seem strange in view of emergent Deist thought and Newtonian science in England, but doubt played a more prominent role in seventeenth-century French culture than it did across the Channel. In France, the philosopher Descartes had used provisional doubt as a technique for arriving at indubitable propositions. Miguel de Montaigne devised a new literary form, the essay, as an instrument for self-discovery in the face of the fallible human mind's inability to reach any knowledge with certainty, except a knowledge of itself. And the society of the Parisian salons, which Pascal frequented, was famous for a cultivated skepticism. But Pascal's doubt was not an epistemological doubt nor was it the chic doubt of the Parisian intelligentsia. It was religious and existential. It was the doubt of mystics, indi-

cating an insecurity about every human existential truth in the face of incomprehensible mystery.

Yet, doubt was not the final word either, for in the words of Pascal's
most famous expression "the heart has reasons of its own, which reason
does not know." However opaque the knowledge of God and the self to
natural reason, divine grace can touch the heart and enlighten the mind.
Of this Pascal had personal knowledge for on November 23, 1654 he experienced a spiritual awakening. The meaning of that awakening he wrote
on a piece of parchment that was found sewn to his clothing at his death.
It read simply:

> God of Abraham, God of Isaac, God of Jacob,
>   not of philosophers and scholars.
> Certainty, certainty, heartfelt joy, peace,
> God of Jesus Christ.
> God of Jesus Christ.
> My God and your God.
> Thy God shall be my God.
> The world forgotten and everything but God.
> He can only be found by the ways taught in the Gospels . . .

Pascal knew from experience how a believer came to a knowledge of
God without the aid of metaphysical proofs. Even his challenge to the cultured despisers of religion was aimed at shaking their intellectual confidence by confronting them with an urgent existential choice. In Pascal's
famous wager, he argued that existence confronts us with a decision of
ultimate concern. We are obliged to wager that God exists or does not
exist. It therefore behooves us to think about the gamble and consider our
gain. To win is to win infinitely; to lose is to lose very little. But neither
Pascal's wager nor proofs that he accepted for Christianity's truth—fulfillment of prophecy and New Testament miracles—create certitude of faith.
Faith comes when God touches and inclines the heart. All else is but preparation.

Pietism in Germany

The seventeenth century saw an inward turn away from the formality
of Catholic and Protestant orthodoxy as well as from the rationalism of
natural religion. In Catholic France Pascal objected to Christian rationalism
and the externalization of morality by Jesuit casuistry. He also disapproved
the neglect of the spiritual in the church's preoccupation with orthodoxy
and ecclesiastical authority. In Spain, Miguel de Molinos (1627–1696) deni-
grated the externals of religion. He favored, as did the Quietist movement
that developed through his influence, a quietistic and mystical fellowship

with God. A similar spirit stirred England. Puritanism's conviction that a vital faith rests upon an experiential knowledge of God's election of the individual believer found warm reception there. Others looked to the Society of Friends, the Quakers, for a setting where inward and spiritual worship could be practiced. But one of the seventeenth century's most impressive spiritual awakenings took place on German soil in the aftermath of the Thirty Years War and was known as *Pietism*.

Emphasizing feeling and life over reason and doctrine, Pietism introduced anew personal, experiential religion into the life of seventeenth- and eighteenth-century German Protestantism. But Pietism was not wholly new; some viewed it as a completion of the Reformation begun by Luther but interrupted by the arid doctrinal debates of Protestant orthodoxy. Certainly,it had deep roots in Luther's thought. But it owed much as well to English and Dutch Puritanism, to the mystical writings of Jakob Boehme, and to the Christ-centered mysticism of the Middle Ages before the Reformation. Pietism also was widely influential and shaped religious sensibility in the Netherlands, England, and North America, where, as a result of the Great Awakening, it left a permanent impression on the American character.

Still, Pietism was foremost a spiritual renaissance within the Lutheran church and reflected very much the conditions of a demoralized Germany in the wake of a war remarkable for its destruction of life and property. It was against the backdrop of the spiritual and moral deterioration that accompanies physical destruction that a Frankfort pastor, Philipp Jacob Spener (1635–1705), made a proposal for spiritual renewal with far-reaching consequences. In a sermon of 1669 Spener exhorted his congregation to come together in the afternoon to review the morning's sermons and engage in devotional reading and conversation. The following year a small group of like-minded people gathered in what came to be known as *collegia pietatis* ("assembly of piety") for Bible reading, prayer, and devout discussion. Pietism was born.

In *Pia Desideria* (1675), a work considered the charter of Pietism, Spener proposed a program for reform. He began by reviewing the low state of the church, criticized orthodox clergy for regarding a conformity to doctrine and the external observance of sacraments as sufficient for the Christian life, took the laity to task for low morals, and disapproved the state's interference in the internal affairs of the church. Experience had taught him the value of small groups, "little churches within the church" (*ecclesiolae in ecclesia*), as a leaven for the larger church. Private reading of the Bible, group study, and family devotion were therefore urged along with public worship as instruments of renewal. Spener also encouraged the recovery in practice of Luther's priesthood of all believers. Christians were to shoulder a common responsibility for one another to be exercised above all in mutual admonition and correction. He set forth a program of university reform aimed at elevating the standard of morality among students and professors. Finally, Spener sought to correct the combative, quarrelsome spirit surrounding theological controversy with an admonition to seek the truth in love.

Spener's program was not welcomed all around, and he was forced from his post in Frankfort and then from Dresden to Berlin, where he lived until his death. The steady progress and triumph of Pietism, however, lead to a weakening of orthodoxy's demand for a rigid conformity in doctrine and an eventual shift in Protestantism's center of gravity from creeds to Scripture. Thanks to Pietism's regard for the Scripture, Protestantism even today looks to the Bible as a principal instrument of edification in the process of growth in personal holiness known as *sanctification*. To this emphasis of Pietism, August Hermann Franke (1663–1727) made the important addition of *personal conversion*. Franke's own experience was sudden. As he described it, sadness, anxiety, and doubt were scattered before a certainty of the Father's grace, and "I was suddenly overcome by a wave of joy, such that I praised and magnified God aloud, who had granted me such grace." Though Pietism regarded personal faith alone as requisite, Franke's conversion—and later John Wesley's—came to be exemplary of one popular Protestant view of the inner struggle with sin leading to a sudden change of heart and a commitment to holy living.

Because Pietism stressed feeling over thought and renewal of the heart above pure doctrine, its contribution to seventeenth- and eighteenth-century theology or religious thought was negligible. On the other hand, it greatly enriched the liturgy and the hymnody of the church, and its stress on an ethic of personal holiness was complemented by a vigorous social ethic. Much was owed to the example of Franke. As the successor of Spener and Pietism's second great leader, Franke set in motion a host of charitable projects from his base at the University of Halle. He established an orphanage with affiliated schools, an infirmary, and a printing press. And of importance for the future of Protestantism, he encouraged a heretofore latent Protestant interest in foreign missions by instituting a school for the linguistic training of missionaries.

Over sixty missionaries had gone out from Halle by the eighteenth century. But the most impressive agents of Pietism's enthusiasm for missionary activity were the Moravian Brethren under the inspiration and leadership of Count Nikolaus Ludwig von Zinzendorf (1700–1760). From Herrnhut on Zinzendorf's Saxony estate, missionaries went out to work in the West Indies, Greenland, Guiana, Egypt, South Africa, and Labrador. No other group in the eighteenth century labored more energetically to spread the Christian message and the influence of "heart religion." Zinzendorf himself came to America and there began missions to the Indians, organized over a half-dozen Moravian congregations, giving the name

Bethlehem to the most famous in Pennsylvania, and sought to promote an ecumenical unity among the Germans in the New World. Despite the energy and scope of their activities, however, the Moravian church was never large and its importance restricted, had it not been for the influence its scattered societies had on others. John Wesley was one of these.

John Wesley's Methodism

In October of 1735, John Wesley (1703–1791) embarked for the new colony of Georgia where he was to serve as pastor to the English settlement in Savannah. This future founder of the Methodist movement had every expectation of success on his first independent ministry. He had shown sufficient academic promise at Christ Church, Oxford to be invited back to the university in 1726 as a fellow of Lincoln College. He also demonstrated religious leadership in a student group known as the "Holy Club." These "Methodists," as they were derisively called by fellow students, had dedicated themselves to a strict "rule and method." Hence their nickname. They covenanted to lead a holy life, to take communion at least once a week, to be disciplined in private devotions, to visit prisons, to spend three hours together every afternoon in the reading of the Bible. A record in Wesley's *Journal* pictured a day begun before dawn with prayer and continuing, at what seems an exhausting pace, until private prayer from five to six, more reading, public worship at seven, and then a meeting of the club for exhortation and instruction before bed at nine or ten.

There can be little doubt about this young Anglican priest's intellectual gifts, discipline, or religious earnestness. Yet, on the sea trip to Georgia, he was distressed at his own lack of courage when confronted with the prospect of shipwreck. After arriving in the colony he sought the counsel of Gottlieb Spangenberg, leader of the Moravian missionaries. Wesley found himself uncertain when questioned about the personal assurance of his faith. With irony turned on himself, Wesley wrote that he had gone to America to convert the Indians but was himself in need of conversion.

Back in England, Wesley again sought out the Moravians. On May 24, 1738, while attending one of their societies at Aldersgate Street in London, he underwent a transforming experience. During the reading of Luther's preface to the Epistle to the Romans, he wrote, "I felt my heart strangely warmed. I felt I did trust in Christ, Christ alone for salvation: And an assurance was given me, that he had taken away my sins, even mine, and saved me from the law of sin and death." Like August Franke, Wesley's conversion was a sudden, complete self-surrender with an accompanying joy. And, like the Pietists, he held that the experience of God, not the reasonableness of believing, was decisive for the Christian life. For religion to be true it must be deeply felt, built on a personal relationship with the Lord, and expressed in personal and social holiness. In these emphases Wesley resembled the continental Pietists, though a visit with Zinzendorf strained his relations with the Moravians. Moravian piety seemed too subjective and quietistic. Wesley's holiness was directed to the world. But then Wesley's genius, and his important contribution to Protestant Christianity, related more to his exceptional talent for preaching and organization than to his theological originality or innovation.

Wesley's preaching career began with an invitation to join George Whitefield in preaching to some three thousand coal miners in a brickyard beside Bristol. At first, he was hesitant to imitate George Whitefield's innovative practice of open-fields preaching. Wesley shared the Anglican conviction that God wished things to be done with regard for due order. But the success of this unconventional ministry soon changed his mind. The saving of souls outside of church buildings was—if not desirable—at least necessary. He even worried over the emotional effect of his preaching on the crowds. Nevertheless, Bristol was to be the beginning of an itinerant ministry that led to Wesley's traveling, largely by horseback, over two hundred and fifty thousand miles and preaching between forty thousand and fifty thousand sermons before his death. The pulpits of England being closed to him because of his unorthodox methods, he preached wherever he could and whenever, sometimes three, four, five times a day, rising to exhort laborers at dawn on their way to work in factories, meeting them at evening on their way home. And Wesley's preaching was always to one end: To produce and reinforce the felt experience of being loved and forgiven by God.

Methodism's early success was attributable to Wesley's preaching and to the preaching of a few Anglican clergy who enlisted in the movement. But, having taken as his parish the world, Wesley was persuaded to allow lay preachers, both male and female, to assist in an enormous work and to function as a parallel and complementary ministry to the sacramental ministry of ordained clergy. Methodist gains, however, are traced also to Wesley's conviction that preaching was only the beginning and conversion a prelude to a life of personal and social holiness. To provide for methodical growth in Christian holiness and perfection, he saw to the formation of small societies ("classes") under the charge of a lay leader for extemporaneous prayer, Bible study, witnessing, mutual encouragement, and the collection of funds for charity. Begun, like the Moravian Brethren within the Lutheran church, as "little churches within the church," these Methodist societies were already becoming independent of the Church of England. When Wesley died, there were eight thousand groups of Methodists in England and Wales, two thousand local preachers, and an emerging Methodist Episcopal Church in America.

SUMMARY

The early modern era dawned with a revolution in mathematics, astronomy, and physics. For some this scientific revolution appeared as a forbidding specter, looming dark on the horizon, calling into question religious belief and traditional certainties. Others demonstrated in their response and work a confidence that the "new philosophy," as Donne called it, confirmed in a fresh way ancient Christian affirmations concerning God, creation, scriptural revelation, and above all Jesus Christ. Those who held this undiminished confidence included no less a figure than the eighteenth century's great scientific architect, Sir Isaac Newton. Yet, it was the philosopher John Locke who, more than any other thinker of the age, established Christian revelation on the foundation of natural reason. But thinkers critical of Christianity, in the name of reason, pressed hard the claim of reason and natural religion against Christian apologists during the age. And, ironically, important beginnings in modern biblical criticism can be traced to Christianity's eighteenth-century Deist opponents. Yet, both apologists for reasonable Christianity and its Deist critics were overmatched by the philosophical skepticism of David Hume which called in question the competency of reason altogether in establishing religious truth. But then, there were Christians during these early modern centuries, philosophers like Pascal and revivalists like John Wesley, who sought religious certainty and Christian truth beyond reason in the regions of the heart, and in important respects prepared the way for the powerful new defenses of religion that followed in the nineteenth century.

REVIEW AND REFLECTION

1. The seventeenth and eighteenth centuries saw the rise of modern science. How was science greeted by religious thinkers? What importance does the scientific spirit of the age have for understanding Christianity?
2. What were the basic tenets of natural religion? Why was natural religion popular during the Enlightenment?
3. How did the defenders of revealed religion support the idea of revelation?
4. Who were the Deists and *philosophes* and what was their attitude toward Christian revelation and Scripture?
5. The Age of Reason was also an age of skepticism. What forms

were given skepticism by philosophical and religious thinkers? How did religious doubt help restore the authority of revelation?

6. How did Pietism develop? What were its main contributions to the story of Christianity in the eighteenth century?

7. Discuss John Wesley's life and ministry. What do we learn of Methodism from its founder's experience? How did Methodism meet the needs of the age?

END NOTES

1. Laurence Binyon, trans., *The Divine Comedy* in Paolo Milano, ed., *The Portable Dante* (New York: The Viking Press, 1961).

SUGGESTED FURTHER READING

BECKER, CARL L. *The Heavenly City of the Eighteenth-Century Philosophers*. New Haven: Yale University Press, 1932.

CRAGG, GERALD R. *The Church and the Age of Reason, 1648–1789*. Middlesex, England: Penguin Books, Ltd., 1960.

CRAGG, GERALD R. *From Puritanism to the Age of Reason: A Study of Changes in Religious Thought within the Church of England, 1660–1700*. Cambridge: The Cambridge University Press, 1950.

CRAGG, GERALD R. *Reason and Authority in the Eighteenth Century*. Cambridge: The Cambridge University Press, 1964.

LIVINGSTON, JAMES C. *Modern Christian Thought: From the Enlightenment to Vatican II*. New York and London: Macmillan Publishing Co., Inc. and Collier Macmillan Publishers, 1971.

McGIFFERT, A. C. *Protestant Thought before Kant*. New York: Harper & Row, Publishers, 1962.

RANDALL, JOHN HERMAN JR. *The Making of the Modern Mind: A Survey of the Intellectual Background of the Present Age*. Rev. ed. Cambridge, MA: The Riverside Press, 1940.

9 | The Modern World

Reason displaced revelation in the eighteenth century; feeling dethroned reason in the nineteenth century. And the cultural movement known as Romanticism that gave ascendancy to feeling and the affections turned out to be a valuable resource for Christian thinkers intent on reformulating the Christian faith in its quest for new foundations. But we discover as we study the nineteenth and then the twentieth centuries that western Christianity was more divided than ever about the nature of its foundations. The Catholic revivals of the Church of England and of Roman Catholicism looked to the Christian past to authenticate Catholic forms of worship and belief. It was to the great ages of the church, to the early church or the church of the Middle Ages, that these Catholic Christians turned for renewal and assurance.

For Protestant Christians, the Bible was the principle source of inspiration and authority, and much of our discussion centers on the ways Protestants sought to recover biblical meaning and reconstitute biblical authority. But liberal Catholic and Protestant attempts at renewal and restoration

Christianity in the Nineteenth and Twentieth Centuries—Key Dates

DATES	PERSONS AND EVENTS
1781 C.E.	Immanuel Kant's (1724–1804) *Critique of Pure Reason* questions the assumptions of natural religion
1799 C.E.	Friedrick Schleiermacher (1768–1834) defends religion as the expression of inner experience in *Speeches on Religion*
1835–1836 C.E.	David Friedrick Strauss (1808–1874) publishes *The Life of Jesus*, a controversial account of the historical Jesus
1822–1889 C.E.	Albrecht Ritschl, pioneer liberal theologian who joined Christian faith and historical scholarship
1833 C.E.	the beginning of the Oxford Movement in England
1864 C.E.	*Syllabus of Errors*, a set of Roman Catholic theses rejecting basic principles of modern society
1869–1870 C.E.	the First Vatican Council, published the decree of papal infallibility
1895 C.E.	conservative Protestants at Niagara, New York issue "five points of fundamentalism"
1906 C.E.	Albert Schweitzer (1875–1965) repudiates nineteenth-century liberal views of the historical Jesus in *The Quest of the Historical Jesus*
1910 C.E.	the beginnings of the modern ecumenical movement
1919 C.E.	Karl Barth's (1886–1968) *Commentary on Romans* signals a new theology emphasizing the otherness of God, revelation, and human sin
1963–1965 C.E.	Second Vatican Council, called by Pope John XXIII (1958–1963) for the renewal and updating of the church

have not always been welcomed by their coreligionists. And conservative Christian reaction had its own contributions to make to the modern Christian experience and to the story this chapter tells. It goes without saying that the story of Christianity in the modern world does not properly end but is a continuing one. For that reason we offer some reflections at the end of the chapter on the Second Vatican Council of the Catholic church, for this ecumenical council inaugurated immense changes with significance for the future of all Christians.

THE SPIRIT OF ROMANTICISM

The *Romantic movement* followed the Enlightenment. Pietism had prepared the way by elevating personal experience and feeling above the prevailing dominance of reason. But the weakening of the Enlightenment's hold on culture came also from within. In Germany, the last of the great Enlightenment philosophers, Immanuel Kant (1724–1804), asked about the nature and limits of reason. In his *Critique of Pure Reason* (1781), he answered that human knowledge of the external world is restricted to phenomena or appearances. A knowledge of things as they are in themselves, however, he thought beyond human capacity; all demonstrations for the existence of God, natural religion, or the nature of the universe he thought pointless. What knowledge we have of God and immortality comes from within and arises in conjunction with our moral sense. And on still another front, the French Revolution weakened reason's grip on European culture. Revolutionary forces set in motion a program to "dechristianize" the new republic. The worship of God was abolished; the Cult of Reason was established; churches were converted into "temples of Reason"; the Goddess of Reason was carried through the streets of Paris. And the thought of French *philosophes* was installed for a time as the republic's reigning theology.

The excesses of the French Revolution in the name of reason, coupled with the more subtle effect of Kant's philosophy, quickened the decline of the Enlightenment and prepared the way for a culture more committed to the heart than the mind. The mantle of prestige and authority that had draped the shoulders of scientist, mathematician, and philosopher now fell to the new heroes of culture: artists, poets, and composers—Goya, Delacroix, Constable; Goethe, Wordsworth, Coleridge; Beethoven, Schubert, Chopin. Rationality had yielded pride of place to the imagination, and the old prejudices against history and tradition vanished as well. It seemed even that the Enlightenment prejudice against revealed religion might disappear as well. At least, romanticism promised to be more receptive to much of traditional Christianity that formerly had been derided as contrary to reason and common sense.

IN SEARCH OF NEW FOUNDATIONS

Catholic Revival

With importance for Catholic Christianity, romanticism stimulated a renewed cultural interest in history, especially in those historical periods like the Middle Ages neglected by the Enlightenment, and in traditional forms of social existence. These new interests were eagerly embraced by both Roman Catholics and the Anglo-Catholic party within the Church of England. It was hoped by both groups that Christian tradition would repair the damage Catholic Christianity suffered in the name of reason. It was believed that tradition would bring an end to the corrosive effect of rationalism in the areas of belief and religious practice. And it was believed that a return to doctrine, liturgical forms of worship, and the notions of religious authority that prevailed during the first Christian centuries and the Middle Ages would provide Christianity with a surer foundation than either reason or Scripture might supply.

On the Continent, the Catholic revival sought to restore the prestige of the church and the power of the papacy. The romantic writer Francois Rene de Chateaubriand (1768–1848) defended the Catholic faith on the basis of aesthetic feeling. French priest Felicite Robert de Lamennais (1782–1854) opposed autonomous reason. A universal consensus of the human race embodied in Catholic tradition was, in his view, a more trustworthy standard of truth and a surer guide in the regeneration of society in the era following the disarray of the French Revolution.

In England the Oxford Movement also exhibited a distrust of autonomous reason. Members of this Anglo-Catholic revival, the most famous of whom was John Henry Newman (1801–1890), believed that "reason alone" results in a destructive skepticism that trivializes the faith's sacred mystery and undermines the church's unity. Where should the church turn for guidance? Should perhaps the church build on the foundation of Scripture? Newman expressed the movement's view that, while the Bible was widely held by Protestants as the standard of faith, "no two agree as to the interpreter of the Bible." The Anglo-Catholics trusted rather in ancient tradition and the corporate teachings of the church. These alone seemed to assure the integrity and mystery of Christianity's ancient faith.

Liberal Protestantism

Catholic Christianity sought to revive church tradition and traditional forms of Christian authority. Liberal Protestantism with roots in eighteenth-century Pietism turned rather to experience. Indeed, the greatest of the nineteenth-century theologians, Friedrich Schleiermacher (1768–1834), regarded experience as the very touchstone for what is genuine in faith and religious practice. But Schleiermacher's trust in experience's authority did not come directly from Pietism. During his years at the University of Halle and his first encounters with Enlightenment thought, he drifted from Pietism. At Halle, he developed an appreciation of critical thought and was exhilarated by the intellectual freedom he found there. Yet, Schleiermacher was to return to the German Pietism of his youth and to the Pietist emphasis on experience and the religious affections. His return, however, was through German romanticism. And it was his years spent in Berlin and his contact there with the future leaders of German romanticism that gave him the language and conceptual tools that he needed if he was to speak persuasively to his "enlightened" contemporaries.

Schleiermacher first addressed his Romantic friends, an audience whom he called "the cultured despisers of religion," in the eloquent and adeptly argued *Speeches on Religion* (1799). Here he hoped to persuade them that religion was not what it is commonly thought to be. True religion does not detract from but rather enhances human freedom and a higher life of the spirit. Schleiermacher began by stating what religion is not. Religion in its essence is neither belief nor morality. Setting himself in opposition to Protestant orthodoxy, he denied that religion can be reduced to an intellectual assent to the truths of revelation. Opposing himself to natural religion and the moral justification of religion that Kant set forth in the *Critique of Practical Reason* (1788), Schleiermacher objected to the idea that religion is a buttress for ethics. Stating his position summarily, he wrote that "Piety cannot be a mass of metaphysical or ethical crumbs." True religion has to do with inner experience.

Schleiermacher spoke of this inner experience as a "sense and taste for the Infinite" and in a later, more famous expression as a "feeling of absolute dependence." Such Romantic phrasings sound vague, but we can be certain that he did not intend by them mere sentiment or momentary emotional stirrings. Sense, taste, and feeling described a unique element of human experience. They pointed to a primal awareness of the Eternal in the midst of time, of the Infinite in the finite. This sense or taste for the Infinite, Schleiermacher believed, is also universal to humans and common to all religion. In this belief, Schleiermacher showed the influence of the Enlightenment's understanding of religion as a historical, human phenomenon. For him, all religions, including Christianity, are concrete expressions of religious experience and all are true to the extent that they manifest and promote this awareness.

But nowhere, Schleiermacher believed, is this fundamental God-consciousness, this "feeling of absolute dependence," more completely realized than in the historical person, Jesus of Nazareth. In this tenet, developed in *The Christian Faith* (1821–1822), Schleiermacher sought to recover the unique, historical character of Christianity which eighteenth-century rational theology had obscured. His teaching concerning Christ can be put simply. Jesus Christ is the pure expression of the immediate feeling of absolute dependence. As such, Christ was the unique Mediator between God and humanity whose mission was to communicate his own perfect God-consciousness to others. All other aspects of the Christian religion are secondary, interpretive responses to this redemptive fact. Faith does not depend on the external authority of the Bible or doctrine for its warrant; it does not require the confirmation of philosophy or science. The touchstone of the Christian life is the inner, experiential testimony of Christian consciousness.

Historical and Biblical Studies

The Bible, subject of literary and historical study during the Renaissance, emerged during the Reformation at the center of intense controversy. Its significance and authority were later the subject of discussion in the eighteenth century. But it was for the nineteenth century to effect a revolution in *biblical criticism* whose importance has been compared to the Reformation itself. Influenced by historical studies, nineteenth-century biblical scholarship was prompted to ask of Christian origins and the life of Jesus the question historians were asking of history: How did it happen? Encouraged by the success of literary studies, biblical studies adopted literary critical tools. To be sure, the textual criticism developed and refined during the Renaissance for the purpose of determining original texts and correcting textual errors was still used. But now Scripture was studied as literary critics studied Homer, Virgil, and Shakespeare. Knowledge about literary form, authorship, authorial perspective, audience, setting, and date of composition were considered essential for interpretation and the construction of meaning. It was one of those curious anomalies then that the publication of Strauss's *The Life of Jesus* (1835–1836), a book notable for its disregard of history and its weakness in handling New Testament documents, should be a signal impetus for biblical studies.

Like Schleiermacher, David Friedrich Strauss (1808–1874) was discontented with the theological heritage of the eighteenth century. He believed that rationalism and supernaturalism both failed to offer adequate understandings of the New Testament and the nature and origins of the Christian faith. As a corrective, Strauss proposed an explanation that he hoped would secure the Christian religion against rationalism's attack, yet provide an account of Christian beginnings that would be believable to rational persons. He argued that Jesus was merely human and that the events of his life occurred in ordinary human history. Yet, the Gospel narratives of Jesus, though with some residue of actual history, transcended history as myth. Having made a powerful impression on the imagination of his followers, Strauss argued, Jesus was taken into the collective unconscious of the apostles and transformed through the process of myth making into the divine and supernatural Christ of the New Testament.

The reaction provoked by Strauss's mythic life of Jesus proved a stimulus for historical criticism and study of the historical Jesus still evident today. Unhappy with the psychologizing of the biblical witness, Strauss's principal theological critics sought to redirect biblical studies away from the New Testament writers' subjectivity toward the objective history behind the New Testament. Ferdinand Christian Baur (1792–1860) and Albrecht Ritschl (1822–1889) were especially important in the effort to locate Christian theology solidly on a historical foundation. Both were confident that historical criticism would yield dependable findings, and in this conviction they were followed by others who embraced what Albert Schweitzer called "the quest for the historic Jesus." Both believed too that it was not only desirable but possible to distinguish what Jesus did and taught from what the apostles and the primitive church taught about him.

No more than Schleiermacher did these scholars believe that faith was the subject of history alone. Ritschl in particular insisted that historical facts became revelation only in so far as Jesus appears to and lays hold of the individual believer. Yet, he and other major nineteenth-century thinkers opposed Schleiermacher's idea that religious experience is the datum of theology. He insisted that the essence and content of the Christian religion was historic fact. The foundation for faith was in short neither tradition nor experience but the historic revelation of God in Jesus Christ.

CHALLENGES TO LIBERAL PROTESTANTISM

Dissent from Within

The nineteenth century represented an opportunity for Christianity to recover ground lost during the Enlightenment. Schleiermacher found in romanticism a new warrant for the Christian religion in experience; advocates of biblical studies discovered in historical and literary studies useful tools for reassessing the meaning of Scripture; and theologians saw in the historical Jesus a teacher and exemplar with immediate relevance for an age that was optimistic, progressive, tolerant, and socially idealistic. In brief, nineteenth-century liberal Protestantism saw opportunities for creative expressions of faith that the eighteenth century had not presented. But, toward the end of the century, a reaction to liberal Christianity had begun within its own ranks.

The new method of biblical study known as *form criticism* cast doubt on the prospect of getting behind the written Gospels to the oral stage of the Gospel tradition. Among other conclusions, form critics believed that the Gospels do not show Jesus himself. They held rather that the biblical record presents us with a Jesus refracted through the mind of the first-century church. And they believed that what the nineteenth century had beheld in the Gospel was not the historical Jesus but only the image of its own mind. And that liberal image, Albert Schweitzer (1875–1965) argued persuasively in *The Quest of the Historical Jesus* (1910), cannot be reconciled with the world to which Jesus belonged.

It thus became more and more difficult for liberal Protestant interpreters of the New Testament to find in Scripture its own progressive, optimistic, tolerant spirit. Schleiermacher's romantic image of Jesus as the archtype of God-consciousness or Ritschl's optimistic view of Jesus as exemplar of the ethical Kingdom of God became increasingly difficult to reconcile with the eschatological outlook of the first century. The progressive transformation of human society central to the social gospel of Walter Rauschenbusch (1861–1918) seemed harder and harder to reconcile with the idea that permeates the pages of the New Testament—that God is about to bring an end to the present age. Against the background of the preceding century's thought, Schweitzer's Jesus must have seemed "a stranger and enigma" indeed. Yet, Schweitzer and other twentieth-century liberal critics of nineteenth-century liberal Protestant thought were not its harshest critics. Much of twentieth-century Protestant theology is in fact built on the thought and on the historical and biblical research of the last century. The severest criticism of Protestant liberalism issued rather from a movement that has been called reactive Protestantism. [1]

Reactive Protestantism

Whereas liberal Protestantism saw opportunity in nineteenth-century secular thought, Protestant conservatism beheld the century with horror. Christianity seemed to them besieged on all sides. The philosopher Ludwig Feuerbach argued in his *Essence of Christianity* (1841) that god was a mental projection whose purpose was to answer human hopes and meet human needs. In *Future of an Illusion* (1927), Sigmund Freud presented religion as an expression of communal neurosis and wish fulfillment. The anthropologist Sir James Frazer assembled data on religious ritual in *The Golden Bough* (1890). There he discovered a continuity in ritual pattern from the most primitive to the most advanced religions. The new discipline of comparative religion also concluded that all religions without exception share common characteristics.

Many Christians also found themselves in a defensive posture with respect to the natural sciences. Geology and zoology explained the formation of the earth and the development of life forms in ways that seemed flatly to contradict Genesis. Charles Lyell demonstrated persuasively in his *Principles of Geology* (1830) that the earth was not recently created but had formed over aeons of geological time. And Charles Darwin's epoch-making *Origins of Species* (1859), followed later by *The Descent of Man* (1871), presented life on earth as an evolutionary process of natural selection. From the conservative perspective, the net effect of these developments was to jeopardize the uniqueness of the Christian religion, and, of serious concern for Protestants who had neither pope nor tradition to fall back on, the authority of the Bible.

Typical of the conservative reaction was Charles Hodge (1779–1878) of Princeton Theological Seminary. In a return to seventeenth-century Protestant orthodoxy, Hodge opposed basing faith on subjective feeling or inward experience. Faith required the assurance of external proof and the certainty of facts. He also rejected the liberal distinction between the facts of science and the judgments and interpretations of theology. Once science is fully known and the Bible better understood, their truths would be found to harmonize. He did not of course accept the findings of contemporary science. Natural selection and the evolution of new species Hodge regarded as mere theories in conflict with the self-evident teachings of Scripture. But then, he believed Darwin had made a serious mistake. He had failed to distinguish his theory from the facts. Hodge was reminded that humans often err in reading the facts but the facts are never in error because "the facts are from God." Or, as Billy Graham put it, "it was man and not the Bible that needed correcting." Hodge did however recognize that science and theology had different objects, if not separable sets of data, and the object of science was the facts and laws of nature. The facts and general truths and principles of the Bible, on the other hand, were the object of theology.

While liberalism looked to experience for confirmation of biblical truth, Hodge sought an objective measure of truth in the very words of the Bible. The Bible's words, as an 1881 article in *The Princeton Review* announced in boldface, "ARE THE WORD OF GOD . . . [and] all their elements and all their affirmations are absolutely errorless." This certainty about the full inspiration and inerrancy of the Bible also became a central article of conservative Protestantism. This bedrock of biblical authority was the objective ground on which the fundamentalists and the contemporary neoevangelicals would be willing to square off against liberal theologians, higher criticism of the Bible, and modern philosophy and science. From here the conservatives would again seek to capture the initiative in affirming the uniqueness of the Christian religion, the validity of the creation story as presented in Genesis, and the reality of supernatural intervention as God's way of dealing with the world. Influenced by *premillennialism* and a renewed sense of the reality of evil, conservatives reaffirmed with new energy the biblical doctrine of sin. They also defined themselves in opposition to liberal social programs and social ethics, and they associated the social gospel and the ecumenical movements as liberal evils. And, heirs to revivalism and Pentecostalism, they have coupled an insistence on doctrinal fundamentals with the need for personal conversion.

Theology of the Word

At the end of World War I, Europe's confidence in material and moral progress had been shattered by the war's scope and sheer brutality. Art and literature, always accurate for taking seismic readings of culture, pictured social and cultural dissolution. The great Irish poet W. B. Yeats, thinking of the medieval art of falconry, likened western civilization to the widening circle of the falcon as it flies too far from the falconer. He feared that western culture, like a falcon without a controlling center, was in danger of being lost. And in *The Waste Land*, a poem that came to stand for the spiritual crisis and malaise of the postwar years, T. S. Eliot foresaw in apocalyptic vision a universal ruin, "Cracks and reforms and bursts in the violet air/ Falling towers/ Jerusalem Athens Alexandria/ Vienna London/ Unreal." The world and human history thus presented a darker, more ambiguous aspect than they had in the nineteenth century, and the need for a new theology for the times became apparent.

The signal that a major shift in Christian perspective was afoot was the *Commentary on Romans* (1919) by the Swiss pastor Karl Barth (1886–1968). Like Protestant conservatives, Barth took issue with liberal theology. He denied, for example, that Scripture is dependent on history or relative to time and place or that it should be accommodated to present circumstances. He cautioned that the Bible is "not the history of man but the history of God." And again, he wrote that the Bible is an open portal to "a strange new world, the world of God." It is easy to understand that this European theologian, perhaps the greatest in the twentieth century, would hearten American conservatives and attract them to Germany and then Switzerland to study with him. Yet, though Barth firmly believed the Bible stood in judgment of human speculations and aspirations, he did not dissociate himself, as reactive Protestantism had, from secular ideas nor did he hesitate to use historical criticism in biblical exegesis. To be sure, he believed revelation to be the foundation of Christian faith and theology. Yet, for Barth and the continental theologians he influenced, revelation was not the words of the Bible. Though the church over the centuries has heard God's Word in the Bible, Barth argued, the Word of God is rather the living incarnate Word to whom the human words of the Bible bear witness.

Barth's "Theology of the Word," was welcomed in America not among conservative Protestants but among an influential group of neoorthodox Protestant theologians. Neoorthodoxy, like its counterpart in Europe, was a response to the quandary of liberalism and the crisis of western culture in the first decades of the twentieth century. Neoorthodoxy's general assessment of the dilemma was wryly expressed in H. Richard Niebuhr's (1894–1962) judgment that here "a God without wrath brought men without sin into a kingdom without judgment through the ministrations of a Christ without the cross."

Richard's brother Reinhold Niebuhr (1892–1971) was neoorthodoxy's greatest spokesperson. But Reinhold's understanding of the cultural and religious situation was as much a matter of personal as it was of intellectual conviction. Before becoming a professor at Union Theological Seminary in New York City, Niebuhr had served as pastor to Detroit auto workers in the days before unionization, and so had firsthand impressions not only of the possibilities and limits of human nature but also of human institutions. Liberalism's optimism about reason and good will provided thin resources for dealing with the institutional evils that Niebuhr addressed in his first major book, *Moral Man and Immoral Society* (1932). Like Barth, he turned for insight to the great sixteenth-century Protestant Reformers, to Augustine, and to the classical creeds. Above all, he turned to the Bible and to the great biblical themes as the source for his theology. Yet, despite his insistence on the transcendence of God, human fallibility, and the need for grace, and despite his disenchantment with the optimism of the social gospel movement, Niebuhr retained a pragmatic, activist orientation that is a feature of the American religious tradition. Though he believed that in God love and justice coincided, his was a "Christian Realism" that allowed for sinners to "toil and sweat to make human relations a little more tolerable and slightly more just."

TRENDS IN ROMAN CATHOLICISM

Papal Authority

If church architecture makes a statement, then, Saint Peter's in Rome announces in the most theatrical terms of the baroque style the Catholic triumphalism of the Tridentine church. Yet, at the dawn of the modern era, the highly centralized Roman church with power concentrated in the pope faced European nation states determined to resist external interference. European prelates and theologians took opposing positions on the issue. On one side, the impetus to limit papal authority materialized in France as Gallicanism and in Germany as Josephism. The opposite view was taken up by the *ultramontanists*, so called because they looked "beyond the mountains" to Rome for direction and authority. Before the French Revolution, the ultramontanists feared that the national churches could too easily be made instruments of state policies; after the Revolution, they saw in a cohesive church linked to the pope a conservative bastion against the social disorder and godlessness associated in their minds with republican forms of government. As it turned out, ultramontanism proved successful in promoting papal supremacy, but not even the popes were able to withstand the modern secular state.

It was ironic that the success of ultramontanism was to accompany the transfer of the pope's temporal estates to a secular state. On July 18, 1870 the delegates of the First Vatican Council (1869–1870), with a terrific thunderstorm outside Saint Peter's, voted 533 to 2 for affirming *papal infallibility*. In *Pastor aeternus* it was decreed that, when the Roman Pontiff speaks *ex cathedra*, that is, in his office as pastor and doctor of all Christians, he is possessed of "divine infallibility" and his definitions on matters of doctrine and morals are irreformable. In practice, only once after this proclamation has a pope exercised this authority and that was in 1950 when Pius XII promulgated the dogma of the Assumption of Mary. Still, it is significant that for the first time in Christian history popes could by their own authority rule on dogma. Some Catholics in the Netherlands, Germany, and Austria left, taking the name "Old Catholics." But, apart from expected objections to the dogma by the Orthodox and Protestant churches, there was little dissent to the ruling. Gallicanism was dead, so too was conciliarism. Still, the victory must have been bittersweet for Pius. Early in September, the Italian armies invaded papal territory and before the end of the month, the city of Rome fell to the new kingdom of Italy. The pope's authority over the church had been greatly magnified, but all that remained of his temporal authority was an ecclesiastical state of 0.15 square miles.

Catholic Modernism

The papacy suffered a loss of prestige, power, and territory to the new secular state that issued from the French Revolution. The church's traditional, largely medieval outlook on Christian authority was also undermined by the new republican form of government. To be sure, there were a few traditionalists who hoped for an alliance between Catholicism and political liberalism. Lamennais espoused the liberal program and wrote in his controversial newspaper, *L'Avenir* ("The Future"), "Let us not tremble before liberalism, let us catholicize it." But Gregory XVI (1771–1846) had a different view of such liberal ideas as freedom of the press and the doctrine of the sovereignty of the people, and condemned them in the encyclical *Mirari vos* (1832). The blow that most stunned the church's progress in making terms with the modern world, however, came during the papacy of Pius IX (1846–1878). In the *Syllabus of Errors* (1864), Pius repudiated much that was fundamental to the modern state, ideas such as the toleration of religious diversity, nonparochial public schools, and the separation of church and state. In all, eighty errors were catalogued; all related to the church's authority and all embodied the mood of the eightieth error: "That the Roman Pontiff can and ought to reconcile himself to, and agree with, progress, liberalism, and civilization as lately introduced."

The papacy also took umbrage at theologians who wanted to bring the tradition of Roman Catholic beliefs into closer relation to modern historical and biblical studies, philosophy, and science. These *Catholic modernists*, as they were called, were critical of many traditional Catholic teachings and were dissatisfied with the dry, dogmatic approach to revelation and dogma of traditional scholastic theology. Instead, they took their lead from liberal Protestantism and advocated a critical study of the Bible and Christian tradition. But they also dissented from liberal Protestantism's negative view of the institutional church and the formation of tradition and dogma that followed the New Testament period.

Whereas Protestant liberalism sought the essence of Christianity in the teachings of the historical Jesus, modernists like Alfred Loisy (1857–1940) sought to demonstrate that the church's tradition and its hierarchy, under the guidance of the Holy Spirit, were the necessary, continuing and full expression of gospel. In so arguing, the modernists had in effect turned Protestant research to the defense of Catholic traditions. Yet, their defense was not welcomed by an increasingly reactive papacy. Leo XIII (1878–1903) warned against weakening the authority of the Bible and the church and in an encyclical of 1879 called for a return to the scholastic theology of Thomas Aquinas. His successor, the conservative Pius X (1803–1914), further closed the doors on the modernist movement. He condemned its ideas, excommunicated Loisy and the English modernist, George Tyrrell (1861–1909), and forced others into submission. Not until the encyclical *Divino afflante Spiritu* (1943) was a window onto modern biblical interpretation opened again for Catholic scholars.

Catholic Renewal

When the seventy-seven-year-old Angelo Guiseppe Roncalli (1881–1963) was elected pope on the eleventh ballot, it was expected that he would be an interim, caretaker pope. When he took the name John XXIII, a name tainted with memories of the Avignon papacy, it might have been guessed that he intended to break new ground. Nevertheless, when he announced three months later his decision to call an ecumenical council, there was surprise—many thought that the declaration of papal infallibility had ended the era of councils. In some quarters there was dismay. Here was a modern pope prepared to depart from the recent tradition, confident, as he announced in his opening address to the delegates of Vatican II (1963–1965), that "Divine Providence is leading us to a new order of human relations." The renewal or "updating" of the Catholic church, however, was not wholly unprepared for. John had established a Secretariat for Promoting Christian Unity in 1960 and had named three official observers to the third assembly of the World Council of Churches. He called also for the updating of Catholic social teaching in the encyclical *Mater et Magistra* (1961). Yet, the work of updating and renewing the church he undertook jointly with the bishops of the council.

Filling the nave of Saint Peter's, over two thousand bishops, with an impressive 42 percent from Latin America, Asia, and Africa, in the presence of ninety-three non-Catholic observers by the final session, the council began a work that would radically alter the face of the Catholic church. Influenced by a group of distinguished theological experts, among whom were Henri de Lubac, Yves Congar, and Karl Rahner, the council followed a course, as these theologians had in their theologies, of affirming both tradition and the modern world. In sixteen documents, the bishops addressed afresh the question of papal authority and found in favor of the principle of collegiality. Without abandoning papal primacy, bishops were considered to participate in the full and supreme authority of the pope over the church.

The council also took significant steps when it revived the ancient image of the church as the people of God, gave greater importance to the common priesthood of all Christians, and undertook a liturgical reform which resulted in the translation of the Latin Mass into modern languages. The council also looked outward to the world religions in its recognition of the common religious experiences and problems of all faiths, and it built bridges to other Christian communions which were now addressed as "divided brethren." In the words of Dutch theologian Edward Schillebeeckx, the Roman church gave up "her monopoly of the Christian religion." Finally, breaking with the "syllabus mentality" of Vatican I, the council affirmed individual conscience and religious liberty, and recognized the positive advances of human culture. Before adjourning, it was clear that this Twenty-first Ecumenical Council, with the pope's blessing, launched a new epoch of the church's history.

SUMMARY

The modern era gave birth to an independent and critical spirit which exempted no authority from critical scrutiny. With good reason, then, Christianity at this juncture in its history is often pictured as defensive or reactive. Yet, we've seen that Christianity was capable also of energetic and creative response to the challenges of modernity. In the wake of the Enlightenment's critique of revealed religion, Christianity produced spirited justifications of Christian revelation, New Testament miracles, and the practical superiority of Christian teaching. It also found creative expression among Christians indifferent to the Enlightenment and its rational arguments for and against religion. Mystics like Pascal believed the heart to have reasons beyond the knowing of reason; Pietists cultivated "heart religion"; and Methodists provided warm, personal religious experience and the fellowship of laity-directed Christian societies to the dislocated urban workers of the Industrial Revolution.

The nineteenth century presented Christianity with new, and in many ways, more critical challenges to the forms of its authority and to its basic convictions about the nature of the world. Yet, once again, Christians discovered in the culture resources for creative redefinition and renewal. Schleiermacher discerned in experience a powerful justification for vital faith requiring the confirmation of neither reason nor history. Traditionalists in the ranks of Roman Catholicism and Anglicanism appealed to a Catholic past—to the Middle Ages or beyond to the age of the church fathers. There they found models for stability, unity, and order in an age of social fragmentation and divisive individualism. Even the tools of nineteenth-century historical and literary scholarship—by some thought to be inimical to Christian revelation and truth—were used by biblical scholars and church historians in the preparation of new defenses for faith. Liberal Protestants sought a surer ground for the Christian faith in the person and teachings of the historical Jesus, and Catholic modernists endeavored to show that the legitimate faith of the church emerged along with the traditions of the early church. To be sure, there were those who sought authority beyond and in opposition to the modern world, and the late nineteenth and twentieth centuries contributed to the forces of reactive Protestantism and Catholicism. But even twentieth-century Christianity, though more cautious about embracing modernity, found in the theology of Karl Barth and the decrees of Vatican II ways to reaffirm traditional religious and theological values.

REVIEW AND REFLECTION

1. How did Romanticism create a more favorable cultural climate for Christianity?

2. What were the objectives of the Catholic revival at the beginning of the nineteenth century?

3. Describe the liberal Protestantism of Friedrich Schleiermacher.

4. What were the objectives of the Protestant biblical scholars who sought the historical Jesus behind the pages of the Gospels?

5. What challenges did the nineteenth-century quest for the historical Jesus meet with?

6. Describe the features of reactive Protestantism and Catholicism. What were they reacting against? What positive program did each advocate?

7. How did Karl Barth and the Niebuhrs seek to go beyond Protestant liberalism?

8. Describe the achievements of the Second Vatican Council. Compare this council with the the First Vatican Council.

END NOTES

1. For a discussion of reactive Protestantism see Martin Marty, *Modern American Religion, Volume I: The Irony of It All 1893–1919* (Chicago and London: The University of Chicago Press, 1986), pp. 208 ff.

SUGGESTED FURTHER READING

BARTH, KARL. *Protestant Thought: From Rousseau to Ritschl.* trans. Brian Cozens. New York: Harper & Row, Publishers, 1952.

CHADWICK, OWEN. *The Secularization of the European Mind in the Nineteenth Century.* New York: Cambridge University Press, 1975.

NEILL, STEPHEN. *A History of Christian Missions.* Rev. for the 2nd ed. by Owen Chadwick. Middlesex, England: Penguin Books, Ltd., 1986.

KNOX, R. A. *Enthusiasms: A Chapter in the History of Religion.* Oxford: At the University Press, 1950.

PITTENGER, W. NORMAN. *Reconceptions in Christian Thinking, 1817–1967.* New York: The Seabury Press, 1968.

RANCHETTI, MICHELE. *The Catholic Modernists.* New York: Oxford University Press, 1969.

ROUSE, RUTH and STEPHEN NEILL. *History of the Ecumenical Movement, 1517–1948.* Philadelphia: The Westminster Press, 1952.

TILLICH, PAUL. *Perspectives on 19th and 20th Century Protestant Theology.* ed. and with intro. by Carl E. Braaten. New York: Harper & Row, Publishers, 1967.

VIDLER, ALEC R. *The Church in an Age of Revolution, 1789 to the Present Day.* Middlesex, England: Penguin Books, Ltd., 1968.

WELCH, CLAUDE. *Protestant Thought in the Nineteenth Century, Volume 1: 1799–1870.* New Haven and London: Yale University Press, 1972.

WELCH, CLAUDE. *Protestant Thought in the Nineteenth Century, Volume 2: 1870–1914.* New Haven and London: Yale University Press, 1985.

10 | Forms of Catholic Christianity

INTRODUCTION

In Part I we explored Christian foundations and beginnings; in Part II we pursued the Christian story in its history and in the development of its traditions. We might say that our purpose to this point has been with the story's conception, formation, and elaboration. Now, however, our objective is to look at Christian traditions synchronically, to examine them as they exist in their integrity and wholeness and without reference to what comes before or what comes after. In this chapter and the following one, we profile representative Christian church traditions taking into account what is characteristic of each.

Each of the Christian churches that we examine is of course rooted in a particular culture and geography, and our approach begins with a review of the circumstances of time and place that account so much for what is distinctive of each. Yet, what is most representative of religious traditions is the way they arrange their thought to express their understanding of ultimate mystery and the way they orchestrate symbols to gain access to that mystery. With this in mind we turn to theological beliefs and doctrines of salvation distinctive of the traditions we examine, and to what is most representative about their worship. Views of Christian community and leadership, then, help us understand the context and agents of the divine/human transaction leading to salvation and central to worship.

Chapter 11 develops these themes in relation to Protestant Christianity. This chapter explores the various forms and meanings of *Catholic* Christianity, though we should clarify our use of the word *catholic*. Here we use the word in two senses. It refers to those Christians in union with the bishop of Rome, Christians called Roman Catholics. We use the word

Orthodoxy's emphasis on worship and monasticism are apparent in priests like this archimondrite and monk of the island of Patmos.

catholic too to identify Christian churches that assign special importance to the ancient creeds as sources of doctrine, to the sacraments as necessary channels of God's saving reality, and to the historic episcopacy (rule of bishops) as the authorized agent of Christ's ministry in succession of the apostles. Among the non-Roman ''Catholic'' churches, Eastern Orthodoxy has claim of preeminence both in antiquity and numerical size, and so we begin with this church tradition. Our discussion of Roman Catholicism follows, and we conclude with the Anglican and Episcopalian churches as a quite different example of the western Catholic tradition.

EASTERN ORTHODOXY

Profile

Often overlooked by the West, the churches of Eastern Orthodoxy worldwide number nearly 160 million, [1] making them the largest Christian tradition next to Roman Catholicism. There are close to 6 million communicants of the Orthodox Catholic church, as they prefer to call themselves, in North America alone. Other countries where Orthodoxy is represented by organized churches include Palestine, Egypt, Syria, Cyprus, Finland, and Japan. Yet the designation *Eastern* indicates the geographical and cultural center of gravity for Orthodox Christianity. Orthodoxy in the first place lays claim to a continuity with the ancient churches of the East, the Greek-speaking churches of the apostle Paul's ministry. After the expansion of Islam in the seventh century, Orthodoxy's center of gravity shifted northward to the countries of eastern Europe where in the Balkans and Russia it continues to be the dominant Christian church. Orthodox cultural legacy comes also from the East. As the Christianity of the Greek-speaking half of the Roman Empire, it evolved a form of Christian life, theology, and worship that distinguished it from the Latin West and from the religious traditions of the church of Rome from which it was formally separated in 1054.

The titular or honorary head of this eastern branch of Christianity is the ecumenical patriarch of Constantinople, but the patriarchate of Constantinople (modern Istanbul) functions mainly as a symbol of Orthodox unity. Effective ecclesiastical authority is decentralized and resides with the patriarchs and metropolitans of the fifteen self-governing or autocephalous and autonomous churches that make up the worldwide fellowship of Orthodox Christians. There exists, as can be imagined, a degree of diversity of centers within Orthodoxy not found in the more centralized tradition of Roman Catholicism. There is found as well a greater identification of Orthodox churches with national cultures and languages. Because of the formative influence of Greek Byzantine culture and thought on its liturgy and theology, for example, Orthodoxy has sometimes been referred to as Greek Orthodoxy. Yet, we know Orthodoxy by other names linked to other nations—the Church of Romania, for example, or the Church of Russia, the largest branch of Orthodoxy. The integrative force of Greek tradition within Orthodoxy not withstanding, national languages and ethnic traditions have given tangible expression to Orthodox diversity.

It can be said, however, that Orthodoxy is a unity-in-diversity, a federation of churches, each of which is distinct yet undivided. We have already observed that the patriarch of Constantinople serves the Orthodox world as a symbol not of ecclesiastical power but rather of Christian unity and cooperation. Other unifying symbols important to Orthodoxy are the Bible, the writings of the church fathers, and the doctrinal statements and decrees of the first seven ecumenical councils (Nicaea [325], Constantinople [381], Ephesus [431], Chalcedon [451], Constantinople [533 and 680], Nicaea [787]).

The acceptance of the ecumenical councils as the supreme and infallible expression of the church's authority particularly distinguishes Orthodoxy from Roman Catholicism. The Roman church recognizes twenty-one general councils, the most recent being Vatican II (1962–1965). For the Orthodox church—sometimes described as the church of the councils—only a truly ecumenical council, where bishops from the whole world have gathered, is empowered to make doctrinal decisions that are irrevocable. To believe as the early church believed and to worship with the creed of the ecumenical councils, the Nicene-Constantinopolitan Creed (381), is to be *Orthodox* in one of the word's essential senses—"right" (*orthos*) "belief" (*doxa*).

Orthodox Christians, however, are quick to observe that *orthodox* means also "right praise or worship," and any who have seen the Orthodox liturgy can understand the remark of the envoys of Prince Vladimir of Kiev on first seeing the liturgy in Constantinople's Church of the Holy Wisdom, "We knew not whether we were in heaven or on earth." Together with ancient belief, the liturgy is for Orthodoxy a distinctive sign of its identity, the basic form its religious experience takes, and a symbol of unity among its churches.

Salvation and Theological Belief

The Genesis story of creation and the fall may be the best point of entry for our discussion of Orthodoxy's view of salvation. In that biblical account, God creates human beings with a special dignity. After having made everything else, the heavens and the earth and the living things that inhabit the earth, God expresses the divine purpose with respect to humans in the words, "Let us make man in our image, after our likeness" (Genesis 1:26). This passage has been interpreted to express a variety of theological meanings, but the words *image* ("icon" in Greek) and *likeness* play a central part in Orthodoxy's understanding of salvation. According to Orthodoxy, Adam and Eve were destined for immortality and communion with God. By virtue of the image or icon of God, the original couple possessed rationality, freedom, and moral responsibility. And had they used these natural endowments properly they would have progressed by degrees to a full participation in the life of God, an assimilation to God that Orthodoxy speaks of as *theosis* or deification. In the natural course of things, humans would have become "second gods." But sin intervened, caused God's icon to be blurred, and subjected Adam and his descendants to corruption and death.

This Eastern theology contrasts with the West's view of Adam's transgression at a number of important points. In the West as far back as Anselm and earlier, sin was thought of in penal or judicial terms as a crime against divine justice. According to this interpretation, humanity's fall in Adam is traceable to a willful, rebellious self-assertion for which humanity is guilty and deserving of divine retribution. The dominant motif of the

West's doctrine of the *atonement* (i.e. reconciliation of God and humanity) is thus Christ's submission to death on the cross; as victim, Jesus mounts the cross to suffer vicarious punishment for a guilty humanity.

Orthodox see rather the divinity beneath the humanity; beneath the suffering and outward humiliation they celebrate *Christus Victor*, Christ the victorious king. Even the note of triumph that marks Good Friday observance and the preference for the symbol of the empty cross in Orthodox churches sounds this triumphal note. And, as the crucifixion marks the conquest of death, Christ's Resurrection from the tomb—which is said to have burst open under the pressure of the divine life—signals the liberation of humanity from the unnatural cycle of mortality. Yet, we cannot appreciate Orthodoxy's view of salvation—or for that matter its attitude toward crucifixion and Resurrection—apart from the central importance of the Incarnation. Taking its themes from the Christological definitions of the early church councils, Orthodoxy holds that the Incarnation of the second person of the Trinity joins in perfect union the human and the divine, an act that restores the sullied icon of God and makes possible once more the progress godward intended for humanity when it was still in paradise.

The Incarnation is thus central not only to Orthodox Christology (doctrine of Christ) but basic to its soteriology (doctrine of salvation). It is by virtue of the unique union of the human and divine in the person of Christ that humans can hope to realize their full potential as persons in mystical union with God. Yet, we must be careful not to think of Orthodoxy's doctrine of *theosis* as involving a dissolution of the self, a loss of personal identity in the abyss of the Godhead. Unlike the Hinduism of the Upanishads, where no ultimate distinction exists between Atman, the Great Self, and Brahman, the Everlasting Spirit, Orthodoxy adheres to normative Christianity's differentiation between creation and Creator.

As in the other biblical faiths, Orthodoxy begins with an affirmation of God's transcendence that precludes any fusion of the self with the Godhead. God in himself is found to be very much the numinous ultimate that we encounter in Otto's *The Idea of the Holy*. He is totally transcendent, utterly incomprehensible, a being before whom religious images and theological concepts fail. For this reason Orthodoxy inclines to greater reticence than the West when it comes to theological speculation or dogmatic definition, regarding as sufficient the irrevocable doctrinal formulations of the ecumenical councils. And theologians of the Eastern church are more apt to employ a "negative" or *apophatic theology*, a theology that uses negation to transcend images and concepts. The goal of this essentially mystical theology is not clarity of thought so much as it is a readying of the mind to enter the divine darkness which discursive thought cannot penetrate.

Nevertheless, the Orthodox hold that, in spite of the inaccessibility of the divine *essence*, there is more to God than essence. God is, of course, revealed in the person of Jesus. He is also manifest dynamically in acts of power or uncreated *energies* which flow from the divine essence and permeate the world of created beings. As uncreated light, the divine energies are associated with the brilliance that shone from Christ's body at the time of the transfiguration on Mount Tabor. And, Orthodox hold, in this life the uncreated energies are also experienced by mystics as an illuminating inward light and by the saints as a transforming bodily radiance akin to the radiance of Christ's transfigured body. Such experiences are, however, thought to be but the first fruit of a fuller transformation that will accompany the general resurrection at the end of time. On the day of the Resurrection, all the redeemed will be transfigured and the inward light will illumine not just their souls but their bodies as well and not just the saved but all of the material world. The process of deification will thus be the fulfillment of God's purpose for his creation. But Orthodox believe that the anticipated transformation of the world is only the culmination of a process already begun in the present life of the church. It is a process that unfolds now in the context of the church's liturgy, its sacraments, the life of prayer and obedience to the Commandments, and the reading of Scripture. It is to these aspects of Orthodoxy that we now turn.

Right Praise and Worship

The first impression people often have of Orthodoxy is of great churches with massive domes or onion-shaped cupolas crowned with golden crosses. For those who go inside, the domed interiors give almost tangible expression to Orthodox belief that the Holy Spirit descends upon the earth, and sanctifies and transforms the material world. The interior (and often the exterior) walls of its churches are covered with bright luminous colors—of red, blue, and green. And, while the frescoes on the walls instruct the faithful with scenes from the Old and New Testaments, they seem also to celebrate material beauty. Certainly, the affirmation of materiality is basic to the use of the painted panels of wood bearing images of Christ, Mary his mother, and the saints. These images, called *icons*, are placed around the church's interior or mounted on a screen, an *iconostasis*, that divides the nave and the worshippers from the sanctuary where the priest consecrates red wine and leavened bread. According to the canons of Nicaea II (787) and great Orthodox theologians like John of Damascus (c. 675–c. 749), the icon is a testament to the Spirit-bearing potential of all material things. It is in this conviction that Orthodox worship makes active use of other material symbols as well—consecrated water and oil, incense and candles, and symbols of physical gesture such as bows, prostrations, the kiss, and the sign of the cross. And within the interior of Orthodox churches corporate worship is celebrated with the unhurried dignity of the ancient Byzantine court ceremony from which it in part derives.

One can see why Prince Vladimir's envoys said of the Orthodox service that they knew not whether they were in heaven or on earth. As others have observed of the *Divine Liturgy*, heaven seems to have come down to the earth as priest and people together rehearse a timeless drama in readings from Scripture, in liturgical gesture, and in sacramental act. The themes of the drama are from the biblical story of salvation and, like the famous ouroboros, the cosmic serpent biting its tail, it begins with the world's creation and circles on itself, ending with the restoration of the world on the day of the Resurrection.

Everything in the Orthodox church seems to speak of this cosmic story—a story of the preexistent Word of God, God's eternal Son who became incarnate, suffered death on the cross, burst forth from the tomb on the third day, ascended to heaven where he is enthroned, and who on Pentecost sent the Holy Spirit as a pledge of his presence to Christians. The frescoes on the church walls tell of this story. The church's calendar of sacred time coordinates the steady progress of the year with it, providing above all for the observance of five great feasts, the greatest of which is Easter, the Feast of Feasts. And the lection of prescribed readings from the Gospels and the Epistles interpret its great themes and provide at the same time for a reading of the entire New Testament (with the exception of Revelation) once each year in the context of liturgical worship. In addition to these occasional readings, some 98 quotations from the Old Testament and 114 from the New Testament are folded into the liturgy, evidence of the importance of Scripture in Orthodox worship and praise. Prayers, symbolic gestures, and chanted hymns, which Orthodox sing without the accompaniment of musical instruments, further orchestrate the symbols of faith that rehearse the sacred Christian story.

Yet, all these features only function as a setting for the liturgy's central sacramental action and the focus of salvation's drama. Out of view behind the iconostasis, the priest stands at the center of the sanctuary before the holy table or throne and consecrates the Eucharistic symbols. He offers thanksgiving (*eucharistia*), recalls (*anamnesis*) Christ's words of institution at the time of his last fellowship meal, and invokes the Holy Spirit (*Epiclesis*). Emphasis on mystery—reinforced by the screen of icons—has made Orthodoxy reluctant to follow Roman Catholicism in giving precise doctrinal formulation to its understanding of the Eucharist. Nevertheless, Orthodox believe that at the *Epiclesis* the bread and wine become the true, objective body and blood of Christ, and it is Orthodox practice to reserve the consecrated bread for distribution to the sick.

They also hold that the Eucharist is a true *sacrifice*. Orthodox do not teach, however, that this "mystical sacrifice," as it is called, is a renewal and reenactment of the oblation of Calvary in which the essence of the sacrifice is the same. After the consecration, the priest brings the consecrated bread and wine—called the holy gifts—through the royal door that pierces the center of the iconostasis, and offers them to the people who receive the sacred food from a spoon. The service ends with a final blessing, and the people approach the priest, kiss a cross that he holds in his hand, and are offered a piece of bread that has been blessed but not consecrated, an act of fellowship reminiscent of the love (*agape*) feasts of the early church.

Orthodox regard baptism as a necessary condition for admission to the Eucharist, and the early church practice of sending the unbaptized from the room at the time of "the breaking of bread" still echoes in the Orthodox liturgy at the deacon's cry, "The Doors! The Doors!" The words, however, reflect more the conservative character of the Orthodox liturgy with its emphasis on continuity with ancient traditions than contemporary practice. In practice, infants are introduced to full church membership shortly after birth through the administration of the rites of baptism and chrismation (or confirmation). They are initiated into the mystical burial and resurrection of Christ through a triple immersion, and immediately are anointed with oil specially consecrated by the patriarch of the church. With the sign of the cross marked on forehead, eyes, nostrils, ears, mouth, then breast, hands, and feet, the newly baptized child receives the Holy Spirit, a sign of the first Christian Pentecost.

In the hierarchy of *sacraments* that include chrismation, penance, holy orders, marriage, and the anointing of the sick, however, Eucharist and baptism are preeminent. Yet, the Orthodox churches do not restrict sacramental action to these rites alone. The blessing of the waters at Epiphany, for example, or such minor blessings as the blessing of the harvest's first fruit and the labor of the home make tangible Orthodox belief in the potential sanctity of matter and material existence, though nothing expresses this religious conviction more than Orthodoxy's attitude toward the icon. Not only is the icon integral to prayer and worship, a sacred object to be censed by priests, carried in procession, kissed by the faithful, an object before which prayer is offered or candles burned or prostrations made. According to Nicaea II and unwavering Orthodox conviction, the icon is a Spirit-bearing piece of material reality with power to sanctify. Whether the icon is honored at home or in the church, Orthodox regard it as a point of access to the sacred, an opening into heaven where the worshipper comes into the presence of the sacred persons there depicted.

Christian Community
and the Church

Orthodoxy puts special emphasis on the doctrine of the *Trinity* as the key to what is fundamental about God. According to its theology, the essential mystery of ultimate reality is the mystery of three divine persons

Icons like this one of the Virgin and child focus Orthodox worship and devotion.

in a perfect union of love—the Father, Son, and Holy Spirit, each God in every sense, yet each fully personal. But for Orthodoxy this ultimate mystery is not just a subject of theological speculation. Because humans are said to bear the stamp of the divine image, as a kind of interior icon, they too are essentially social, personal beings whose human potential is only realizable in the context of community. Orthodoxy's Trinitarian theology thus shapes its understanding of Christian community as a fellowship of diverse individuals united in freedom, mutuality and love. But Christian community, conceived as the church, is also a hierarchical and sacramental society presided over by a bishop. A symbol of unity and authority, the bishop within his own diocese is charged with teaching, discipline, and pastoral care. A priest with sacerdotal powers, the bishop is the chief celebrant at the church's Eucharistic worship.

It has been said that, where the bishop is in the midst of his people, there is the church. Certainly, the twofold emphasis on bishop and people is an important characteristic of Orthodoxy's view of the church and one that it shares with such early Christian leaders as Ignatius of Antioch (c. 35–c. 107). Like Ignatius, Orthodoxy believes that the local congregation where the people assemble around their bishop and celebrate the Eucharist constitutes the church in its full integrity. Yet, the local bishop is not a bishop apart from his fellow bishops. Reflecting the *ecclesiology* (teaching about the church) of another early Christian church theorist, Orthodoxy holds with Cyprian of Carthage (d. 258) that "the episcopate is a single whole, in which each bishop enjoys full possession." There is, Cyprian believed, but one collective ministry in the church, yet the bishops severally possess and exercise that single authority.

For Orthodoxy, therefore, governance of the church does not reside in any one bishop, a bishop of the bishops such as the pope in Roman Catholicism. Church governance is entrusted rather to the collective wisdom and decision making of the assembly of Christian bishops in *synod* or council. Only such a collectivity, guided by the Holy Spirit, is guarantor of the church's continuity, unity, and holiness. History and practice have established, however, that Orthodox monastic communities like the famous communities of Mount Athos in Greece also function within Orthodoxy as a source of spiritual and moral authority. Historically, monasticism has been Orthodoxy's first line of defense against attacks on its faith and practice. It continues to be the setting for the development and cultivation of the mystical prayer that permeates Orthodox religious experience and even its understanding of worship. And it is to monastic communities that Orthodox churches turn when they require persons to serve as their bishops.

ROMAN CATHOLICISM

Profile

The word *catholic* was used by Augustine in the fourth century to differentiate normative from sectarian Christianity. The Catholic church, the bishop of Hippo held, is a universal church whose members are geographically dispersed throughout the known world. The fifth-century monk, Vincent of Lerin, further elaborated the word's meaning according to the triple standard of ecumenicity, antiquity, and consensus. In the formula known as the Vincentian Canon, *Catholic* was said to be that faith held always, everywhere, and by everyone. And, when we judge Roman Catholicism by this standard, it is clear why Catholics have taken this name for themselves. Not only is the Catholic church an ancient church whose beginnings are at the dawn of the Christian religion and whose first bishop, according to Roman tradition, was none other than Peter, the first of the apostles. Roman Catholicism approaches more nearly than any other Vincent's test of ecumenicity and consensus. With over 900 million baptized members, Roman Catholics are more numerous than the Orthodox, more numerous than the Protestants taken together, more numerous than even Islam, the largest world religion after Christianity. Nevertheless, Catholicism's demographic center even today coincides with its historic center of gravity in central and southern Europe and in the countries or regions of South and North America where Europeans successfully transplanted it. In Asia, on whose margins Christianity began, Catholics make up only 3 percent of the population and only 1 percent if we exclude the Phillippines. And in Africa, where Catholic missions have been more successful, it remains a minority faith with less than half the number of Muslims on that continent.

The designation *Catholic*, as it is commonly applied, has still another—and for Roman Catholics indispensable—meaning. To be Catholic is to be a Christian in union with the *pope*. Indeed, for many non-Catholics the pope is the most familiar symbol of the faith; for many others he is all that is known of Catholicism. Yet, it must be admitted that for many non-Catholics this figure is as enigmatic as the religion itself. Even Ronald Eyre, narrator of a popular film series on the world religions titled *The Long Search*, seems unable to make much of this religious leader who combines in a curious way the roles of spiritual leader and absolute sovereign of a tiny independent state in the heart of Rome, Vatican City. Yet, this blending of roles in a figure who is quite clearly basic to Catholic religious experience is not unprecedented. The Dalai Lama, spiritual leader of Tibetan Buddhism, was virtual ruler of Tibet until 1959 and even today is the political head of the Tibetan government in exile. As the reincarnation of Avalokitesvara, the bodhisattva (a fully enlightened being) who personifies the Buddhist virtue of compassion, he is also the object of devotion and the focus of religious experience. Though Catholics make no claim that the pope is a divine being, it is clear that he too is viewed as something more than another religious leader, albeit the leader of the world's largest religious fellowship of believers. For Catholics, the pope focuses and embodies in a special way Christ's presence and continuing activity on earth.

For a devout Catholic, a journey to Rome can prove to be a pilgrimage. A papal blessing before Saint Peter's or a papal audience within the Lateran Palace is a religious act. Yet, as the Dalai Lama presides over the religious and temporal affairs of Tibetans, so the pope exercises supreme authority over the affairs of the church of which he is head. By virtue of his unique episcopal office, he possesses "full power of jurisdiction over the universal church both in matters of faith and morals and in matters of discipline and government." He is bishop of Rome but among bishops he is a bishop of bishops, in the words of one Catholic theologian "a bishop of the whole church."

Yet, the pope exercises his oversight of the church with the advice and through a hierarchy of patriarchs, archbishops, and bishops who reside as a rule in geographically defined areas known as dioceses. The synod of bishops, a geographically representative body of bishops, also assists the pope in carrying forward the church's worldwide mission. Much of the day-to-day work of the church, however, is conducted by the Roman Curia, the resident Roman *cardinals* who make up the pope's personal staff and function as agents of papal government. Described as the right hand of popes, the Curia conducts church business, reviews candidacy for episcopal office, monitors Catholic doctrine and practice, and promotes dialogue with other Christian churches and with non-Christians among its many formal tasks. And in keeping with the political character of the papacy, the Curia also assists with the government of Vatican City's internal and external affairs.

Salvation and Theological Beliefs

The interior of a Catholic church has its focal point in an altar and, above the altar or behind it on the wall, a crucifix. As the symbol of Christ's suffering and death, the crucifix underscores the sacrificial character of the *Mass*. Carried in procession, worn by members of religious orders as a part of the habit, attached to the rosary, used in administering liturgical blessings, displayed in Catholic hospitals, schools, charitable establishments, and in Catholic homes, the crucifix testifies also to the prominence of sacrificial suffering in popular Catholic devotion. The symbol for this suffering also compresses, as only symbols can, the essential Catholic understanding of redemption. In a drama that opens with the world's creation and Adam's fall, the crucifix stands at the center, regarded by Catholics as an emblem of both God's creative love and of his eternal justice. According to Anselm's classical theological formulation, God's loving purpose, a purpose evident in the creation of the world, is steadfast, yet eternal justice will not be deflected. Adam's disobedience, his affront to God's infinite honor, thus incurred an infinite debt requiring infinite satisfaction. It was for this reason, according to Anselm, that God became incarnate "as Jesus Christ. As human, Jesus was able to offer the "satisfaction" that humans owed and that only a human can make, but as God, Jesus was great enough to pay humanity's infinite debt. And thus in the suffering of the incarnate God, God's righteousness and infinite justice were vindicated; his creative purpose, manifest decisively as a redemptive love that offers itself in perfect obedience, was fulfilled.

Anselm's is a classic statement of the Catholic conception of the Incarnation and its role in salvation. Augustine was also immensely influential in the formulation of the western church's belief that salvation is the *justification* of sinners, according to Paul in his New Testament letters an act whereby God forgives and reconciles sinners to himself. We should recall that the East selected other New Testament redemption themes. Among the Orthodox churches, salvation is a process of deification and transfiguration, and original sin is a condition leading to death, a sickness or an infection of being. But influenced by early Jewish-Christian legalism and by the judicial orientation of ancient Roman thought and religious practice, the Roman church tended to formulate its doctrine of salvation much as Anselm had in *Cur Deus Homo*, in judicial terms appropriate to a court of law. Adam's sin had been a grievous fault, a defiance of God's justice, a primal crime against God's honor, and salvation required justification as a condition of a renewed fellowship between God and human beings. On this, Roman Catholics and Protestants agree, resembling one another more than they resemble the churches of Eastern Orthodoxy. But Protestants differ from Catholics in their understanding of the meaning and terms of justification.

Catholic theology emphasizes that the process of being made right with God entails the removal of sin and the regeneration of the soul which makes the believer holy and pleasing to God. This new life is imparted to believers by the Holy Spirit who is the agent of a sanctifying *grace* that blots out sin and renews life. This grace, which Catholics regard as a free and unmerited gift of God, is responsible for the new and higher disposition of the Christian. It is the vital principle of Christian holiness or *sanctification* and is the possession of the whole person, of the mind, will, and affections. It is this sanctifying grace that causes Christians to turn to God and away from sin, but with a characteristic Catholic emphasis—which Roman Catholics share with other Catholic traditions—this conversion or turning is gradual and progressive, a movement from "grace to grace." It is in this spirit that the Catholic Reformation's Council of Trent rejected Luther's claims that salvation is by faith alone and that justification entails a radical and sudden conversion.

Catholics insist that the human response to grace is progressive and mediated in and through the human response to it and that sanctification is a lifelong endeavor. Yet, the Catholic position on the importance of salutary works is misrepresented if we do not recognize that grace is operative in the effect as well as in the cause. Catholics, for example, think of *faith* as one of the effects of grace, a theological virtue along with hope and charity. According to the classic definition formulated by Thomas Aquinas, faith is an intellectual assent given under the impulse of the will to revealed truth. Yet, the provision made for this assent helps us see better just how Catholics hold grace and works, and reason and revelation, in a creative and cooperative union. According to Catholic theology, the mind does not embrace revealed truth because it is intrinsically evident to the natural light of reason, even though there are certain religious truths like the existence of God that are open to ordinary human reason. Knowledge of revealed truth is supernatural knowledge and the faith that apprehends such truth is attributable to grace and the authority of God who is the revealer. It is by grace that faith—the virtue considered by Catholics to be the beginning of salvation—enlightens the mind as to what is to be believed and what is to be done on the Christian's journey heavenward. But progress in holiness, leading ultimately to a heavenly vision of God and irrevocable union with him, comes too through participation in the sacraments of the church.

Worship

Liturgical worship, the official public worship of the Catholic church, is the special title used for the administration of the Eucharist and the other six sacraments. As such it is the instrument Catholics most frequently employ in expressing and communicating their experience of God. Through a rich, varied, and often complex pattern of ritual gesture, word, and material symbol, the liturgy is capable of expressing the whole range of religious sentiment and of commemorating every significant event of human life. Birth, adolescence, marriage, religious vocation, sickness and death—all the great moments of human passage or decision are marked by the church's sacramental rites and carried forward with the assistance of sacramental grace. Thanksgiving, praise, adoration, petition, intercession, penitence, and forgiveness—all are voiced in the church's liturgical services.

Yet, of the seven official sacraments of the Roman church, the premier act of worship and public prayer is the Eucharistic service of the Mass. Here is the touchstone of Catholic religious experience and the key to the Christian drama as the Roman church embodies it. Here, above all, is God's redemptive activity in the self-oblation and sacrifice of Jesus, an offering that the church regards as contemporary to Christians in the Eucharistic sacrifice of the altar. On the altar, Catholics believe and openly declare that the bread and wine are made from the same body broken on Calvary and the same blood spilled, and in this bloodless form the unique self-offering of Golgatha is reenacted.

In this central Catholic sacrament, Christ is thus held to be actually present in the symbols of bread and wine—in a manner Catholics explain as *transubstantiation*—and in this form Christ receives the worship of the faithful. The faithful are able to approach him in the reserved sacrament of consecrated bread outside the context of Eucharistic worship as well. Kept in a receptacle called the tabernacle, the Eucharistic bread provides a focus for meditation and prayer. Offered for public viewing in a receptacle called a monstrance, it is carried in procession. Placed on the altar during ceremonies known as the Benediction of the Blessed Sacrament and the Exposition of the Blessed Sacrament, the sacramental bread is the object of devotion and adoration. Catholic worship also invites participation in the sacrifice made visible on the altar. Of course, there are Catholics with a special calling to a life of sacrificial devotion, members of the church who are pledged by monastic vows to the religious life. Yet, the offering of alms or money gifts assimilate the lay Catholic to the sacrifice of the Mass. And the bringing of the bread and wine to the altar by representatives of the people symbolizes for all Catholics a vocation to obedient sacrifice.

The Eucharist is also a sacrament, a spiritual food that nourishes the whole body of believers and strengthens each member in the divine life on which each embarks at baptism. And, together with baptism, this sacrament is the church's principal one. Yet, Roman Catholicism regards five other sacramental rites and signs as instrumental in advancing the Christian life in its progress toward ultimate salvation. Confirmation is a rite of initiation and regeneration along with baptism and Eucharist; reconciliation (or penance) is the rite for the forgiveness of postbaptismal sins and is sometimes called the second baptism; the anointing of the sick is offered for spiritual strengthening and health; the sacrament of orders requires the imposition of the bishop's hand and confers the grace and powers of priesthood; marriage is the sacrament of the Christian family, whose model is Christ's unity with and love for the church. Authority for these seven sacraments, Catholics believe, derives directly from Christ's institution; their validity requires the administration of an official agent of the church. Priests, as authorized ministers, are empowered by holy orders to preside at these sacramental rites, though the efficacy of the rite is independent of the spiritual worthiness of the minister. Catholic sacraments, it is believed, communicate God's grace when they are duly performed because God is working in them.

The liturgical changes instituted at the Second Vatican Council are very much a part of the story of Catholic worship today. And, while the council held that no substantive alterations of "ancient doctrine" were made, it revived elements of early Christian worship which inevitably brought about significant shifts in emphasis. The restoration of certain classical forms of early church worship, for example, moved Roman Catholic worship closer in theory to Orthodoxy. The council's assigning Scripture a more extensive role in Christian devotion and in the church's preaching together with its disposition to speak of faith as an act of loyalty to Christ affirmed elements of worship congenial to Protestants.

The reforms that affected the way lay Catholics worship on a continuing basis were the most apparent and often the most controversial of the council's achievements. The Mass, formerly celebrated uniformly throughout the Catholic world in Latin, was now recited or sung in the language of the people by priests who faced the people. And the people, for whom a more passive role had earlier been assigned, were now encouraged to be active participants. To this end, congregational singing was reinstituted; the ritual "kiss of peace," indicated in modern usage by a handshake, was reintroduced as a communal gesture; and the custom whereby representatives of the community presented the bread and wine at the altar renewed the corporate character of the Eucharistic offering and oblation. The sacrament of reconciliation was also restructured to allow for a common confession set within the framework of Scripture reading, a homily, and hymns. These, and other changes, had the effect of bringing Catholic sacraments and worship into a more direct relation to the life of the people where they function more evidently as instruments for a gradual conversion and transformation of the Christian existence.

Vatican II and the Church

The monarchical and judicial ideas so important in the social organization of imperial Rome left a deep imprint on the Roman church's historic self-understanding. Reflecting this understanding, Catholics conceived of the church judicially as a hierarchically structured society, professing one faith and administering divinely instituted sacraments under lawful pastors, chief of whom was the bishop of Rome. We saw in Chapter 6 that there were those who wished the western church to adopt a conciliar form of church order and authority; others like Wycliffe and Huss sought to define the church in terms of its spiritual rather than its governmental function. Yet, the concept of the church as a visible society in which judicial and spiritual functions coincide won favor at the Council of Trent. At the First Vatican Council in the last century, the declaration of papal infallibility further contributed to the pyramidal conception of the church as a visible, supernatural, and "indefectible society" presided over by the Roman Pontiff.

The twentieth century, however, signaled a desire to restore elements of Catholic ecclesiology obscured by the definitions of Trent and Vatican I. The effect of Pius XII's encyclical *Mystici Corporis* (1943), for example, was to reaffirm the church's spiritual character as a sacramental reality, a source of divine grace through its teachings, laws, and rites. A still more revolutionary shift in Catholicism's view of the church was set forth in the deliberations of the Second Vatican Council convened by John XXIII on October 11, 1962. Making use of the biblical image of the church as the people of God, the council fathers stressed the equality, dignity, and common vocation of all by virtue of baptism and the priesthood of the faithful—both grounds for an expanded lay role in the church's worship and mission in the world. And, together with the image of the people of God, the ancient image of the pilgrim church popular since Vatican II enhanced further the historical nature of the church as a sign of God's Kingdom in the midst of the present age.

Of importance too, was the enlarged role given the bishops in governing and guiding the church. Evidently intended to counterbalance the First Vatican Council's exclusive preoccupation with the papacy, Vatican II advanced the principle of episcopal collegiality and the right of bishops to participate in full papal authority. Though none of the Roman Pontiff's prerogatives were abridged and no claim was made for equality between pope and the college of bishops, the important conciliar document *On the Constitution of the Church* (*Lumen Gentium*) corrects an earlier tendency to view the pope in isolation from his fellow bishops. The council declared rather that the pope, together with the other bishops, has supreme authority and power over the universal church, a declaration with the potential of broadening decision making within the church and extending that decision making to the bishops of the whole world.

ANGLICANISM

Profile

Christianity arrived in England probably not later than the early third century, and historian Steven Neill speculates that there already may have been Christians among the Roman soldiers there in the second century. We do know that three British bishops traveled to the Council of Arles in 314 and that Pope Gregory the Great dispatched the Roman monk Augustine to Kent in the sixth century. On his arrival, Augustine gained the support of King Ethelbert and his Christian queen and in Kent founded Canterbury and became its first archbishop. Yet, in spite of close ties with the church of Rome from its inception, the church of England exhibited an independent national spirit which characterizes it still, now some four and a half centuries after King Henry VIII severed relations with Rome. And it is this English spirit that accounts for the temper or mood that stamps Anglican churches in North America, Asia, and Africa as peculiarly and recognizably Anglican.

A global family of autonomous churches, Anglicanism is perhaps best thought of along the lines of the loose association of countries that make up the British Commonwealth of Nations. [2] As a worldwide communion, Anglican churches are united in shared traditions and a common loyalty to the honorary head of the Church of England, the archbishop of Canterbury. And the closest one comes to an official definition of Anglicanism comes from the 1930 international Lambeth Conference of Anglican bishops. The bishops described their communion as "a fellowship within the One Holy Catholic and Apostolic Church." They further described their church tradition (called Episcopalianism in the United States) as a federation of national and regional churches in fellowship with the See of Canterbury, dedicated to the faith and worship set forth in The Book of Common Prayer, and bound together by the counsel and guidance of its bishops in conference. Within this broad definition, there is a patience among Anglicans with diversity of religious practice and opinion, a fact which makes it difficult to generalize about this communion of Christians.

Worship

Essentially a conservative church tradition, inclined to "make haste slowly," Anglicanism has pursued a middle course, a *via media*, between Roman Catholicism and Protestantism. The result is a blending of traditions in a national church that is at once Catholic and Protestant in its theology, ecclesiology, and worship. Its Protestant heritage is evident in its love of the Bible, its use of the Bible as the standard of faith and preaching, and the role the Bible plays in the devotion and prayer of its members. The evangelical movement of the eighteenth century represented by revivalists like John Wesley (himself an Anglican priest) also left an enduring impression on Anglicanism, especially among those Anglicans identified as low church. Among other features, these Anglicans assign importance to conversion, to the experience of personal reassurance, to a personal relationship with God through Jesus Christ, and to dedicated Christian service in the world. The high church or Anglo-Catholic party represents the end of the Anglican spectrum that most nearly approaches Roman Catholicism. Anglicans of this persuasion especially esteem the institutional life of the church. They regard church authority and the episcopacy as essential Catholic features of the Christian church; they believe that the liturgy and the sacraments are the indispensable elements of public worship; they make use of ascetic practices like fasting; and they regard meditation and mystical prayer as important devotional forms.

Anglicans of all persuasions, however, are agreed on the Book of Common Prayer as the principal instrument of public worship. The official and prescribed book of services, the Prayer Book was first prepared by Archbishop Thomas Cranmer in 1549 and has been subsequently revised, most recently by a 1955 liturgical commission of the Church of England. It contains forms for the administration of the sacraments, the daily offices of "Morning and Evening Prayer," the Psalter, and instructions for the three cycles of prayer used in connection with daily offices, saints and feast days, and the seasons of the Christian year. Yet, the Prayer Book is for Anglicans much more than a religious service book. It embodies the spirit of Anglicanism; it is a repository of basic Anglican values; and it is a source of Anglican doctrine.

The English are famous as well for music and composers of religious music, and the beauty of Anglican worship is enhanced by a distinguished and rich tradition of hymnody and choral music. The use of the ancient creeds, prayers, and liturgical patterns of worship express the Catholic heritage of the early church to which Anglicanism aspires. The two sacraments that Anglicans regard as necessary to salvation are baptism and the Eucharist, though the other sacramental rites are used as well. Like the Roman Catholics, the practice of infant baptism is customary and the form is by infusion, that is, by the pouring of water over the head. The structure of the Eucharistic rite follows closely the Roman Catholic rite, but Anglicans do not ordinarily employ the doctrine of transubstantiation to explain Christ's presence in sacrament or conceive of the rite as a sacrifice along Roman Catholic lines. Like the Orthodox whom they resemble in many respects, Anglicans are less concerned than Roman Catholics with dogmatic clarity and theological definition, and are more inclined to inclusive formulas that allow for a comprehension and diversity of theological perspective.

Church Unity

The catholic spirit is best described as inclusive and comprehensive, and the history of the English church gives special meaning to that spirit. From its beginnings in the sixteenth century, the Church of England combined elements of Protestantism with its ancient Catholic heritage. Yet, as Anglicanism spread abroad to English colonies in North America, Africa, India, and the Far East, it became clear too that the English genius for comprehension had applicability to the federation of autonomous Anglican churches in diverse national cultures. It was thus that in 1888 the bishops of these churches, meeting at the Lambeth Palace on the Thames, agreed on four principles which served subsequently as the basis of fellowship among Anglicans around the globe. Known as the Lambeth Quadrilateral, these articles of conviction affirmed Scripture as the standard of faith, the Apostles' and the Nicene Creeds as the sufficient statement of belief, baptism and the Lord's Supper as necessary for salvation, and the historic succession of bishops as the true constitution of the church. On this last point of church polity, Anglicanism resembles Orthodoxy more than Roman Catholicism in its view that the bishops have independent jurisdiction within their dioceses and that the clergy and laity are active partners with the bishops in the governance of the church.

Anglicanism's understanding of itself as a comprehensive tradition, standing between Catholicism and Protestantism and embracing a diversity of the autonomous churches within its own communion, may account as well for the early and active role it played in this century's *ecumenical movement*. It was, for example, the Anglican bishop Charles Henry Brent (1862–1929) who persuaded the General Convention of the Protestant Episcopal Church to convene a World Conference on Faith and Order at Lausanne, Switzerland in 1927. Brent served as president of the conference that numbered more than one hundred delegates from Protestant and Orthodox churches and which became a part of the World Council of Churches in 1948.

Anglicans have also entered into interchurch relations with a number of other churches—with the united churches of South India, of North India, of Pakistan, and of Sri Lanka, and with the Old Catholic churches in Europe and the United States, the Lusitanian Church of Poland, the Spanish Reformed Episcopal Church, the Philippine Independent Catholic Church, and the Mar Thoma Syrian Church in India. Finally, Anglicans have actively sought dialogue partnerships with the Lutherans, and in 1966 Pope Paul VI met with the archbishop of Canterbury, Michael Ramsey, to lay the foundation for the Anglican-Roman Catholic International Commission which initiated and continues conversation on matters of doctrine and practice basic to Christian unity.

SUMMARY

Catholic Christianity includes several different church traditions and reaches back in time to the church of the first centuries. Indeed, all the Catholic church traditions understand themselves as being in some way a continuation and a contemporary expression of this ancient Catholic heritage. All, for example, claim a continuity of ministry through a succession of bishops with the ministry of the apostles and their successors, the bishops of the earliest churches. Roman Catholicism stresses the ministry of the apostle Peter as the first bishop of Rome; Orthodox and Anglicans hold to a corporate, collegial ministry of bishops as successors of the apostles.

All also take the doctrinal formulas and creeds of the first ecumenical councils as sources of authoritative Christian teaching. Orthodox assign special importance to the first seven ecumenical councils and believe that what the council fathers taught is infallible and unalterable Christian truth; Anglicans regard the Apostles' and the Nicene Creeds as sufficient statements of belief. Roman Catholics adhere to ancient creeds but teach that papal infallibility also empowers the popes to define doctrine in matters of faith and morals.

Finally, all the Catholic church traditions assign a special prominence to sacramental worship. Roman Catholics restrict the number of sacraments to seven and are more definitionally precise in specifying the manner in which Christ is present in the consecrated bread and wine of the Supper. Orthodox, on the other hand, have a less exact, more fluid understanding of sacraments and of the capacity of all material existence to communicate holy reality. Anglicans look on baptism and the Eucharist as the sacraments necessary for salvation, though Anglo-Catholics in particular use all the traditional sacraments and sacramentals.

We found that theological perspective gave further variety to Catholic Christianity and the forms its worship assumes. Orthodoxy takes the icon to be central and sees salvation as a process of deification and transfiguration. Roman Catholicism finds in Christ's sacrifice the model for Christian living and in the sacraments the beginning and nourishment of a supernatural life commenced at baptism. And, as a bridge church standing between Catholicism and Protestantism, Anglicanism manifests the Catholic principle of comprehension which it expresses particularly in its quest for Christian unity and its work for interchurch cooperation, fellowship, and dialogue. Alike and different, in short, the church traditions discussed in this chapter are a witness to the variety of forms Catholic Christianity assumes. In the next chapter we examine Protestant Christianity, a form of Christianity, if anything, still more varied.

REVIEW AND REFLECTION

1. In what countries are the churches of Orthodoxy largely found?
2. Describe Orthodoxy's understanding of redemption as deification. How is this idea of deification related to Orthodoxy's views on creation, the fall, the Resurrection, and other key Christian doctrines?
3. What are the major features of Orthodox worship? What role do Orthodox assign the icon in worship?
4. How does the doctrine of the Trinity help us understand Orthodoxy's view of Christian community and the church?
5. What are several meanings of the word *catholic* as they apply to Roman Catholicism?
6. In Roman Catholicism the pope functions in several different capacities. Can you describe this religious figure and his central importance for Roman Catholicism?
7. Why did we say that the crucifix is so basic to Roman Catholic experience and to its understanding of salvation?
8. What is the Roman Catholic understanding of grace and sacra-

ments? Compare this understanding with Orthodoxy's view on sacraments.

9. What changes did Vatican II institute?
10. Why did we say that Anglicanism is a bridge church?
11. What is Anglicanism's contribution to Christian unity? What makes this church tradition especially suited for this role?

END NOTES

1. The source for membership statistics is *Britannica Book of the Year, 1988* (Chicago: Encyclopedia Britannica, Inc., 1988).

2. The comparison was suggested by Stephen Neill, *Anglicanism*, 4th ed. (New York: Oxford University Press, 1978), p. 402.

SUGGESTED FURTHER READING

BENZ, ERNST. *The Orthodox Church: Its Thought and Life.* trans. Richard and Clara Winston. Garden City, NY: Anchor Books, 1963.

CUNNINGHAM, LAWRENCE. *The Catholic Experience.* Crossroad Publishing: New York, 1985.

CUNNINGHAM, LAWRENCE. *The Catholic Heritage.* Crossroad Publishing: New York, 1983.

FOUYAS, METHODIOS. *Orthodoxy, Roman Catholicism, and Anglicanism.* New York: Oxford University Press, 1972.

HATCHETT, MARION J. *Sanctifying Life, Time and Space: An Introduction to Liturgical Study:* New York: Seabury Press, 1982.

MCKENZIE, JOHN. *The Roman Catholic Church.* Garden City, NJ: Doubleday, 1971.

NEILL, STEVEN. *Anglicanism.* 4th ed. New York: Oxford University Press, 1978.

WARE, TIMOTHY. *The Orthodox Church.* Rev. ed. New York: Pelican, 1980.

ZERNOV, NICOLAS. "Christianity: the Eastern Schism and the Eastern Orthodox Church." in *The Concise Encyclopedia of Living Faiths.* ed. Robert Charles Zaehner. Boston: Beacon Press, 1967.

11 | Forms of Protestant Christianity

INTRODUCTION

Protestantism is remarkable for its variety as well as for its adaptability to diverse historical, social, and cultural circumstances. It would be a mistake, therefore, for us to attempt to specify a single pattern of belief, worship, church order, ministry, or life that is characteristic of all Protestant groups. There is in fact a great variety of Protestant churches, some of which we examine in this chapter. But so that we do not get lost in the diversity of churches and traditions, the church traditions have been arranged into groups that share a common history or that bear a family resemblance. We include in one group, for example, the classical Reformation churches because of their common sixteenth-century heritage. We bring Methodists, Holiness, and Pentecostal churches together because of family traits.

It is possible to speak of all these variations as Protestant only if we can discover certain normative beliefs and values that are common to them all and that can be said to be distinctly and distinguishably Protestant. And so we need to ask ourselves also about the principles that shape this form of Christianity. We need to ask, for example, what is meant by the phrase ''the Protestant spirit''? When we read of the central Protestant principles of faith, grace, and Scripture, we need to ask how these principles help us understand what is basic to Protestantism's understanding of sin and salvation. How do these principles help us discover what is basic to Protestant worship? These questions guide our discussion of Protestant diversity in two ways. They help us identify and isolate what is characteristic about Protestantism. And they help us locate the normative center of Protestant Christianity, thereby providing our discussion of individual Protestant churches and church families a stable point of reference.

PROFILE OF PROTESTANTISM

The Protestant Spirit

Protestantism is the second major form of Christianity within the tradition of the western church. Yet, Protestantism is not today nor has it ever been a denominator for a single church group. Just as we spoke of Catholicisms in the last chapter, we will speak of Protestantisms in this one, for Protestantism is the name used for a group of very different church traditions which nevertheless share a common history and ethos. For the most part, we can say that Protestantism's history began with a reform movement and a schism within the sixteenth-century Roman Catholic church. When Protestants celebrate this heritage on Reformation Sunday, they remember in particular the German monk whose name is perhaps most often associated with this form of Christianity. They commemorate Martin Luther and his defiance of pope and emperor in the name of the Bible and personal conscience. Yet, fairness requires that the reformer Ulrich Zwingli receive credit as well for launching an independent reformation among the Swiss. Others like John Calvin joined the revolt against the Roman church, and before two decades had lapsed from the time of Luther's Ninety-five Theses (1517) much of northern Europe, England, and Scotland had separated from Roman Catholicism. The reformation churches also divided among themselves into four major church traditions—Lutheran, Reformed, Anabaptist, and Anglican (see Chapter 5). Much that we know as Protestant today derives directly or indirectly from these churches.

These early Protestant churches commonly referred to themselves as evangelicals or reformed, but the name *Protestant* has come to be the most frequently applied name for the Christians who set themselves in opposition to ecclesiastical and papal authority. Originally, the name was applied to the Lutheran princes and burgers who objected to the limitations imposed on the new evangelical faith at the Diet of Speyer (1529). At that imperial legislative assembly, six Lutheran princes and fourteen Lutheran cities formally "protested" the proceedings that prohibited the propagation of their faith within the Catholic territories of the empire. These Protestants, as they were subsequently called, followed Luther's example when at Worms he refused to renounce his teaching though church and emperor pressed him to do so. And, in what on the surface seems but a political gesture from which Protestants derive their name, the evangelical party at Speyer demonstrated the meaning of what is regarded as a fundamental "Protestant principle." They exemplified the critical spirit of Hebrew prophecy that says no! to human authority and institutions in the name of a transcendent God.

For Protestantism the recovery of this prophetic heritage as a basic feature of the Christian faith also led to Protestantism's commitment to reform and renewal—a commitment that explains Protestantism's vitality and its tendency also to splinter and form new church groups. It was, for example, a belief that reform was progressing too slowly that prompted the Anabaptists to separate from the Reformed church of Zurich. It was a Puritan impatience with the Church of England that gave birth to the seventeenth-century *free churches*—the Congregationalists, the Baptists, and the Quakers. Methodism developed as a corrective to the cold formalism of the eighteenth-century English church. And in nineteenth-century America the Protestant spirit and frontier expanse combined as a powerful stimulus to new church groups, utopian Shakers, restoration movement churches like the Disciples of Christ, and millennialists like the Seventh-Day Adventists.

True also of Protestantism's prophetic no! is its obverse, the yes! that is a witness to the living revelation of God in Jesus Christ. This yes accounts for the conviction with which Protestants endeavor to bring the Christian message into a creative relation with changing historical and cultural circumstance. It helps us understand, for example, Protestant liberalism's efforts to accommodate the Christian gospel to current forms of thought and experience. It is the "yes" that stands for the creative protest registered by the social gospel movement at the beginning of this century and a little later by the neoorthodox Protestant thinkers who sought to balance liberalism's affirmation of contemporary experience with a biblical sense of sin and judgment. The insistently vigorous Bible preaching of modern evangelicals and fundamentalists is in its own way also a Protestant affirmative. But there is no more evident expression of the Protestant commitment to profess or witness than that of the early Protestant settlers to these shores, and somewhat later the Protestant missionaries of the last century.

It was because of a commitment to witness that Protestantism first found its way in the seventeenth century to North America, a continent that was to be its second home. Today, with nearly 95 million in North America, Protestantism has a slightly larger concentration of these Christians than the Europe of Protestant beginnings. But it was in connection with the efforts of missionaries like William Carey (1761–1834) in India, Adinoram Judson (1788–1850) in Burma, James Hudson Taylor (1832–1905) in China, and David Livingston (1813–1873) in Africa that Protestantism, until the nineteenth century an essentially western and European/American form of Christianity, became a genuinely worldwide religious movement with some 332 million members.

In the mission field, however, Protestants learned that the historic differences in theology and church order meant little to the nonwestern peoples they sought to convert. And thus in the interest of preaching and teaching the gospel of Christ, Protestant churches began to rethink their confessional differences and church orders in the interest of cooperation and Christian unity. Christened the ecumenical movement, this quest for unity became an institutional reality at the World Missionary Conference at Edinburgh in 1910. The missionary conference at Jerusalem (1928) and the one at Madras, India (1938) further contributed to the shape of world Protestantism by making the "new churches" of Asia and Africa full partners in the ecumenical enterprise. Then in 1948 at Amsterdam, Protestants established the World Council of Churches and thus put the ecumenical desire for interchurch cooperation on a permanent institutional base. Yet, it is important to keep in mind that Protestantism even in this ecumenical key is a unity of diverse churches. What they have in common is important, but no more important for our discussion than what differentiates and defines these churches.

Salvation and Related Beliefs

Protestantism is associated with the personal dimension of religious experience. Protestant hymns evoke a personal devotion to Jesus. The Jesus of popular Protestant art invites love, trust, intimacy, and fellowship. He is often pictured in the quiet of a garden, a setting associated with intimacy and divine presence in both the Old and New Testament; or he is portrayed as one who approaches and is near, as one knocking at the door. The Protestant fondness for the "praying hands" indicates too the importance of personal prayer. The open Bible points to the central role of private devotional reading and to the importance of a personal encounter with God's Word. Even when Protestants worship together in a church or at a football stadium, surrounded perhaps by hundreds or thousands, they conceive of worship in personal terms as an inward hearing of the gospel publicly proclaimed, as a personal decision for Christ publicly announced, or as a personal conviction of salvation attested to openly. And, though Protestant churches differ in form of worship, *church polity*, and theology, there is a virtual consensus that the rescue from the unsatisfactoriness of human existence is a profoundly personal experience. Deliverance from sin and the wages of sin, Protestants hold, is the effect of a divinely initiated forgiveness and a relationship of intimacy and trust with a personal savior, Jesus Christ.

Redemption from sin, a personal conviction of forgiveness, and a sense of having entered into communion with a holy presence are emphases deeply rooted in Protestant experience. John Wesley discovered them in his own conversion at a religious meeting in Aldersgate Street, London. Wesley noted in his journal that "I felt my heart strangely warmed. I felt I did trust in Christ, Christ alone for my salvation; and an assurance was given me that He had taken away my sins, even mine, and saved me from the law of sin and death." The repeated emphasis on the first person singular is typical of spiritual rebirth as Protestants experience and talk about it.

Typical too is Protestantism's paradoxical association of unworthiness and acceptance with the revivifying power of a holy presence. As in Wesley's case, the experience of the holy combines elements of amazement and surprise as well as a profound sense of gratitude. And, by contrast to a Catholic emphasis on a gradual growth in grace through priestly mediation and ritual word and gesture, Protestant conversion is sudden, unexpected, and often dramatic. It comes rather with the feeling of being personally and powerfully addressed by Scripture and gospel. It is through God's revealed Word enshrined in the Bible that sinners are ushered into the presence of the Holy and know themselves to be loved and accepted. It is by the force of the written and spoken word that the gospel of Jesus' life, death, and resurrection becomes real to the individual Christian. In our example above, Wesley felt the tide of God's grace rising within him while listening to a reading from Luther's preface to The Epistle to the Romans. And Luther was meditating on Romans 1:17 when he came to the conviction that "the righteousness of God is revealed by the gospel, namely, the passive righteousness with which merciful God justifies us by faith."

Those familiar with Protestant diversity will remind us that there is no one way that Protestants speak of or give doctrinal formulation to their experience of holy reality. And they would be justified in pointing to our own examples of Wesley and Luther. Whereas Wesley's conversion came as a gently rising tide, Luther's conversion arrived as a flood burst, breaking in on his consciousness, sweeping away all sense of defilement and guilt. And there are other striking variations on Protestant religious experience. The charismatic Pentecostals, to take a notable example, testify that the experiential knowledge of a holy presence arrives with explosive force, a baptism of fire manifest visibly in spontaneous movement and audibly in ecstatic speech. Doctrinal emphases vary as well, with some Protestants giving prominence to forgiveness and justification, others to acceptance and sanctification or personal holiness.

Yet, for all its diversity, basic Protestant experience and teaching point to a shared theological affirmation arising in connection with the awareness of personal sin and dependence that we have been speaking of.

Protestant theology holds that God is above all a transcendent, majestic, and sovereign reality. The Protestant intuition about the holy begins with the conviction that God is a mysterious, awesome, and holy reality in whose presence sinners are stricken with a personal sense of helplessness and unworthiness. In the preceding section we described how this theology has been formulated as the Protestant principle. There we said that God stands in judgment on every human authority and every institution. To this we should add that the belief that God is beyond every temporal limitation is also the cause of the Protestant suspicion of symbols and symbolic actions in worship and devotion and of persons and institutions as mediators of salvation. But finally, this suspicion comes back to the personal and experiential conviction that God exposes the human illusion of self-sufficiency. It was the pretension that human effort counted for something in salvation that prompted Luther to attack the Catholic belief that works must be added to grace for salvation. It was the belief that humans can contribute anything at all to salvation that spurred Calvin to elaborate his doctrine of predestination. For these Protestants and their modern-day descendants, salvation itself is a mystery whose source is the inscrutable will of God. What counts, Protestants over the centuries have held, is God's initiative and the trusting response of the believer.

Protestants use the word *grace* to describe this divinely initiated salvation. It is by grace that sin is forgiven and that sinners are brought into a new, personal relationship with the divine. Yet, Protestants teach that God not only initiates forgiveness but restores fellowship with humans. Salvation is by grace alone, that is, by grace and not by reason of any human effort, merit, or worth. Protestants hold also that, since grace is a spiritual gift freely bestowed on sinners, it is not a possession of the church and cannot be bound to the sacraments. Grace is pictured rather as something beyond human calculation, something that is surprising, wonderful, even bewildering. It is, in the words of a well-known Protestant hymn, an "amazing grace," amazing because it makes known at once human deficiency and helplessness, divine power, generosity, mercy, and love.

But, if grace is for Protestants essentially the expression for divinely initiated salvation, faith is the attitude of trust that expresses confidence in the power of grace. According to Protestantism, it is by grace through faith that salvation comes to sinners. It is by faith alone that sinners accept the gospel of Jesus Christ as a personal, saving gospel. It is by accepting grace and acknowledging God's initiative that sinners are liberated from the illusion of self-sufficiency, the root cause of sin and humanity's alienation from God. And thus freed from a compulsive preoccupation with personal salvation, a compulsion which Protestants associate with monasticism, the Christian is at liberty to turn outward in a loving concern for the needs of others.

The simplicity and natural light of this New England Church reflect a puritan emphasis on the spoken word.

Worship and Sacraments

Visit a Protestant church on any Sunday—or Saturday for the *sabbatarian* Protestants. You will have to go on Saturday to join the Seventh-Day Adventists for their corporate worship services. In all likelihood you will be greeted with a smile, an offered handshake, and a friendly welcome. Look around as you enter the space assigned for worship. What you see will vary from denomination to denomination, yet there will be clear clues that you are in a Protestant church. If you have found your way to a Quaker silent meeting, first impressions might be of natural light (Quakers tend not to use stained glass windows), of simplicity, and of facing rows of benches—qualities reminiscent of the sixteenth-century Flemish oil paintings of Jan Vermeer. You will discover many of these same qualities if you find your way to a white clapboard New England Congregational church. Natural light through transparent glass, a simplicity of furnishing, the orderly rows of pews oriented toward a pulpit—space here is nicely adapted to worship whose purpose is a personal, inward fellowship with God. The uncluttered interiors of these churches also create a space perfectly suited to preaching and hearing the word of Scripture. Standing in the pulpit, the minister's voice is easily audible as the Bible's meaning and truth are expounded and its application to daily life made apparent. Other Protestant churches are not as austere and as characteristically "puritan" as New England Congregational churches. Lutherans make more liberal use of liturgical colors, objects, and symbols in their churches and worship. All except the Quakers, however, regard Scripture as vital to worship and to the personal relationship with God that is the foundation of Protestant worship.

Protestant services of worship also may give the impression of confusing variety. Among the *free church* Protestants, worship is less structured, more spontaneous and informal, characterized by spirited preaching, lively congregational singing, free prayer, witnessing, and personal testimonials. The Pentecostal family of churches believe that a charismatic experience—a baptism of the Spirit and the gift of ecstatic speech—is an essential and authentic feature of Christian worship. Traditional, established Protestant churches, on the other hand, incline to set orders of worship. They do, of course, encourage congregational participation in worship through the singing of hymns, and in this they resemble the free churches. But, among the established churches, services of worship are more regular and formal. Characteristically, prayer is offered or led by the minister; Scripture from the Old and New Testaments is read, often according to a cycle prescribed by the lectionary; a prepared sermon probably substitutes for the *ex tempore* preaching of the free church; the offering is collected; a benediction said; and a closing, recessional hymn is sung. The observance of the Lord's Supper (the preferred Protestant name for the Eucharist) is also a part of the weekly service of worship among Protestant churches like the Disciples of Christ. Yet, frequency varies from a weekly to a monthly or quarterly or even an annual observance, and only a few Protestant churches like Quakers and the Salvation Army do not observe the rite at all.

From what we have said so far, however, it is not evident that even the majority of Protestants who make use of sacraments regard them as basic to Christian worship. We have seen, for example, that Protestants are more sparing than Catholics in the use of material symbols. The rich materiality of Orthodox worship, evident in the prominence of sacraments and *sacramentals* in the extensive use of nature symbolism, is not found here. For Protestants the primary medium of grace is the word of Scripture, confirmed inwardly by the Spirit and received in faith. What might be called the principle of parsimony [1] seems also to have application to the traditional seven sacraments of Roman Catholicism. Protestants recognize only baptism and the Lord's Supper as valid sacraments, and the two "gospel" sacraments, it is held, were expressly instituted and commanded by Jesus.

Protestants disagree with Roman Catholics on other issues as well. They reject Catholicism's doctrine of transubstantiation and the practice of reserving the consecrated bread. The Catholic beliefs that the Mass is a sacrifice that appeases God and that the celebration of the Mass fulfills a commandment and so is a meritorious act pleasing to God are regarded as unacceptable. Salvation, Protestants are quick to observe, is by grace alone. The Catholic teaching that grace is objectively available by reason of the sacrament's enactment (i.e. *ex opere operato*) is also unacceptable to Protestants. They teach rather that grace is free, surprising and always personal.

Yet in spite of the rejection of Roman Catholicism's sacramental theology, in spite even of Protestantism's orientation to auditory rather than sacramental worship and experience, most Protestants do believe sacraments to be basic to Christian worship. To be sure, they are firm in the belief that grace cannot be bound to sacraments. The grace that reconciles humans to God is deemed to be prior to and independent of every ritual action; the grace of the gospel of Jesus Christ is a free and unmerited gift, a gift that manifests the priority of God's action to every human response. It is thus in connection with God's gracious action as the revealed Word, the Word made flesh in Jesus and the word of Scripture, that sacraments have efficacy; only when sacraments are united with the Word are they instrumental in salvation. In the sacrament of the Lord's Supper, for example, the church proclaims the gospel of Jesus' death and resurrection, though not so much with words as with visible action. As Protestant theologian Robert McAfee Brown describes it, "the church does not just talk. It acts. It acts in the way its Lord acted. Since 'the Lord Jesus took bread . . . ' so does the church" [2].

We have seen that Protestants are far from unanimous over the meaning and application of the action. Lutherans understand communion as a rite for penitents. Others like the Disciples of Christ think of the act as a commemorative meal and a communion with Christ and in Christ with one another. Reformed and Presbyterian churches regard the sacrament as a declaration of God's good will toward forgiven sinners. Yet, in every instance, even among Lutherans who believe that Christ's body and blood are present "in, with, and under" the bread and wine, the Word takes precedence over the material symbolism of the rite.

The priority of the Word to sacrament is apparent also in Protestant baptism. Whereas Roman Catholicism teaches that the baptismal water has intrinsic regenerative power, that baptism conveys sanctifying grace, removes sin, and opens the way to further grace, Protestantism holds that baptism's power is the power of the Word. Even Luther, who believed that the rite itself is efficacious, did not isolate the sacrament from his evangelical theology. Baptism, Luther taught, brings the forgiveness of sin, deliverance from death and the Devil, the gift of eternal life—but not apart from

God's Word. The Reformed and Presbyterian churches reflect John Calvin's belief that salvation is an invisible covenant between God and the individual person. To this covenant of grace baptism makes no material contribution, but it does ratify God's covenant of grace with sinners. It affixes a seal on the inward covenant of grace by which the elect are engrafted into Christ and his church.

What is known as a believer's baptism, a baptism by immersion according to the example of the New Testament, is a third major form Protestant baptism assumes. Practiced by Anabaptists, Baptists, Disciples of Christ, and other Protestants, the believer's baptism features the new Christian who, having already been brought to faith, makes a public profession of that faith as a condition of admission to the community of faith. Yet, what is fundamentally true of these churches is true of the Protestant majority that practices infant baptism. The sacrament reflects Protestantism's basic principles—that salvation is by grace, faith, and Scripture alone. To God's initiative and Christ's gospel, baptism adds nothing, yet it attests to both grace and the gospel through ritual enactment.

Churches and the Church

An early Lutheran statement of belief, the Augsburg Confession, defines the church as a community of believers among whom the Word is rightly taught and the sacraments properly administered. As we saw in our discussion of sacraments, Protestants have not always agreed on what constitutes the right understanding and administration of baptism and the Lord's Supper. The radically divergent understandings of Scripture found among liberal and fundamentalist Protestants show how difficult it is for Protestants to arrive at consensus about the right teaching and preaching of the Bible. Yet, Scripture and sacraments are regarded as essential signs of the church by nearly all Protestant groups. But what of the Christian community brought together by the Word and sacraments? How do Protestants conceive of the visible church? One possible answer is that Protestantism thinks of itself over against the Roman Catholic church. Against the expanded role of the papacy and the Roman clergy, sixteenth-century Protestantism sought the democratization of the church by placing clergy and laity on equal footing. They sought too to place their churches under the direct authority of Scripture. The church, it was held, is "a group called out" or "set apart" by God—as the Greek word for church, *ecclesia*, suggests—in obedience to the gospel.

But, having rejected the Roman church and taken the Bible as the standard of Christian life, Protestants still faced the problem of giving institutional form to their common life. How should the Christian church be organized, and on the basis of what principles? Basing their redefinition of church organization on Scripture and the example of the early church, Protestants elaborated three major types of church polity. The polity found among the Reformed and Presbyterians was developed by the sixteenth-century reformer John Calvin who believed the New Testament indicated a *presbyterian polity*. A pattern of religious authority apparent in the early church, pastors and a representative council of elders together provide leadership and guidance to local congregations. Pastors are charged with preaching and religious instruction; the elders (a name derived from the New Testament *presbyteros*) are responsible for selection of ministers and for the supervision of worship, membership, and church property. According to presbyterian government, however, final authority resides in representative associations of congregations known as presbyteries, synods, and general assemblies.

Still more democratic are the churches that subscribe to a *congregational polity*. For this group of churches, religious authority ultimately resides in the congregation. According to congregationalist theory, the church exists wherever the disciples of Jesus gather in response to the Holy Spirit and in obedience to Christ's gospel. A community of personally committed individuals, each of whom is a fully responsible member of the community, the local congregation possesses the power to call its ministers, make rulings on questions of doctrine, practice, and discipline, and manage its own internal economic affairs.

The third type of church government appears at least superficially more Catholic than either the presbyterian or congregational church patterns. It involves the rule of bishops and so is called an *episcopalian polity* (from Greek *episcopos* meaning bishop). Though an essentially Catholic form of church order, episcopal order is not deemed by Protestants to be an essential sign of the church. The Lutheran and Methodist churches that employ this type of church government think of it rather in functional terms as useful and beneficial.

The external, structural form the church takes is one way Protestants have of defining themselves as churches, and Protestants for the most part regard this visible church as basic to the meaning of Christian community. Yet, Protestants also believe that the true church is an invisible society whose essential nature is one, holy, catholic, and apostolic. But, whereas Roman Catholicism thinks of the pope as a visible symbol of unity, its historic episcopate as proof of apostolicity, its sacraments as grounds for holiness, and its universality as evidence of catholicity, Protestantism establishes its claim to these four properties by appealing to basic evangelical principles. The unity of the church, Protestants believe, resides not in the visible church, though some Protestants feel that it is incumbent on them to work toward a visible unity of the churches. It rests on Christ alone in whom all Christians are joined. The church's catholic character derives from the universal validity of its message. The church is apostolic not by reason of an apostolic ministry but because the church teaches and preaches the same gospel that the apostles proclaimed. And the holiness of the church is the holiness of forgiven sinners who bear witness in their lives to the grace and mercy of a holy God.

Ministry and Christian Vocation

A common term for Protestant clergy is simply minister. From the New Testament word *diakonia*, a word from which "deacon" derives and that means one who waits on tables, a minister is literally one who serves. The Protestant minister first and foremost is a servant, a servant of the community of believers, and above all else a servant of God's Word. This emphasis on serving and proclaiming is expressed too by the popular titles preacher and pastor—a preacher (Latin *praedicator,* one who speaks forth) is one who proclaims, and a pastor (Latin *pasco,* to feed) is one who provides spiritual sustenance. The title *priest* used commonly by Catholic Christians of a priestly caste possessing special sacramental powers is not generally used by Protestants.

In a wider application of the idea of the priestly office, however, Protestants do speak of a *priesthood of all believers.* Every Christian, it is said, has a priestly authority to appear before God to pray for others, to teach and bear witness to the gospel, and to confess, repent, forgive, and be forgiven. In Luther's words, all are "worthy to appear before God to pray for others and to teach one another the things of God." In theory too, all baptized Christians are called to be ministers of the Word and all are charged with the upbuilding of the church through mutual assistance and encouragement. Among some Protestants in the Anabaptist and Quaker traditions, a radical application of this principle led to the abolition altogether of the functional distinction between clergy and laity. Most Protestants believe, however, that a professional clergy is advisable, though it is best understood as a functional ministry. It is the business of the clergy to see to the orderly conduct of worship and the efficient and effective operation of the church.

An important theoretical formulation, the priesthood of all believers has significant practical implications for the role Protestant laity have assumed in the church. We noted in an earlier section that Protestants sought ways to involve laity in worship through the translation of the Bible and the liturgy into the language of the people and through the introduction of congregational singing. The free churches encourage testimonials, spontaneous prayer, and ecstatic speech to the same end.

We saw too that Protestant churches introduced democratic and representative forms of church government. Laypersons were charged with responsibility for calling ministers, the oversight of worship, the application of spiritual and ecclesiastical discipline, and the formulation of doctrine. And beyond the local congregation, laity exercised leadership along with the clergy in associations of churches like the presbyteries, synods, and general assemblies of the Reform and Presbyterian churches. Laypersons have been instrumental in church-related benevolent societies, in mission fields, and in movements for interchurch cooperation. Extraordinary laywomen like Mother Ann Lee, Mary Baker Eddy, and Ellen G. White have been inspired founders of new churches. And in recent years advocates of women's ordination have challenged Protestant churches to rethink and enlarge the application of their basic belief in the one priesthood of all believers.

The priesthood of all believers is also the theoretical basis for the Protestant view of *vocation*. By vocation, we should note, Protestants do not mean what we ordinarily mean by the term—a profession or an occupation. A vocation in its religious and biblical sense is a "holy" calling. But, if we are to understand what is distinctive about the Protestant doctrine of vocation, we need to understand that it is not, as in some religious traditions, a calling to a separate life of holiness or ascetic discipline. Protestantism rejects the polarity of a sacred and a profane realm of existence that, for example, is at the heart of Judaism's emphasis on ritual purity and separateness. Protestantism rejects also the idea inherent in monasticism that religious obligations can best be fulfilled by withdrawing from ordinary society in pursuit of a superior holiness. From the Protestant perspective all Christians have the same status; all have a common ministry and a common vocation. And, except for functional differences, there is no difference in value or merit between a Christian calling pursued within the church, say as a professional minister, and other vocations outside it. Every useful service has an equal dignity before God. Every human work, every task, every occupation is a holy calling if it witnesses to faith. Every vocation has the potential to manifest what might be called a worldly holiness on condition that it reflects God's glory in the concrete circumstances of social life.

PROTESTANT DIVERSITY

Overview

So far we have discussed the character of Protestant Christianity in the broadest terms. We have identified what Protestants have in common. And so we have concentrated on the beliefs, forms of worship, church polity, and ministry that are closest to the center of the Protestant faith. Now we want to move the discussion from the center outward in order to survey the concrete variety of Protestantisms. Of course, some of the Protestant groups that we survey are nearer to the normative center of Protestantism in belief, worship, and polity. Other groups are more obviously farther from that center. And some groups often identified as Protestant seem to have traveled so far from the center toward the margin that their Protestant identity is no longer clearly apparent. Contemporary Unitarian-Universalist churches, for example, retain the features of congregational polity as well as some religious values that reflect the New England Protestant ethos from which they arose in the nineteenth century. They do not, however, subscribe to the central Protestant tenets about God, the Bible, grace, and faith. Mormonism can also be offered as an example of a religious group with clear historical ties to Protestantism which has so reexpressed basic Christian beliefs and symbols that some scholars have begun to think of the Mormon churches more as an instance of a new, emergent religion than just another form of the Christian religion.

Still, we need to find a way or ways of bringing order to this often bewildering array of churches that we call Protestant, and so we propose the following scheme of identifying church traditions and families. We begin with the classical Reformation churches, Protestant churches that trace their origin to the dawn of Protestantism in the sixteenth century. Next we examine the free church family of Protestant churches. These churches, many of which arose during the seventeenth century, began in protests against the dominant Reformation churches, regard themselves as true witnesses to the Reformation, and stress the principle of voluntarism in church order and life. Related to the free churches are the Methodist churches, and the Holiness and Pentecostal churches that stem from Methodism. These churches emphasize an inward conversion and a personal sanctification that is manifested outwardly in the desire for moral perfection. We conclude our discussion with two distinctly American religions, both of which help us appreciate how varied Protestantism can be and how far Protestantism has pressed beyond its normative center.

Classical Reformation Churches

The Protestant churches that originated in the sixteenth century have much in common. They all regard the Bible as instrumental in salvation and as the final court of appeal in matters of doctrine, worship, church order, and the Christian life. They hold that salvation is by grace through faith alone. And they subscribe to a believer's priesthood, formulated as the priesthood of all believers. Yet these churches differ among themselves as their sixteenth-century founders differed over the interpretation and application of basic Protestant principles. Lutherans, for example, reflect

Luther's conservative attitude toward theology and tradition. And, while they view the Bible as the sole source of faith and doctrine, they follow Luther in preserving elements of tradition that are not proscribed or forbidden by Scripture. Consequently, a rich liturgical and sacramental tradition distinguishes Lutheran churches and gives to them a more nearly Catholic appearance than any of the other Protestant churches. Lutheran churches retain as well the traditional creeds, though they regard the Augsburg Confession, the Formula of Concord, and Luther's two catechisms as normative statements of belief. And, since Lutherans regard church polity as a functional rather than a doctrinal matter, we find among them a variety of polities, everything from the congregational to the historic episcopalianism of the Church of Sweden.

Lutheranism arose in Germany and spread to Scandinavia and America. The Reformed and Presbyterian churches spread to France, Holland, Hungary, Scotland, England, and America, but their birthplace was Switzerland. Ulrich Zwingli and John Calvin were this tradition's greatest architects. And much that is distinctive about the Reformed churches derives from their theologies, especially their theology of God as transcendent, holy, and surprisingly merciful. This view, for example, lies at the heart of the Reformed doctrine of predestination. It explains the importance the Reformed tradition attached to gratitude and praise as fundamental religious attitudes of life and worship. The belief that praise is directed to a holy and utterly transcendent God explains also the austerity and puritan character of Reformed worship. Among these churches, the externals of worship are minimized; actions, gestures, expressive forms of art, music, vestments, and material symbols are not thought to be effective or suitable instruments for expressing religious truth or communicating holy reality. Even Reformed sacraments are given a spiritual rather than a material and objective interpretation. Words rather are the instruments of Reformed worship, and the revealed Word, read or preached from the pulpit, is the essential form given this oral and aural experience of worship and praise. One further quality of this experience: Reformed preaching is designed to enhance understanding rather than to quicken the emotions. It is preaching that makes plain what Scripture teaches by the clear and careful exegesis of the biblical text.

The Lutheran and Reformed churches have been called the Reformation's magisterial churches because their reform went forward under state sponsorship. The Protestant churches that constituted themselves as autonomous congregations of believers were known by the name Anabaptist and represent a third sixteenth-century Protestant tradition. A family of free churches that includes today Mennonites, Amish, Hutterites, and Brethren, the Anabaptists regard personal decision and a believer's baptism as essential conditions for church membership. They also believe that separation from the state and society is a condition for a strict adherence to the pattern of Christian life found in the New Testament. Amish plain dress, black buggies, and traditional, nonmechanized practices of farming are perhaps the most familiar signs of Anabaptist separateness. Yet, a literal application of biblical principles dictated that all Anabaptist churches restrict their contact with the world. All of these churches, for example, renounce war, involvement in civil government, the use of courts, and the taking of oaths. And, though they refuse to use violence against persons, they do reserve to themselves the right to discipline their own members. This they accomplish according to the counsel of Matthew 18:15–17 by a practice of excommunication known as the ban. Their other basic convictions are published in the Schleitheim Confession.

English Free Churches

The free church principles basic to the Anabaptists were adopted as well by dissenters on English soil and institutionalized as Congregationalism, the Baptist church, and the Society of Friends (Quakers). Like the continental Anabaptists, these English-tradition free churches exhibit a "puritan" spirit in worship and life, a democratic character in church polity, a noncreedal biblicism in theology, and a separatist drive in church and state relations. Yet, with the exception of the Quakers, the strict prohibition on involvement in public life and a religious objection to war were dropped. Early Congregationalism was in fact divided over the issue of state establishment, with the nonseparating party of the opinion that the church ought to have intimate ties with government (see Chapter 6). Yet, even the nonseparating Congregationalists thought the church to be a gathered and covenanted community of believers, a community of sinners each with the covenant of grace. And, though these churches practiced infant baptism, a profession of faith is deemed a necessary condition of full church membership.

Possible Anabaptist influence on John Smyth, founder of the first Baptist congregation, may be behind the Baptists' rejection of infant baptism. Baptism by immersion as a sign of the believer's faith thus became a hallmark of these churches. Anabaptist influence may help account too for the strong Baptist conviction that the church is a gathered, autonomous community of believers. That meant in practice that the church has an organizational status independent of the state—an idea the Baptists promoted in their colony of Rhode Island and worked to institutionalize in the Constitution of the American nation. Baptists differ from the Congregationalists at least in one other important respect. Whereas Congregationalist preaching tends to be expository and cognitive, Baptist preaching is evangelistic in its appeal to the emotions, and it is revivalistic in its call for repentance and personal decision. Mention at this point might also be made of the Disciples of Christ and the Christian Churches. Though not technically of the Baptist family, these churches reflect Baptist influence. Both church traditions are congregational and democratic, practice adult baptism by immersion, and interpret the Lord's Supper as a commemorative meal. Yet, the historic commitment to Christian union, a union on the basis of doctrinal flexibility and open, weekly communion, has always given the Disciples a decidedly ecumenical character.

Of the English free churches the Quakers are perhaps most like the continental Anabaptists. Together with the Mennonites, Amish, and Brethren, theirs is one of the historic peace churches. They also oppose the practice of oath taking and have been instrumental in bringing the American court system to accept "affirming" as an alternative to swearing on the Bible. They witness against the use of tobacco and alcohol. They live lives of self-conscious simplicity, evident notably in plain dress. Quakers have not, however, sought to disentangle themselves wholly from society and politics. Two American presidents in this century—Herbert Hoover and Richard M. Nixon—have been Quakers, one of whom was an active member of the Society. And Quaker commitment to social activism and reform has involved them in prison reform, antislavery, and in this century in international relief work for which the American Friends Service Committee is famous. Yet, Quakers depart from Anabaptists (and most other Christian groups) on baptism and the Lord's Supper, which they do not practice. Also peculiar to Quakerism is its teaching of the Inner Light. Even though Quakers hold that the Bible is a source of faith and life, they believe that the divine Spirit speaks directly to and daily illumines the believer's heart—a belief around which Quaker silent worship is centered.

Methodism, Holiness, and Pentecostalism

With historic ties to the seventeenth-century Pietist movement, the Methodist and the Holiness churches are distinctive for their cultivation of heartfelt religious experience, a zealous moral commitment to Christian living, and warm Christian fellowship. Of the churches discussed in this section, the Methodists are the oldest and the largest of the groups treated here, and the United Methodist Church (1968) is the largest of the Methodist group. Deriving from the theology and the organizational effort of John Wesley, the Methodists manifest many of their founder's religious values. Like Wesley, Methodists give less weight to doctrinal formulation, more weight to the practical and experiential dimension of religion. Methodist preaching, for example, aims at arousing in sinners a consciousness of their sin and forgiveness. It is preaching intended to evoke in the believer a lively sense of Christ's holy presence. Hymn singing, for which Methodists are famous, contributes too to the believer's heightened awareness of that permeating presence. Methodism also reflects Wesley's belief that assurance of forgiveness is followed by a lifelong growth in personal and social holiness, a growth Wesley called *Christian perfection*. One side of this Wesleyan perfectionism is Methodism's dedication to moral living; its flip side is Methodism's strong commitment to charitable and benevolent work.

The religious values that gave rise to Methodism were transferred to the holiness movement that began in the nineteenth century. Originally loose associations within Methodism, these early holiness Methodists—increasingly disaffected from the worldliness and moral laxity of the established churches—formed independent groups of "come-outers." Today, Holiness denominations include a whole array of groups, among them such denominations as the Church of God (Anderson, Indiana), the Church of the Nazarene, and the Salvation Army. These churches generally accept Wesley's doctrine of sanctification, but they differ from Wesley and Methodism in holding that sanctification is instantaneous. Sometimes calling this *entire sanctification* a second blessing, Holiness groups teach that it comes after the experience of being born again (justification) and involves an inward cleansing of sin, the indwelling of the Holy Spirit, and the empowerment of the believer to live a life of perfect holiness. For Holiness churches, personal sanctity manifests itself especially in conservative social attitudes and in codes of moral conduct, in a religious style of life that might be described as a worldly asceticism. Among Holiness groups like the Salvation Army, sanctity is a primary motive for a ministry of service to the poor and disadvantaged.

In the early twentieth century Pentecostalism established itself as an independent family of churches. Like the Holiness churches from which it emerged, the Pentecostal churches believe in personal sanctity, a strict holiness code, a divine healing, the plenary inspiration of the Scripture, and the expectation of Christ's imminent Second Coming. What differentiates the Pentecostals is their conviction that beyond justification and sanctification there is a third blessing—a baptism of the Spirit and the gift of tongues, "glossolalia." Pentecostals are, however, a fissiparous family of churches prone to dividing over theology and practice. The largest Pentecostal group, the Assemblies of God, dissent from the third blessing doctrine, affirming rather that Spirit baptism is a second and final grace after a first blessing that both justifies and sanctifies. The Jesus Only, or Jesus Name, Pentecostals discover biblical grounds for what might be called a unitarianism of the second person. They baptize, according to the example of the apostles, in Jesus' name only and teach that the names Father, Son, and Holy Spirit are but titles of the one God, Jesus Christ. A "sign preaching" involving the handling of snakes and the drinking of poison

(Mark 16:17–18) is thought by another group to be visible evidence of faith and the presence of the Spirit. And, though the 1906 revival at the Azusa Street Mission in Los Angeles launched Pentecostalism as an interracial movement, its churches were soon to divide along racial lines—the largest black Pentecostal group being the Church of Christ in God founded by Charles H. Mason. Yet, in spite of all, Pentecostalism has grown remarkably in recent years and has spread as neopentecostalism to many mainline Protestant, Episcopalian, and Roman Catholic churches.

Millennialists

The Christian belief that Christ is to come a second time can be traced to the New Testament and the early church. A fervent belief (see Revelation 20:1–10) that Christ promised his followers a thousand-year reign of peace and blessedness upon his return is the peculiar hope of millennialist-oriented churches like the Adventists. In America, for example, a millennial hope for the Advent, that is, for Christ's imminent return, mounted as tens of thousands prepared for the world's end when a lay Baptist preacher, William Miller, published his conviction that Christ's thousand year reign was to begin in 1843. A little over a half century later, Charles Taze Russell made a similar prediction about the year 1914. From a remnant of Miller's followers sprung the first American Adventist churches, the largest and most influential of which is the Seventh-Day Adventists. Around Russell's predictions developed a group that became the Jehovah's Witnesses. Of the two churches, the Seventh-Day Adventists stand closest to the mainstream of Protestantism and within that stream nearest to the Baptists. They take the Bible as a literal, authoritative source of Christian faith. They adopted the Baptist view that baptism and the Lord's Supper are *ordinances* rather than sacraments. They use immersion to perform the baptismal rite; they perform foot washing in connection with the observance of the Lord's Supper. What distinguishes them is their worship on the seventh day, the Jewish Sabbath, and their adherence to Old Testament dietary restriction on impure foods such as pork and shellfish. And they think of Ellen G. White as a prophetess and meditator through whom God spoke and view her writings as inspired and authoritative.

The Seventh-Day Adventists are known to many Americans through their schools, health programs, and hospitals and medical centers like the one at Loma Linda in California. It may be that even more Americans have encountered the Jehovah's Witnesses through their house-to-house visitations and distribution of *Watch Tower* literature. Jehovah's Witnesses are well known too for their social and political stand against registration for the military draft, saluting the flag, and reciting the pledge of allegiance, and for refusing to permit their children to receive blood transfusions. For the Jehovah's Witnesses, such radical separatism is but a behavioral expression of a deeply felt millennial belief. The present age, according to their teaching, is in the control of Satan, and government is a tool of evil, as are the churches and other religious organizations. Yet, the Witnesses believe that the present age is transient and the ascendancy of satanic forces only temporary. Witnesses take hope in the confidence that Christ will soon return in visible form to rule the earth. In a great battle, the prophesied battle of Armageddon, he will defeat the Devil and his forces and together with the saints will rule the earth for a thousand years.

Protestantism on the Margin

We began our discussion of Protestantism with European churches. Many of the Protestant groups that we surveyed, however, are what might be called home-grown American varieties. The Disciples of Christ, for example, came into existence and reflected the circumstances of the American frontier. The Holiness churches sprung from American Methodism, Pentecostalism spun off from the holiness movement, and the Adventist churches developed out of the millennialist fervor that swept America in the middle of the nineteenth century. Yet, two American churches have special claim to being really new. They also are farther from what we have defined as normative Protestantism than any of the churches surveyed in this chapter.

The first of the two that I have in mind is popularly known as Mormonism. Its founder Joseph Smith taught that he was called to revive the ancient church established by Christ among the peoples of North America. To his church, which Smith called the Church of Jesus Christ of Latter Day Saints, Smith entrusted the Book of Mormon as a record of God's revelation in addition to the Bible. Other distinctive features of this church group include a belief in the plurality of gods, a denial of original sin and an acceptance of free will, a doctrine of marriage for time and eternity, the necessity of baptism by immersion for salvation, and the efficacy of baptizing the living for the dead. The second uniquely American church group was founded in Boston by Mary Baker Eddy as the Church of Christ Scientist. Eddy's Christian Scientists teach that the perfection of human nature comes through a knowledge that God is an all-pervading divine Spirit and that sin, sickness, and ignorance are caused by the illusion that material existence is real. According to Eddy's *Science and Health with Key to the Scriptures,* divine healing was basic to Jesus' ministry and the message of the New Testament. It is the means Scripture teaches for overcoming sickness and sin, and it includes the principle of spiritual perfection and eternal life.

SUMMARY

Protestant Christianity began as a reformation within the western church. Yet, the Protestant Reformation did not work for the renewal of inherited religious traditions. It called rather for a radical rethinking of Christian foundations. It sought a basic reformulation of Christian experience. Beginning with Luther, Protestants substituted the authority of Scripture for tradition. Scripture, it was held, is a sufficient standard in matters of belief, worship, church order, and the Christian life. Protestants appealed to Scripture as well to interpret their experience of holy reality. According to this new understanding of the divine/human transaction, it is through the preaching of the Bible that believers experience God's grace in faith. It is through the proclamation of the gospel and through the Spirit's inward confirmation that believers know themselves to be forgiven and restored to new life in Christ. Yet, the identification of Protestantism's central values is not to isolate a representative pattern of Protestant worship or church order or experience. The history of Protestantism is the story of bewildering variety in church order, forms of worship, and distinctive beliefs. The outsider—a Hindu or a Muslim student, for example—might wonder even that the name *Protestant* is used of religious groups with so many apparent differences. Yet, Protestantism's vitality is in part attributable to its remarkable capacity to reform itself and reexpress its central values to meet the religious needs of new historical and social circumstances.

REVIEW AND REFLECTION

1. What is the meaning of the phrase "the Protestant spirit"? What does it reveal about the nature of Protestantism?
2. What are the two meanings of the word *Protestant*?
3. Describe the basic elements of the Protestant experience of salvation.
4. In what sense is Protestant worship essentially auditory? What reason can you give for this observation?
5. How do Protestants view sacraments? How does the Protestant view differ from the Catholic idea of sacraments?
6. Discuss the features of the three major types of Protestant church polity.
7. How do Protestants justify the belief that theirs is also the one, holy, catholic, and apostolic church?

8. Describe the Protestant view of ministry. How does this view of ministry help us understand the notion of Protestant vocation?

9. Be familiar with shared traits of the Protestant groups discussed in the final section of the chapter.

10. How did we evaluate the various Protestant churches in relation to the normative center of Protestantism? Are some closer to the center than others?

END NOTES

1. The phrase "principle of parsimony" was suggested to me by Robert S. Ellwood, Jr., *Many Peoples, Many Faiths* 2nd ed. (Englewood Cliffs, NJ: Prentice-Hall, 1982), p. 316.

2. Robert McAfee Brown, *The Spirit of Protestantism* (New York: Oxford University Press, 1965), p. 46.

SUGGESTED FURTHER READING

BACH, MARCUS. *The Inner Ecstasy: The Power and the Glory of Speaking in Tongues.* Nashville, TN: Abingdon Press, 1969.

BROWN, ROBERT MCAFEE. *The Spirit of Protestantism.* New York: Oxford University Press, 1965.

DILLENBERGER, JOHN and CLAUDE WELCH. *Protestant Christianity: Interpreted through Its Development.* 2nd ed. New York: Macmillan Publishing Company, 1988.

FORELL, GEORGE WOLFGANG. *The Protestant Faith.* Philadelphia: Fortress Press, 1960.

MARTY, MARTIN E. *Protestantism: Its Churches and Cultures, Rituals and Doctrines, Yesterday and Today.* Garden City, NJ: Doubleday & Company, Inc., 1974.

RAUSCH, DAVID and VOSS, CARL HERMANN. *Protestantism—Its Modern Meaning.* Philadelphia: Fortress, 1987.

SCOTT, WILLIAM A. *Historical Protestantism: An Historical Introduction to Protestant Theology.* Englewood Cliffs, NJ: Prentice-Hall, Inc., 1971.

12 | Christianity in the World Today

OVERVIEW

Every age has its special challenges and opportunities, its unique problems, and its characteristic way of formulating a response to those problems. And every religion exists within a cultural horizon, shares the perspective and values of its surrounding social world, and so forms, renews, and reforms itself in context of the historical, social, and intellectual possibilities of its age. This is not to say that religion can fairly or adequately be understood in social or cultural terms alone. At the heart of religion is an experience of that which lies beyond history and culture. Religion is in the first instance an encounter with sacred mystery. And so the study of religion—our study of the Christian religion—leads to an evaluation of the sacred symbols, stories, and rituals that give form to that encounter. But religious studies leads as surely to an assessment of religious heritage and history. Our study of the Christian religion began with Christianity's biblical heritage, a heritage which it shares with Judaism and Islam.

We started our survey of Christianity with a sketch of the values and beliefs which the first Christians inherited from Hebrew Scripture and the religious matrix of ancient Israel. But, with the early Christian communities, our story moved forward in time from the new faith's founding events. The early years of the church, we saw, were occupied with the task all religious traditions face. Christian communities sought to define the normative form that the new faith would take. They had to decide which of the competing views of salvation would be orthodox belief, which collection of writings would be scripture, which group of persons would be authorized to defend and transmit Christian traditions and preside at Christian worship. And, at least until the reign of Constantine, Christians performed these tasks in a hostile political environment. But, with its improved social standing in the fourth century, the Christian church found itself called upon to negotiate the terms of its existence in relation to culture and society. Perhaps the greatest achievement of the ancient ecumenical councils was the success with which Christian bishops and theologians used Greek language and philosophical categories to reexpress basic Christian belief. The accomplishment of the Middle Ages was the creation of a Christian society, known in the West as Christendom. Then, when Christendom collapsed, Christians of the fourteenth, fifteenth, and sixteenth centuries set about reforming their faith and institutions to accommodate radical political, social, and intellectual realignments in European life. Protestants perhaps better than Catholics realized the profound nature of the change because their reform was nothing short of a reconstitution of Christian authority, faith, and life. Yet, the question of religious authority and Christian foundations was raised anew in the eighteenth and nineteenth centuries. The scientific challenge to the Christian world view forced Roman Catholics and Protestants alike to rethink Christian foundations and the nature of Christian authority.

Though the problem of authority persists, today Christians face what religious thinkers are calling a new pluralism. Because of technological advances in travel and communication, the globe has become smaller and peoples of diverse religions and cultures find themselves living in the presence of others whose beliefs, practices, and values seem strange, perhaps even threatening. In the face of this newest challenge to Christianity, some have taken refuge in exclusivism. Threatened with a bewildering variety that appears to call into question basic Christian truths, many Christian groups have drawn their wagons into tight formation. They identify their religious truth with absolute truth; they identify their way as the exclusive path to salvation or liberation. But then all religions—and not just Christianity—have always privileged their own scriptures and sacred traditions. What has changed is the pervasive and irresistible fact of pluralism as a feature of contemporary existence.

Today, it seems, the menace of the foreign, the alien, the "other" cannot any longer be contained outside a magic circle. The question, therefore, has become not *whether* we are going to live with other profoundly different religious traditions but *how* will we live in their presence. In the words of Wilfred Cantwell Smith, former director of Harvard's Center for the Study of World Religions, "The religious life of mankind from now on, if it is to be lived at all, will be lived in the context of religious pluralism." [1] But Smith is not alone in his perception. Other Christians too have recognized that religious diversity is one of the most pressing problems of contemporary religious life. And so in this final chapter I want to examine its causes and conditions, to look at selective ways it is being given Christian expression, and to consider the example of one Christian theologian who is exploring the opportunities and pitfalls of religious diversity for the Christian faith.

EXPANDING HORIZONS

The Missionary Movement

Human beings seem naturally inclined to think of the boundary of their own social, cultural, and intellectual world as the world's boundary. And, because religious boundaries are established by what Protestant theologian Paul Tillich called "ultimate concern," it is perhaps even more natural that religious groups should have deeply entrenched assumptions about the rightness of their scriptures, beliefs, rituals, and institutions. Yet, by the end of the eighteenth century English novelist Henry Fielding could treat religious parochialism in his comic novel *Tom Jones* as a subject of mild ridicule. He could have the country parson, the Reverend Mr. Thwackum, remark that by religion he meant "the Christian religion; and not only the Christian Religion, but the Protestant Religion; and not only the Protestant Religion but the Church of England." I suspect that today it would be difficult to find an Anglican who would not regard this opinion as archaic. But in Fielding's day the exclusivist assumption about one's own religion had only just begun to be questioned. By the end of the next century, however, and in the wake of that century's intellectual and social ferment traditional religious certainties had become less tenable. And, as we saw in Chapter 9, Christian thinkers began the often controversial process of reevaluating traditional claims about Scripture, belief, ritual practice, and Christian institutions. In the face of successes in the nineteenth century's missionary effort, it became apparent to many Christians that the time had also come to reassess relationships among the competing Christian churches and to reevaluate Christianity's relationship to the non-Christian religions of the world.

We can reasonably assume that the original impulse of nineteenth century missionary activity was not prompted by a desire to establish what Tillich described as "a community of conversation." Interest in the theological implications of the encounter of Christianity with the world religions developed slowly, in part because of the personal experiences of missionaries in foreign mission fields, in part because of the developing academic discipline of comparative religions. The basic motive for Christian missions was the New Testament command to "make disciples of all nations" (Matthew 28:19). More often than not, the passion of early Christian missionaries was the same passion that inspired the spiritual awakenings and revivals of the eighteenth and nineteenth century. Missionaries sailed from England, Europe, and America so that they might share the light of Christ's gospel. Yet, we know too that the cultures, values, and even religions of indigenous peoples among whom Christian missionaries lived and worked have often won the admiration of the missionaries. Modern missionaries have even identified with the aspirations of national independence of their host countries. But even an early nineteenth-century figure like Baptist lay preacher William Carey illustrates this principle. As a Protestant Christian, of course, Carey energetically took it upon himself to translate the Bible. Together with Joshua Marshman, he prepared translations of Scripture in Bengali, Hindi, Sanskrit, and other languages and dialects. But it is significant that, in addition to Bibles, dictionaries, and grammars, the two prepared an English edition of the Hindu epic poem, *Ramayana*.

The picture of Christian missions is of course a complex one. Missionaries have not always been advocates of indigenous cultures, nor have they all been careful students of indigenous religion. African missionaries, for example, used Unkulunkulu to translate God into Zulu, thinking no doubt that Unkulunkulu was a rough equivalent of their own biblical God. In Zulu myth, however, Unkulunkulu is not the Zulu Sky God. He is rather the first man who, having come from the sky, was the creative source of all other human beings. [2] Yet, movements of national liberation and a resurgent cultural pride among Third World peoples are making western cultural provincialism of this kind untenable in the mission field. The rapid maturing of the younger churches and the emergence of an indigenous leadership is effecting important shifts in the character of Christian missions. Already at the World Missionary Conference held at Edinburgh in 1910, the presence and importance of the Third World church were being felt. At subsequent meetings sponsored by the WMC, delegates from the younger churches saw their numbers and their influence rise steadily. At Madras, India, the delegates called for a rethinking of Christianity's relation to other world religions; at the Whitby meetings in England, conference participants redefined missions as a two-way arrangement, with emphasis on the contributing role of the younger churches; at the Ghana meetings in West Africa, the delegates wrestled with the questions of unity and service.

It was becoming evident that the churches in countries that were once missionary lands were emerging as partners in the church's work in the world. The indigenous churches have also begun to function as self-sufficient churches with a significant percent of their personnel drawn from their own populations. Shifts of such magnitude, of course, are bound to excite fears and surface tensions. When, for example, the Zambian archbishop of Lusaka, the Right Reverend Emmanuel Milingo, persisted in an unconventional ministry of spiritual healing and exorcism, European critics accused him of practicing tribal magic and of being a Catholic witch doctor. And the Vatican summoned him to Rome—in spite of the vocal protest of Zambian Catholics—for what was called a period of "rest and reflection."

But what Archbishop Milingo speaks of as the "inculturation" of Christianity is producing striking results in Africa, Asia, and Latin America. Liberation theology and the concept of *base communities* of lay Christians committed to Bible study, prayer, and social action has come from the South American churches; a spiritually vigorous art is developing in Africa, translating biblical stories and motifs into African settings; the Church of South India has long offered First World churches a model of Christian reunion. We find too that the younger churches are sending personnel to staff hospitals and schools in the West, theologians to teach at American seminaries and theological schools, and clergy to fill parish pulpits. Indeed, a small rural midwestern town of nine hundred near the university where I teach now has as minister of one of its two churches an African from Sierra Leone. The tide of Christian missions, having gone out, is now returning; the receiving churches have become the sending churches.

Worldwide Christianity

Ecumenism, a word from the Greek meaning "inhabited world," emerged in this century as a movement for Christian cooperation, unity, and dialogue across denominational and then across cultural boundaries. As we saw in the last section, a major impetus for the ecumenical movement was Christian "foreign" missions. International missionary organizations and commissions provided significant forums for Christians from around the globe to meet, discuss matters of common concern, and work together. Important stimulus for ecumenism came also from the gathering of Catholic bishops at Vatican II. The presence of Protestant, Anglican, and Orthodox observers indicated how deeply committed Pope John XXIII was to fellowship and conversation with the non-Roman churches. In the period following the Second Vatican Council, Catholics became more active in the World Council of Churches; Catholic theologians joined the WCC's Faith and Order Commission; and the Roman church initiated bilateral conversations with the Lutherans, the Anglicans, the Reformed, and the Orthodox. Vatican II in many ways spelled the end of the era of Roman Catholic exclusivism and the historic Catholic view that "outside the church [the Roman church] there is no salvation."

The spirit of Vatican II and its important *Decree on Ecumenism* prompted Catholic theologian Edward Schillebeeckx to write that "the Roman Catholic Church in this Council has officially given up her monopoly of the Christian religion or of Christianity." [3] The presence of bishops from Asia, Africa, and Latin America prompted another Catholic theologian to remark that the Second Vatican Council represented "the first major official event in which the church actualized itself as a world church." [4] Even though the Roman church under John Paul II has taken a conservative turn, a shift from an essentially European to an authentically ecumenical Catholicism, a Catholicism of the "inhabited world," seems inevitable as Third World churches insist that their voice be heard and their independence of western domination be acknowledged. Indeed, among the Third World churches in general, there has been an increasingly vocal insistence that their churches not be evaluated or judged by the ethical, cultural, and religious standards of the West. Some, like Choan-Seng Song, have even proposed that the ghost of "foreign" missions should be put to flight—by firecrackers and drum and cymbal if need be. Certainly, most would agree with Japanese theologian Kosuke Koyama that the new regional churches need "family time" for discussing and formulating their own theologies, mission strategies, and forms of worship.

Theologians Song and Koyama have taken the position that Christianity cannot be a religion of the "inhabited world" in the garb of western civilization. They seem to be saying that before the church can become truly universal it must be genuinely regional. And to this end the younger churches have begun to evolve their own regional associations, associations like the East Asian Christian Conference, the All-African Conference of Churches, and the organization of Latin American Catholic bishops (CELAM). These organizations combine an ecumenical purpose with a determination to encourage the development of indigenous patterns of Christian thought and worship. They have evolved theologies that endeavor to express Christian belief in images and forms recognizable to Asians or Africans or Latin Americans. In *The Compassionate God*, for example, Choan-Seng Song is adamant that only as the "flat-nosed Christ" of contemporary Asian and African art can Christ be brought to the people of those continents. Song writes that "the Word becomes flesh, not just in Bethlehem two thousand years ago, but *now* in *Asia*." [5] Third World theologians are also insistent that religious thought and worship should be linked to regional economic, social, and political realities. Like the influential liberation theologians of Latin America, Third World religious thinkers believe that theological, biblical, even sacramental worship should take form in response to the concrete situation of the poor and oppressed. They believe in particular that only when the Lord's Supper is conceived in relation to the mission and ministry of Jesus among the poor, when it is brought in relation to "the reality of life-situations" of the people, only then can it again be a symbol that unites rather than divides the churches.

The Holy Family in this example of popular Indian art is conceived as a pious Brahman family.

ALTERNATIVE VOICES IN AMERICA

Theologies of Liberation

Asia, Africa, and South America are coming to new understandings of Christianity. As we saw in the last section, there is a recognition among the younger churches that, if Christianity is to come to the peoples of those continents, it must come in a form they can recognize. It must come not as the religion of Europe but as a religion also of Asia, Africa, and Latin America. According to this perspective, that means too that normative western ways of doing theology must give way to a theology that reflects indigenous experience. Theology, Third World theologians tell us, must be expressed in terms of indigenous values and cultural heritages. It must make sense in view of the social, political, and economic realities of actual life-situations on those continents. Above all, it must be a liberating theology—a theology that asks about the gospel of liberation among peoples still dominated by the West.

Understandably, liberation theologians are critical of the normative theologies of Europe and North America and have set for themselves the task of reenvisioning Christianity in the light of their own experience. And, rejecting the dichotomy of Christian and non-Christian culture as false, they have found in their own cultures themes and images with power to express biblical truth. Above all, liberation theologians take the experience and social reality of politically and economically marginalized groups as the primary referent for their theology and biblical exegesis. In Latin America in particular these theologians have made use of Marxist thought much as theologians of the thirteenth century adapted Aristotle for their theologies. [6] Theology, these theologians believe, should speak to the sort of people Jesus himself addressed in his public ministry. It should provide for the needs, aspirations, and dignity of those whose lives have been marginalized through cultural, social, economic, or political circumstances beyond their control. The experience of marginality, however, is not restricted to the Third World or the time of Jesus. Liberation theologies are also found in the First World and among the established churches of the West.

Black Theology

The year 1963 was a watershed year for the civil rights movement. In April of that year, a black Baptist minister from Montgomery, Alabama went to Birmingham where he marched arm in arm with blacks and whites. His purpose was to call national attention by street demonstrations and mass arrests to the segregation of Birmingham's public facilities. August of the same year found that same minister, the Reverend Dr. Martin Luther King, Jr., in Washington. There in the nation's capital beside the Lincoln Memorial, King spoke in almost millennial terms of his dream of freedom in America: ''We will be able to speed up that day when all God's children, black men and white men, Jews and Gentiles, Protestants and Catholics, will be able to join hands and sing in the words of the old Negro spiritual, 'Free at last! Free at last! thank God almighty, we are free at last!'''

The following year the Civil Rights Act was passed by the United States Congress; the Voting Rights Act followed in 1965. Yet, when King was assassinated in 1968, it had become clear to most black church leaders that more radical measures were required if black Americans were to attain full social, political, and economic freedom and dignity—measures signaled by the first Black Manifesto of 1969. In that manifesto, adopted by the National Black Economic Development Conference, the white Christian churches and Jewish synagogues were in particular called to task for their responsibility for racism in American society, and a demand was made that a $500 million reparation be paid for past injuries. The manifesto also made clear that the leaders of the black churches were becoming more critical of their white counterparts, more skeptical in fact of white Christianity as a source for black religious thought and experience. The time had come for a distinctly black theology.

In a 1969 statement of the Committee of Black Churchmen, black theology is described as a theology rooted in the history and spiritual heritage of blacks. The statement goes on to say that it is also a theology of liberation. In the same year theologian James H. Cone published *Black Theology and Black Power*. Here and in the books that followed, Cone was influential in presenting a black theological agenda. Finding traditional Christian theology too abstract, academic, and remote from the actual life-situation of black people, Cone and other black theologians argued that the only theology relevant for blacks is a theology that arises from the crucible of black suffering. The only understanding of Christian Scripture faithful to biblical meaning is one that takes the history of black oppression as its principle of interpretation. The great events of the Bible, they held, are witness to God's identification with those whose lives have been marginalized, who exist beyond and are victims of society's political and economic establishments. God in the Old Testament does not side with pharaoh but with pharaoh's Hebrew slaves; Israel's prophets do not serve the king but champion the victims of the king's policies; Jesus comes not to the haves but to the have-nots. Theologian Albert Cleage goes even further in his revisioning of biblical meaning. He not only repudiates traditional normative Christian theology—a theology that he associates with slave Christianity. He rejects the image of Jesus that evolved during the course of European history, the image of "a white Christ sitting in heaven at the right hand of a white Father." How is it possible, he asks, that such a God can be "champion of the Black man's cause"? [7]

This question is framed in much the same way as Choan-Seng Song framed the question about the shape of Jesus' nose. Just as Song claimed "a flat-nosed Jesus" for Asians and Africans, so Cleage evokes "a Black Messiah, the son of a Black woman, a son of a Black Israel." [8] Other black theologians and historians have begun the task of reconstructing the historical record of black religious heritage. Black theologians and historians have worked to correct and restore the record about the role and significance of black history and the black church. They have contributed to our knowledge of black leaders and to our appreciation of the heroes of black history. And books like Cone's *The Spiritual and the Blues* (1972) have made it possible for us to get the story of black spirituality straight.

With new studies like Cone's book, we can see how far from the mark was the view of the Negro spiritual as merely an opium of an oppressed people. The spirituals, Cone argues, are replete with images of resistance, freedom, and liberation. And, when they evoked images of Canaan and the Promised Land and the River Jordon or when their theme was to "steal away," heaven was not the only, sometimes not even the primary referent. The spirituals pointed to the North or to Canada or to Africa. For Frederick Douglass, Harriet Tubman, and others who had been or were slaves, 'de promised land on de oder side of Jordon' was not just a transcendent reality" [9], nor was the singing just a wistful hope for heaven. The singing of spirituals gave voice to a historical aspiration for liberation. Yet, Cone remarks, the spiritual also expressed a "black eschatology." For black slaves, heaven meant that they were God's elect, an election that "bestowed upon them a freedom to be." [10] Heaven provided American black slaves—much as Zion provides contemporary South African victims of aparteid—ways "to affirm their humanity when other people were attempting to define them as nonpersons." [11]

Christian Feminist Perspective

Like other liberation theologies, feminist theology originates as a marginalized group's protest of injustice. The injustice women have suffered in western societies, of course, is not restricted to religion. Its causes are historical, social, cultural, and economic. Yet, religious history, institutions, thought, and expression are as responsible as any other cause for having consigned women to the status of what Simone de Beauvoir called "the second sex." Though women have been religious founders, mystics, prophets, martyrs, they have been systematically excluded from the liturgical and teaching offices of the church. Women have not been at liberty to pursue priestly or clerical vocations within any of the major Christian church traditions. Feminist theologians point out too that the language of the church is alien to women's spiritual experience. Scripture and normative Christian theology speak of God as male and patriarchal—as a Father, a King, a Ruler, a Judge, a Shepherd, as the God of Abraham, Isaac, and Jacob. Old Testament stories are stories of the faith and example of Noah, Abraham, Isaac, Jacob, Joseph, Moses, and David. And the New Testament pictures woman as responsible for Adam's fall (1 Timothy 2:13–14); certainly Paul's letters bear responsibility for the belief that women are to play a subordinate role in the family, society, and the church (Corinthians 14:34–35; 1 Timothy 2:11–15). And in Christian history women have received not better but worse treatment. It is not surprising that some feminists feel that Christianity is irreformable and have found in prebiblical religions or postChristian women's experience profounder, more authentic symbols for women's spirituality.

Other feminists, however, have adopted a prophetic stance within the Christian tradition. These "reformist" theologians, as they have been called, take their task to be in the first instance the utterance of a prophetic no! to the distortions and corruptions that have betrayed the original core of the Christian faith. They are critical of normative theology, its methods, and its hermeneutical (i.e. interpretative) principles. They reject the ways traditional Christian institutions have excluded women from the exercise of authority. They object to the negative image of women encouraged by a selective reading of the New Testament and reinforced culturally by the influence that classical dualism exercised on Christian thinking, a dualism that associates males with spirit, soul, reason, and transcendence and females with body, flesh, nature, and immanence. Christian feminists have been especially critical of the sexist character of Christianity's symbols for ultimate reality. They observe that worship of Jesus as the God-man translates the Incarnation into a doctrine of maleness. And feminist theology beginning with Mary Daly's *Beyond God the Father* (1974) has advanced the view that the image of God the father ruling in heaven became a divinely authorized model for authoritarian, male-dominated rule on earth.

But, like sixteenth-century Protestantism, the Christian feminist critique of religion is not exhausted in its call for repentance, reform, and restoration. Christian feminists have also committed themselves to reinterpreting and providing alternate models for religious and cultural experience from the perspective of women's experience. They are conscious that theirs is not an easy undertaking. They know that the historical record with which they must work has been constructed and mediated to the present through the interpretative perspective of male theologians, biblical exegetes, and church historians. They are conscious that even the categories (e.g. patristics or the study of the early church fathers) used to describe the Christian past biases the Christian story in its telling.

Yet, the results are impressive as women scholars of religion have undertaken foundational work in biblical studies, the history of Christianity, the sociology of religion, and the history of religions. Work on Christian foundations—on the New Testament and early Christianity—has especially yielded impressive results. Both Elizabeth Schussler Fiorenza and Elaine Pagels are notable examples of scholars who have been instrumental in the reevaluation of the agency and experience of women in the ministry of Jesus, the early church, and among the Gnostic sects of the first and second centuries. They have both contributed to our understanding of the inclusive character of Jesus' message and movement in the period before Christian churches began to accommodate Christianity to its patriarchal environment. Much work, of course, still needs to be done before the historic record is reconstructed and the Christian story can be told from "her" point of view. Nevertheless, it is reasonable to conclude with Elaine Pagels that "the history of Christianity will never be told in the same way again." [12]

AN INDIGENOUS AFRICAN CHRISTIANITY

Much of the vitality within contemporary Christianity is coming from groups whose cultural traditions, values, and experiences differentiate them from the historic European forms of Christianity. As we now turn to sub-Saharan Africa, we discover that the introduction of traditional religious functions, motifs, and patterns of worship also results in vigorous new forms of the Christian religion. Of course, the exchange of cultural and religious symbols is by no means limited to Christianity. It is occurring as well among Muslims in the countries south of Africa's Sahara Desert. Nor is this process of interpenetration of indigenous and Christian religious traditions unique to Africa. Flowers, water, and fire have symbolic meaning and association for Christians of India that they do not have for European or American Christians. Yet, with seven thousand indigenous or independent churches claiming the allegiance of more than 32 million Africans, the African continent has special interest for the student of Christianity.

There is, of course, great variety among these churches and movements. Some of the indigenous churches of Africa began as movements to Africanize Christianity within established churches. The movement known as Jamaa arose as an expression of African Catholicism within Roman Catholicism but hostility to the movement forced many of the movement's members to form a separate church. Some of these churches developed around a charismatic leader outside the context of historic Christianity and the mission churches. The Kimbanguist church of Zaire is an example of such a movement. Yet, however diverse these churches, they are remarkable for integrating African and Christian rituals, symbols, and offices in the creation of new patterns of religious experience. And none was more creative in evolving an inherently African Christianity than the Zulu prophet and founder of the amaNazaretha Baptist Church, Isaiah Shembe.

Like other African religious movements, Shembe's amaNazaretha church blends traditional African religious elements with Christian ones. The Nazarites, as Shembe's followers are called, characteristically attach special importance to visions and dreams, to healing and exorcism, and to the significance of high places for religious activity. They believe that their founder, whom they regard as a "messiah," possessed supernatural power which was communicated through a series of commissioning visionary experiences. It was because of this experience that Shembe was called "the servant" of the Lord among his Zulu people. According to one account, Shembe described a summons by a heavenly voice to enter a mountain cave where in a dream he surveyed the world, saw his own death, and was warned against sexual sin. From this dream, he said, he awoke exclaiming, "I have seen Jehovah." On another occasion, Shembe tells of how he felt compelled to climb a mountain called Inhlangakazi where he was tempted by mysterious powers and then ministered to by angels who brought him heavenly food in the form of bread and wine. At the end of this twelve-day mountain retreat he knew that he had acquired a new identity and new powers of healing and casting out demons.

Shembe's visionary experiences are striking for their biblical parallels. He quite obviously thought of himself as a prophet-liberator sent to the Zulu as Moses was sent to the Hebrews; he just as obviously associated his ministry of healing the sick and casting out demons with the ministry of Jesus. Yet, what is equally interesting is how closely Shembe's experience and role resemble that of the Zulu "heaven-herd" (*izinyanga zezulu*), the one who is called to mediate between the God of the Sky and the Zulu people at times of crisis. [13]

Much about the amaNazaretha church that is distinctly Zulu and African originates in Shembe's singular personality and visionary experiences. He was, as we have said, a charismatic leader whose person assumed a mythic significance for the Nazarites. For them he was a holy man and divine healer, a mediator and messenger of God, a messianic liberator who brought hope to an oppressed people. The Nazarite church is evidence too of Shembe's genius for incorporating authentic Zulu sound and movement and traditional Zulu ritual functions, symbols, and forms of worship into amaNazaretha. Because high places are traditionally the locus of religious activity among the Zulu, places of special approach to the God of the Sky, Shembe's decision to build his first church atop a hill and call it The High Place was a significant one. He chose another high place, the Nhlangakazi Mountain, as the site of one of his first pilgrimages and established there an annual festival with Zulu dress, dance, and song. It is interesting too that Shembe's other holy center at Ekuphlakami is a place of paradiselike harmony and peace which betrays no trace of the Zulu's history of social dislocation and uprootedness from tradition and the land. At festival times the faithful, dressed in white and wearing icons of their prophet, move among the trees, meditate, and sing hymns by Shembe himself—hymns that came to him during his sleep and that have been described as the "heartbeat of Zulu."

A WIDER ECUMENISM

We began our study of Christianity with Jaroslav Pelikan's remark that Christianity came to the nations of the world as "a religion of Europe both in the sense of a religion from Europe and, often, a religion about Europe as well." Women and black theologians have made it clear too that Christianity began this century as a religion whose normative symbols, values, and experiences are predominantly white and male. Yet we have also seen that, during this century, marginalized groups and the younger churches of Asia, Africa, and Latin America have called for basic changes in the historic character of the Christian religion. Blacks and women have criticized traditional Christianity as being too restrictive and exclusive. Asians, Africans, and Latin Americans have challenged the geographical boundaries of historic Christianity as too provincial. These critics urge their fellow Christians to recognize that, until Christianity includes blacks and women in its community of conversation and until it enlarges its cultural boundaries, Jesus' ecumenical charge to be "witnesses in Jerusalem and in all Judea and Samaria and to the end of the earth" (Acts 1:8) will be unrealized.

Still, there have been important advances toward a genuinely ecumenical Christianity, a Christianity of the inhabited world. The circle of conversation has been widened as a result of the efforts of black and feminist theologians within the established churches of the First World. And, starting with the international missionary conferences of this century, Christians have been drawn together in a global ecumenism of mutual respect, conversation, and cooperation. Yet, because of the geographical shrinkage of our world and the global perils facing all peoples of the earth, there has been an awakening to the need for a still wider ecumenism. Christians like Trappist monk Thomas Merton were undoubtedly instrumental in preparing the way for significant dialogue between Christians and members of the other religions. Gatherings like the World Conference on Religion and Peace have over the last two decades brought Christians together with Hindus, Jains, Buddhists, Sikhs, Shintoists, Jews, and Muslims. And dialogues like the one at Washington and Lee University that we spoke of in the first chapter have promoted understanding.

Yet, the drafting of *The Declaration on Non-Christian Religions* by the Catholic bishops at Vatican II deserves special mention for its significance and potential importance in enlarging the boundaries of ecumenism. It is perhaps telling that the declaration was originally to be a part of the *Decree on Ecumenism*. Without doubt, it expresses an ecumenical spirit in its early affirmation that all peoples form a single community. From here the document goes on to acknowledge the existence of a religious sense common to all peoples from ancient time to the present. Though that religious sense takes diverse forms among Hindus, Buddhists, Muslims, and Jews, the declaration states that the Catholic Church "rejects nothing that is true and holy in these religions" [14], but rather encourages an understanding of the other religions and dialogue with their representatives. The World Council of Churches has taken a similar position in commending dialogue and cooperation with peoples of other faiths and ideologies.

Just what shape this latest chapter in the Christian story will take is still to be determined. Yet, there is little doubt that it is in the process of definition. There are even some Christians, with more than an academic interest in the story, who are even now working to think through what is involved in taking serious the koan for Christians that we spoke of earlier. And the Catholic theologian Hans Kung is among those Christians.

In his *Christianity and the World Religions*, Kung provides in his words "a contemporary paradigm" of a Christian theology in serious dialogue with those from other than Christian religious traditions. To accomplish this, he arranged for a series of three extended dialogues with academic colleagues who are experts respectively on the religions and cultures of Islam, Hinduism, and Buddhism. Each dialogue begins with a presentation of the essential ideas and teachings of the other religion. Kung rightly observes that "we cannot know enough about one another," [15] and perhaps this is Kung's reason for starting dialogue with western experts of religion and culture rather than with believing adherents of Islam, Hinduism, and Buddhism—the three religions featured in his book. In any case, Kung follows the narratives on each of the three religions with his own Christian response. And, though he believes the narratives indispensable for deepening our knowledge of the other religions, the principles guiding his own responses are more directly revealing about Kung's understanding of the possible form interreligious dialogue might take.

According to Kung, the theologian in dialogue with other faiths has to steer a course between twin perils—absolutism on the one hand and relativism on the other. Absolutism, he argues, encourages an exclusivism that condemns and a superiority that looks down on what I have called the vital truths of other persons. A superficial relativism that equates all values or an arbitrary pluralism that approves without discrimination trivializes religious truth and encourages a "cheap tolerance." From Kung's perspective, the Christian theologian must cultivate an attitude toward the other religions that is at once empathetic and critical, that is open and guided by standards.

The dialogue that Kung advocates in many respects resembles Paul Tillich's ideal dialogical pattern involving a dialectic of acceptance and rejection. Kung states that he wishes to bring to his "Christian Responses" a "Christian self-criticism in the light of the other religions" and a "Christian criticism of the other religions in the light of the Gospel." [16] There are, of course, risks in such a procedure, and he acknowledges them. He knows that some will find him not Christian enough and others will find him too narrowly Christian. Yet, with the risks there are important gains. Though tension and uncertainty are inherent in the process, Kung believes that dialogue leads to a better understanding of other religious persons with whom our lives in today's world are linked. The encounter gives us as well a better understanding of our own vital truths. And, because religions contribute to the world's conflicts and magnify the misunderstanding and hostility between peoples, Kung argues that ecumenical dialogue is "an urgent desideratum for world politics." As he puts it in a concluding word:

There will be no peace among the peoples of this world
without peace among the world religions.
There will be no peace among the world religions without
peace among the Christian churches.
The community of the Church is an integral part of the world
community.
Ecumenism *ad intra*, concentrated on the Christian world,
and ecumenism *ad extra*, oriented toward the whole
inhabited earth, are interdependent.
Peace is indivisible: it begins with us. [17]

In our first chapter we posed a koan. We asked whether it is possible
to be open to the religious truths of other people without diminishing loyalty to our own vital truths. Perhaps we should ask not whether in our
study of Christianity and other religions it is possible, but whether we can
safely avoid the responsibility for an openness that leads to a wider ecumenism.

REVIEW AND REFLECTION

1. How did the missionary movement contribute to the emergence
   of the ecumenical movement in the twentieth century?

2. What changes in normative Christianity are being called for by
   members of the younger churches of Asia, Africa, and Latin
   America?

3. What are the major themes in liberation theology? How are those
   themes expressly articulated in black theology and feminist theology?

4. What is the constructive agenda of black theology and feminist
   scholarship?

5. Characterize indigenous Christianity in Africa using the amaNazaretha church to illustrate your discussion.

6. What did we mean by a wider ecumenism? What forces are bringing it about?

END NOTES

1. Wilfred Cantwell Smith, *The Faith of Other Men*. (New York: Mentor
Books, 1965), p. 10–11.

2. E. Thomas Lawson, *Religions of Africa: Traditions in Transformation* (San
Francisco: Harper & Row, Publishers, 1985), p. 48.

3. Quoted in James C. Livingston, *Modern Christian Thought: From the Enlightenment to Vatican II* (New York and London: Macmillan Publishing Co. and Collier Macmillan Publishers, 1971), p. 496.

4. Quoted in John Dillenberger and Claude Welch, *Protestant Christianity: Interpreted Through Its Development,* 2nd ed. (New York and London: Macmillan Publishing Company and Collier Macmillan Publishers, 1988), p. 275.

5. Choan-Seng Song, *The Compassionate God* (Maryknoll, NY: Orbis Books, 1982), p. 4.

6. This analogy was suggested to me in Lawrence Cunningham's discussion of liberation theology in *The Catholic Heritage* (New York: The Crossroad Publishing Company, 1983), p. 125.

7. Albert Cleage, Jr., ''The Gospel of Black Liberation,'' in Patrick H. McNamara, ed., *Religion American Style* (New York: Harper & Row, Publishers, 1974), p. 298.

8. Ibid., p. 298.

9. James H. Cone, *The Spirituals and the Blues: An Interpretation* (New York: The Seabury Press, 1972), p. 89.

10. Ibid., p. 91.

11. Ibid., p. 91.

12. Elaine Pagels, ''What Became of God the Mother?'' in *Womenspirit Rising: A Feminist Reader in Religion.* ed. by Carol P. Christ and Judith Plaskow (San Francisco: Harper & Row Publishers, 1979, p. 117.

13. See E. Thomas Lawson's discussion of Shembe's vocation as heavenherd in *Religions of Africa,* pp. 43 ff.

14. Walter M. Abbott, S.J., ed. *The Documents of Vatican II* (New York: Herder and Herder and Association Press, 1966), p. 662.

15. Hans Kung and others, *Christianity and the World Religions,* trans. Peter Heinegg (Garden City, NY: Doubleday & Company, Inc., 1986), p. xix.

16. Ibid., p. xvii.

17. Ibid., p. 443.

SUGGESTED FURTHER READING

WALTER M. ABBOTT, S.J., gen. ed., *The Documents of Vatican II.* New York: Herder and Herder and Association Press, 1966.

CHRIST, CAROL P. and JUDITH PLASKOW. ed. *Womanspirit Rising: A Feminist Reader in Religion.* San Francisco: Harper & Row Publishers, 1979.

JAMES H. CONE. *The Spirituals and the Blues: An Interpretation.* New York: The Seabury Press, 1972.

HANS KUNG and others. *Christianity and the World Religions: Paths to Dialogue with Islam, Hinduism, and Buddhism.* trans. Peter Heinegg. Garden City, NY: Doubleday & Company, Inc., 1986.

OXTOBY, WILLARD G., ed. *Religious Diversity: Essays by Wilfred Cantwell Smith*. New York: Harper & Row, Publishers, 1976.

RUETHER, ROSEMARY RADFORD. *To Change the World: Christology and Cultural Criticism*. New York: The Crossroad Publishing Company, 1981.

RUETHER, ROSEMAY and ELEANOR MCLAUGHLIN. ed. *Women of Spirit: Female Leadership in the Jewish and Christian Traditions*. New York: Simon and Schuster, 1979.

CHOAN-SENG SONG. *Christian Mission in Reconstruction: An Asian Analysis*. Maryknoll, NY: Orbis Books, 1977.

Key Terms

academic study of religion: the descriptive, comparative, analytic study of religion whose purpose is to promote the understanding of religion.

apocalyptic: concerning the end of the present age; **apocalypses:** Jewish and Christian writings using symbolic imagery to speak of the impending destruction of the powers of the present age and the imminent beginning of a new age of the righteous.

Apologist: one of a group of early Christian writers known for their intellectual defenses of Christianity against Christianity's critics and detractors.

apophatic: the negative way to God.

apophatic theology: a theology that speaks of God in negative terms because of the incomprehensibility of God.

apostles: refers to the original Christian missionaries and founders of churches and to the twelve disciples chosen by Jesus as primary witnesses.

ascetic: a person committed to the attainment of higher spiritual virtue through self-denial.

atonement: the teaching that reconciliation between God and human beings is achieved through the sacrificial death of Jesus.

baptism: the Christian rite of initiation.

base communities: small groups of lay Christians in Latin America and elsewhere which apply the gospel to the social, political, and economic circumstances besetting the poor and oppressed.

biblical criticism: the use of literary and historical methods in the study of the Bible.

canon: an authorized list, especially a list of inspired books or sacred writings such as the New Testament; **canonization** is the formation of a canon.

canonization: see *canon.*

cardinal clergy: the principle clergy of the Roman Catholic Church who serve as special assistants to the pope.

cardinals: see *cardinal clergy.*

catholic: meaning universal. Often applied in a restrictive sense as a name for Roman Catholicism; more broadly used to describe Eastern Orthodoxy, Anglicanism, and other churches that claim an institutional continuity with the early church through apostolic succession.

Catholic: see Roman Catholic

Catholic modernists: a group of liberal Catholic thinkers who sought to bring Catholic belief into closer relation to modern thought.

cenobite: used to describe monks living in community.

Christian perfection: a teaching important in the Wesleyan tradition to describe the wholehearted devotion to Christ or the state of being in Christ.

Christological: see *Christology.*

Christology: teachings or doctrines about Christ.

church polity: church structure or organization.

common era: (C.E.) corresponds to the traditional designation A.D., a Christian designation from *anno Domini* meaning "from the year of our Lord"; before the common era (B.C.E.) corresponds to B.C. meaning "before Christ."

conciliarism: a movement that regards the ecumenical or general councils of the church as authoritative in matters of discipline, doctrine, and practice.

conciliarists: see *conciliarism.*

congregational polity: a democratic form of church government wherein authority resides ultimately in the local congregation.

congregational principle: a theory of church governance that posits religious authority in the local congregation.

covenant: a promise, contract, or agreement between two parties; the Old Testament covenants are promises or agreements between God and Israel.

Deism: a seventeenth- and eighteenth-century movement which conceived of God according to the age's scientific world view as the world's architect.

denominationalism: a theory of the church that regards rival church traditions as denominations or names of the one true church.

denomination: a particular church tradition united in polity and belief.

deposit of faith: the tradition of revealed truth concerning faith and works.

diachronic: the study of something through its history.

Divine Liturgy: the name for the worship service of Eastern Orthodoxy.

Divine Office: the Psalms, hymns, prayers, and biblical and spiritual readings formulated by the church for chant and recitation at prescribed times each day.

ecclesiology: teaching or doctrine about the church.

ecumenical council: a general council of the whole church.

ecumenical movement: a modern movement for Christian unity and interchurch cooperation.

energies: the Eastern Orthodox term for the reality of God expressed in creation.

Enlightenment: the early modern period characterized by the dominance of reason and science in all aspects of society and culture.

entire sanctification: the teaching that sanctification is instantaneous rather than gradual and involves an inward cleansing of sin, an indwelling of the Holy Spirit, and a life of Christian perfection.

episcopalian polity: a form of church governance wherein authority resides in bishops.

epistemology: the study of the nature and grounds of knowing.

eremite: a monk living apart from community; a hermit or recluse.

eremitical: see *eremite*.

eschaton: pertaining to the final things.

eschatology: the doctrine of the last things or the end of the world.

essence: the Eastern Orthodox term for the unexpressed reality of God.

established churches: churches whose authority, doctrine, and practices are officially supported by the state.

Establishment: the principle of an officially recognized and state supported church.

Eucharist: a word that means "thanksgiving"; a term used by Christians for their sacred meal commemorating Jesus' final fellowship meal, his death, and resurrection. Other names for this meal are the Lord's Supper, Holy Communion, and Mass.

excommunication: an exclusion from communion, church office or Christian fellowship.

faith: an assent to the church's teachings and creeds or an attitude of trust in God's forgiveness of sinners.

form criticism: a method used by New Testament scholars for studying the oral sources of the Gospel traditions.

free churches: a family of churches which hold that the church is a "free" association of adult believers.

future hope: the Christian hope for God's coming reign and the new age at the end of time.

Gnosticism: a complex religious movement that stressed the importance of a secret wisdom for salvation; Gnosticism in its Christian form exerted important influence on the church during the second century.

gospel: the essential core of Christian revelation regarded as the good news of redemption.

Gospel: usual reference is to the New Testament Gospels of Matthew, Mark, Luke, and John.

grace: the unmerited gift of divine favor or supernatural assistance.

Great Awakening: a spiritual revival and quickening that swept through the American colonies in the middle of the eighteenth century.

Hesychasm: an Eastern Orthodox tradition of mystical spirituality known for its use of inner silence, rhythmic breathing, and the Jesus Prayer.

hierophany: an appearance or manifestation of the sacred.

Holy Thursday: the Thursday before Easter commemorating Jesus's last fellowship meal and his institution of the Last Supper. This day of Holy Week is called Maundy Thursday, a name deriving from the Latin *mandatum novum*, "a new commandment" (John 13:34).

Holy Week: the week preceding Easter, beginning with Palm Sunday and concluding with Holy Saturday.

icon: a stylized representation of Jesus, the Holy Mother, the apostles, or the saints used in devotion and worship among Eastern Orthodox Christians; theologically used to refer to the image (i.e. icon) of God bestowed on humans at creation and restored by Christ.

iconostasis: the screen of icons separating the altar in an Orthodox church.

Incarnation: the doctrine that God's eternal Word was embodied ("took flesh") in the person of Jesus of Nazareth.

indulgence: a remission of the temporal penalties of sin.

investiture: the custom of installing bishops by presenting them with the emblems of episcopal authority.

investiture controversy: the medieval dispute between pope and emperor over the power of investiture.

Jesus Prayer: the prayer, "Lord Jesus Christ, Son of God, have mercy on me, a sinner" which is widely used among Eastern Orthodox Christians.

justification: the teaching that sinners are made just by the virtue of God's action in Christ's sacrificial death; justification is communicated to sinners by grace.

kerygma: the message or proclamation of the good news of Jesus Christ.

laity: those not ordained to the priesthood or ministry.

Last Supper: the last fellowship meal which Jesus celebrated with his inner circle in Jerusalem and the paradigm for Christianity's Eucharistic meal or Lord's Supper.

lay: see *laity*.

lectionary: prescribed readings from Christian Scripture followed in regular sequence through the Christian year.

Logos: the preexistent Word of God about whom John speaks in the prologue of his Gospel.

Marcionism: a second-century Christian movement which sought to separate Christianity from its Jewish heritage by claiming the nonidentity between the God of Christians and the God of Israel.

martyr: those who bear witness to their belief; in the early church the term *martyr* was reserved for those who died witnessing to their faith.

Mass: the name for the Eucharist used most frequently by Roman Catholics.

mendicant friars: members of religious orders who are not bound to one monastic house or establishment and who beg or work for their material needs.

Messiah: denotes a person who has been sent by God to restore Israel and to establish a reign of righteousness. Christians considered Jesus to be a Messiah according to the pattern of the suffering servant of Isaiah.

millennialism: the belief in a future age or millennium (i.e. a thousand-year period) when righteousness and peace will be established.

monks: those with a special vocation to a religious life of poverty, celibacy, and obedience in imitation of Christ's sacrificial life.

mysticism: a direct, unmediated knowledge or experience of ultimate mystery.

natural religion: refers to the religious beliefs that are attested to by reason and religions generally.

normative Christianity: the standard form that Christianity assumed particularly during its formative period.

numinous: the word coined by Rudolph Otto to describe the ineffable character of the religious experience of the holy.

ordinance: a rite followed in obedience to God's commandment. Some Protestants look on the Lord's Supper as an ordinance.

original sin: the sin of the first couple, Adam and Eve, which Christians believe to be the inheritance of the human race.

orthodox: a belief, attitude, or practice that is correct or normative.

Orthodoxy: the name for Eastern Orthodox Christianity.

papal infallibility: the Roman Catholic teaching that popes are preserved from error when they make solemn pronouncements on faith and morals.

Paschal Candle: a special candle lighted on the eve of Easter symbolizing the triumph of the Resurrection over darkness and sin.

Passion: the term used to speak of the suffering and death of Jesus.

penance: an act of self-abasement that expresses sorrow or repentance for a sin committed; one of the seven Roman Catholic sacraments also known as the sacrament of reconciliation.

personal conversion: a change of heart and of life as a consequence of forgiveness and the experience of Christ's redeeming presence.

phenomenological method: a descriptive method of studying religion which endeavors to be faithful to the intentions that lie behind religious practice and belief.

Pietism: an eighteenth-century Protestant renewal movement that emphasized personal conversion and inward religious experience over right belief and the externals of public worship.

pilgrimage: a holy journey to a place deemed sacred often undertaken in fulfillment of a vow or some other sacred obligation.

pope: a word meaning "father" and originally used as a title for any important bishop; Roman Catholics use the title exclusively for the bishop of Rome.

postmillennialist: one who believes that the millennial age will precede and prepare the way for Christ's Second Coming.

premillennialist: one who believes that the millennial age will follow the end of the present age the return of Christ to the earth.

presbyterian polity: a representative form of church order wherein authority resides in a group of elders or presbyters.

priesthood of all believers: a teaching especially central to the Protestant belief that every Christian is a priest and by virtue of baptism has direct access to Christ.

Priestly Writer: the anonymous author of a large block of material found in the Pentateuch.

Psalmist: the reputed author of the Book of Psalms.

relic: the material remains of a martyr or other saint or some object associated with a saint.

religion: the human response to sacred mystery that seeks to comprehend that mystery in symbol, ritual, story, and theology, to give expression to its moral authority in prescribed patterns of behavior, and to stabilize, preserve, and transmit its meaning in canonical writings and sacred tradition.

religious tradition: the rites, practices, doctrines, and ecclesiology that are peculiar to a religious community and its history.

religious vision: the essential understanding a religious tradition has of salvation or enlightenment.

Renaissance: a literary and cultural revival from the fourteenth through the sixteenth centuries beginning in Italy and spreading to northern Europe.

Renaissance humanist: a member of the fifteenth- and sixteenth-century literary movement aimed at the discovery and restoration of ancient texts.

revelation: a word for the content of God's self-disclosure in Jesus Christ and for the process of that self-disclosure.

revivalism: meetings to promote and encourage the personal experience of sin and forgiveness through evangelistic preaching.

ritual purity: the avoidance of spiritual pollution or contamination by a scrupulous observance of the boundaries that separate the sacred from the profane.

Roman Catholic: a Christian who in faith and practice is in communion with the bishop of Rome.

Romantic movement: a nineteenth-century cultural movement important for its renewed emphasis on experience and history.

sabbatarian: used to describe Christians who observe Saturday as the Sabbath day.

sacramentals: religious actions, gestures, and objects akin to sacraments, though without the same authority and efficacy as sacraments.

sacraments: Christian rites regarded as channels of God's grace; Catholics recognize seven sacraments while Protestants acknowledge only baptism and the Lord's Supper.

sacred mystery: refers to the nonordinary, ineffable presence of the holy that is central to religious experience.

sacrifice: an offering of a gift to God for a benefit received or an injury committed.

sanctification: a process of entering upon a new life of holiness made possible by the justification of sinners by God's grace.

Second Great Awakening: a nineteenth-century spiritual revival that spread across the United States.

sermon: a distinctive form of address whose purpose is to expound Scripture and apply its meaning to contemporary circumstances.

Separatist: the name used of the Puritans who separated from the Church of England to form independent congregations.

sin: the act of disobedience that alienates humans from God.

skepticism: a philosophy of radical doubt concerning what can be known.

summae: comprehensive summaries or theological compendiums of Christian belief.

synchronic: the study of a phenomenon in terms of its complexity within a limited period of time and without reference to its historical antecedents.

synod: the official meeting of church leaders from a particular region for deliberation about church teaching, discipline, and reform.

synoptic Gospels: the name for the Gospels of Mark, Matthew, and Luke, which present similar portraits of Jesus and share sources and material.

theology: the disciplined, systematic reflection on the meaning and contemporary expression of the Christian faith.

theosis: the Orthodox teaching that salvation is a process of deification or union with God.

Torah: the first five books of the Bible, known also as the Five Books of Moses or the Pentateuch, containing instructions for the entire range of Jewish life.

transubstantiation: Roman Catholicism's Eucharistic doctrine that the whole substance of the bread and wine become the body and blood of Christ.

Trinitarian: the doctrine that God is a Trinity of three persons.

Trinity: the Christian dogma that there is one God, yet three persons—the Father, the Son, and the Holy Spirit.

typology: a method of interpretation employed by Christians to discover Christian meaning in the figures and events of the Old Testament.

ultramontanists: Roman Catholic proponents for the centralization of church authority in the pope.

unsatisfactoriness: a term used to describe the problematic character of the human condition which Christians speak of as sin.

vital truths: the truths that people live by, though not necessarily our own truths.

vocation: the word in Christian usage can designate either a call to a distinctive life of holiness in the church or a call to a life of holiness in the world.

Word of God: the reference is to the eternal Word (*Logos*) of God revealed in Jesus Christ; **Word of God** also is used of the Bible.

world view: the basic assumptions a people or a culture bring to their understanding of the world of time and space.

Yahweh: the Hebrew name for God, translated *Kyrios* in Greek and the Lord in English.

Yahwist: the anonymous author of the earliest literary source in the Old Testament books of Genesis through Numbers.

Index